TEACHING THE SEVERELY HANDICAPPED,
VOLUME II

edited by

NORRIS G. HARING, ED.D.

Director, Experimental Education Unit
Child Development and Mental Retardation Center
University of Washington
Seattle, Washington

LOUIS J. BROWN, PH.D.

School of Education
Department of Studies in Behavioral Disabilities
University of Wisconsin
Madison, Wisconsin

GRUNE & STRATTON
A Subsidiary of Harcourt Brace Jovanovich, Publishers
New York ☐ San Francisco ☐ London

Library of Congress Cataloging in Publication Data

Main entry under title:

Teaching the severely handicapped.

"The papers . . . are outgrowths of presentations made at a seminar in Kansas City in November 1974."
Includes bibliographies and index.
1. Mentally handicapped children—Education—Congresses.   I.   Haring, Norris Grover, 1923-   III.   Brown, Louis J.
LC4601.T43   371.9 '284   76-25992
ISBN 0-8089-0945-2 (v. 1)
ISBN 0-8089-0980-0 (v. 2)

Grune & Stratton, Inc.
111 Fifth Avenue
New York, New York 10003

Library of Congress Catalog Number 76-25992
International Standard Book Number 0-8089-0980-0
Printed in the United States of America

CONTENTS

Contents

CONTRIBUTORS

GEORGIA ADAMS, Experimental Education Unit, WJ-10, Child Development and Mental Retardation Center,* University of Washington, Seattle, Washington 98195

ROBIN BECK, Experimental Education Unit, WJ-10, CDMRC, University of Washington, Seattle, Washington 98195

LOUIS J. BROWN. Ph.D., School of Education, Department of Studies in Behavioral Disabilities, 427 Education Building, University of Wisconsin, Madison, Wisconsin 53706

NICHOLAS J. CERTO, 111 South Hancock Street, Madison, Wisconsin 53703

LYNN CHANDLER, Experimental Education Unit, WJ-10, CDMRC, University of Washington, Seattle, Washington 98195

PEGGY COYNE, Madison Public Schools, 545 West Dayton Street, Madison, Wisconsin 53703

MARC W. GOLD, Ph.D., Research Associate Professor, Institute for Child Behavior and Development, University of Illinois, South First Street Road, Champaign, Illinois 61820

NORRIS G. HARING, Ed.D., Director, Experimental Education Unit, CDMRC, University of Washington, Seattle, Washington 98195

FRAN JOHNSON, Madison Public Schools, 545 West Dayton Street, Madison, Wisconsin 53703

SIDNEY M. LEVY, M.A., Institute for Child Behavior and Development, Children's Research Center, University of Illinois, South First Street Road, Champaign, Illinois 61820

*Hereafter referred to as CDMRC.

SANDRA SCOTT LIVINGSTON, Experimental Education Unit, WJ-10, CDMRC, Univerity of Washington, Seattle, Washington 98195

DENNIS MITHAUG, Experimental Education Unit, WJ-10, CDMRC, University of Washington, Seattle, Washington 98195

DAVID J. POMERANTZ, M.A., Institute for Child Behavior and Development, University of Illinois, South First Street Road, Champaign, Illinois 61820

NANCY SCHEUERMAN, Madison Public Schools, 545 West Dayton Street, Madison, Wisconsin 53703

RICHARD SCHWARTZ, Madison Public Schools, 545 West Dayton Street, Madison, Wisconsin 53703

DEBRA D. SMITH, Ed.D., Acting Director, Office of Research Administration, Assistant Professor of Special Education, George Peabody College, Nashville, Tennessee

JAMES O. SMITH, Ed.D., Professor and Chairman, Department of Special Education, George Peabody College, Nashville, Tennessee

JANE STEPNER, Madison Public Schools, 545 West Dayton Street, Madison, Wisconsin 53703

BARBARA A. SWETLIK, M.S., Demonstration Teacher of the Trainable Mentally Retarded, Madison Metropolitan School District, Madison, Wisconsin; Active Participant in University of Wisconsin Teacher Training Program; Guest Lecturer at University of Wisconsin-Madison

JAMES W. TAWNEY, Ph.D., Project Director, College of Education, Department of Special Education, University of Kentucky, Lexington, Kentucky 40506

WESTON WILLIAMS, Assistant Professor, Coordinator of Training and Curricula Development, Center for Special Education, Room EDG-408, University of Texas, Austin, Texas 78712

ROBERT YORK, Associate Director, Center for Special Education, College of Education, University of Vermont, Burlington, Vermont 05401

I

Introduction

Norris G. Haring

Welcome Address to the Second Annual AAESPH Conference Kansas City, Missouri November 12–14, 1975

I welcome you as participants of the Second Annual Conference of The American Association for the Education of the Severely/Profoundly Handicapped.

The purpose of this meeting is to provide a forum for discussion, interaction, and exchange to promote the achievement of the goals of the organization that were approved last year at this time. These goals are:

1. To serve as a separate entity in advocating:
    (a) the development of relevant and efficient preservice and in-service teacher training programs, and
    (b) the development of highly specialized doctoral-level preparation, teacher training, research, and instructional design personnel.
2. To develop, refine, and disseminate training and instruction programs and materials for the severely handicapped, including:
    (a) curriculum packages, and
    (b) a teacher training program.
3. To facilitate parent involvement in all program services of the severely/profoundly handicapped.
4. To advocate the full range and high quality development of services for the severely handicapped, following extension and development of community resources available for the total population, beginning at birth.

3

The organization serves as an advocate in securing all local, state, and federal resources needed to achieve these services and, if necessary, enter into litigation or the development of legislation.

The format of this conference is varied to provide alternative forms of interaction. You have already enjoyed the pleasantries of our cocktail party, thereby exploiting the informal communications channel. We are also going to have a keynote address by Ed Sontag, followed by a keynote panel of sages assembled to discuss some of the more difficult philosophical and practical issues related to education of severely handicapped children.

Following this session, we will break into discussion groups, and you will be able to shop around for a group relevant to your interest and needs. Tonight we will have our first Association business meeting with the presentation of the Executive Board, the Association Officers, a Treasurer's Report, and an opportunity for all of you to make suggestions and amendments. Tomorrow a number of task forces will be working to develop papers and generate research issues, and then are charged to report back in a year on their research at our third annual conference.

GROWTH OF ASSOCIATION: "THEY SAID IT COULDN'T BE DONE"

I would now like to digress to recall the time one year ago when 60 of us met in Kansas City to present important research findings, to begin to relate as a group of professionals concerned with the quality of life of the severely/profoundly handicapped, and ultimately to formalize this relationship with the formation of the American Association for the Education of the Severely/Profoundly Handicapped.

Shortly after we formed, the critics emerged: "Why do we need a separate association? This group will be a conglomeration of an Old Boys Club composed of professors. There is not enough interest in the nation to support an association of this type." And ultimately came the criticism of "Why should we waste our time on the severely handicapped? They will never amount to anything."

Well, I am happy to stand here and respond to our critics. I am happy to report that for every criticism we have faced we can respond with information to offset these doubts.

CHART DISPLAY OF GROWTH

This association has seen an unbelievable amount of growth since we initiated membership in June. For that month of June, we solicited a modest thirty three memberships.

Well, as you can see by this chart, in less than six months we have enrolled over 1000 active members in AAESPH. We are also not an association of professors only.

The chart demonstrates that individuals from a variety of professions have joined us in our endeavors: Public school administrators, teachers, institutional professionals, students, and parents have all come into the organization to provide strength through diversity.

The membership response is even more remarkable when you consider that the formation of AAESPH has been largely by word of mouth. Only recently have announcements of AAESPH appeared in *Exceptional Children,* the *NASDSE Newsletter, Insight,* the *CASE Newsletter,* and other professional information exchanges.

In addition, we process numerous requests for information on curricula, training packages, instructional guides, and assessment techniques. It is not uncommon, upon opening mail, to find a brief note: "Please send me one of everything you have."

This chart represents the amount of mail that we respond to each month. Its progression is obvious.

In concert with membership growth and the growth of information has come the growth of centers—training, telecommunications, and demonstration—serving the severely handicapped.

This map demonstrates the response to the needs by BEH in supporting telecommunications centers, demonstration centers, and just a sample of the training centers that are now producing teachers and teacher/ trainers of the severely handicapped.

COMMITMENT TO WORK WITH THE SEVERELY HANDICAPPED: "THEY SAID IT SHOULDN'T BE DONE"

We have organized our efforts despite critics who have said that we really should not even be working with this population.

CRITICS OF WORK WITH SEVERELY HANDICAPPED

Just a month or so ago, a medical practitioner who was an early developer of amniocentesis insisted, in a *Psychology Today* article, that educating even a Down's syndrome child is a futile exercise: "You show me just one mongoloid that has an educable I.Q. . . . . I've never seen even one in my experience with over 800 mongols in the District of Columbia" (Jacobson, in Reztak, 1975).

Our own National Institute for Education has prepared a report to present to Daniel Moynihan, as he assists President Ford with gathering intelligence on the school desegregation issue, and that report contains some distressing implications about the effectiveness of *any* intervention:

> We have a growing knowledge of educational intervention—when to inter-vene, and so forth; but school interventions tried to date in early childhood (3–5 years old) have strong short-term cognitive effects but little long-term influence on achievement. Some compensatory intervention can change short-term achievement scores in a dramatic fashion, but theory is primitive and long-term effects are unknown.

Conclusions like this point up the sharpness of the controversy that is likely to surround any effort to intervene, particularly as the target population exhibits more and more severe degrees of handicap. And this controversy is not new. The ancient Spartans in Greece used to dispose of their handicapped infants by exposing them on a hillside.

Now, I do not intend to stand before this group today to deliver an extended appeal concerning the *rightness* of providing services to the severely handicapped. That would be an example of "preaching to the converted," indeed. For most of us, the right of every child to an education suited to his abilities, regardless of handicap, is simply not a questionable proposition. We value the right of every individual—we insist on a bare minimum, at least, of assistance for those who cannot insist on it for themselves.

But we must recognize that what is a closed issue for us is not at all settled for others. In a tight money economy where resources are limited, the old, the helpless, and the culturally different always have an unmistakably hard time. If we cannot answer some of the more vocal critics, we may find ourselves deprived of resources (particularly financial resources) to provide appropriate services.

There is some comfort to be derived from the realization that so far as the *virtues* of work with the severely handicapped are concerned, the legal trend is currently in the direction of championing the values.

NEED TO SHOW EFFECTIVENESS OF OUR INTERVENTIONS

But what is necessary to us before anything else is to work on the other side of the question—because the critics attack our efforts not only on the grounds that they *should not* be undertaken, but because they are *ineffective* when they do occur.

At least we can show that we do something (and perhaps demonstrating effectiveness will in itself contribute to the conclusion that our efforts are worthwhile. If the severely handicapped young person begins leading a more nearly normal life and appears happier at it, that will tend to win over the skeptics as little else could do.)

Our goal should be, then, to make demonstrable gains with the severely handicapped—gains that are clearly the results of our interventions.

HOW TO SHOW GAINS

What are the first steps in doing this? We have taken several of them already.

1. We have influenced legislation that is either enabling or demanding with regard to funds.
2. We have established organizations like this one to provide for an easy exchange of information and expertise.
3. We have identified experienced leaders who have exerted themselves to establish appropriate training and technical assistance where it is needed.

DOCUMENT GAINS IN QUANTIFIED TERMS

What we must do now—now that the intervention machinery is in place and beginning to turn—is to document its output in precisely specified terms. We must be able to *quantify* the gains made by the severely handicapped pupils in our charge and to pinpoint the antecedents and consequents which were functionally related to the changes we produced.

When we have done this, we may not have provided complete answers to our critics who have said that we "ought not" to spend our time with handicapped, or that we would have been better advised to expend society's resources on a normal child—but at least we will not be vulnerable to the charge that we've wasted our time because we "didn't really do anything" at all.

And yet the need to show that the severely handicapped should be served is vital, too.

NEED TO SHOW THAT THE SEVERELY HANDICAPPED SHOULD BE SERVED—EXCLUSION FROM EDUCATION

For too long, individuals labeled severely and profoundly handicapped have been *excluded* from obtaining those services and rights taken for granted by other members of society. Arguments supporting the denial of such rights and services have been based upon fear, ignorance, and expense.

School authorities have traditionally had the right to exclude from the public schools any child so seriously handicapped as to "impede the progress of other pupils, disrupt classroom discipline, and present an undue number of problems for the teacher" (Dunn, 1973).

The unfortunate alternative to provision of educational and other services to the handicapped population has been institutionalization. Viewed in many instances as an immediate solution to provision of short-term relief for a familial crisis, institutionalization has become in most cases the long-term solution, and the severely handicapped individual has become a lifelong resident who no longer adversely impacts on other members of the family or society at large, but one who also loses all opportunity to participate meaningfully in society.

INSTITUTIONALIZATION NO ANSWER

Institutionalization, the major "answer" to the severely handicapped population, has not been a satisfactory answer; regardless of the good intentions administration and staff might have.

Typically, institutional facilities have been understaffed, under-financed, and overcrowded. Under such conditions, the provision of even minimal education in basic life skills has been all but impossible, and a lifelong, comprehensive program out of the question.

COMPREHENSIVE ECOLOGICAL APPROACH NEEDED

That solution, long found to be economically feasible, is today in many ways indefensible. A growing number of concerned parents, professionals, and politicians are coming to realize that what is needed is a comprehensive, ecological approach. Such an approach not only guarantees that the severely handicapped enjoy those rights considered to be theirs as a matter of ethics and law, but also makes it possible for that population to make some contribution to society.

LEGISLATIVE AND JUDICIAL RULINGS HELP
DEMONSTRATE THAT THE SEVERELY HANDICAPPED
SHOULD BE SERVED

As I mentioned earlier, the first steps have already been taken. By requiring that states provide each individual, no matter how severely handicapped, with full educational services, legislation and judicial rulings have taken a giant step in returning rights to the severely handicapped individual.

Those of us here, representing a broad range of concern—on the part of parents, physicians, educators, institutional administrators, staff, and a number of professions other than education providing services to the handicapped—have already made a personal commitment to improving the quality of life for the severely handicapped through educational programs. Education, normalization, and in some instances deinstitutionalization are concepts which possess extremely positive value characteristics for us.

ECONOMIC QUESTIONS

There are many, however, who would still argue that education for the severely handicapped individual is not only a costly, but most often useless endeavor, and that our efforts to ensure a "quality" existence for such individuals could be better spent elsewhere.

We have obviously only begun to answer the emotional argument against education for the severely handicapped.

In order to persuade others and to ensure that we carefully examine the effects of our efforts, our own commitment must be more than purely emotional. There is strong evidence based on fact—yes, even economic fact—which we can muster to support the enterprise we have just begun: to provide education and thereby an improved quality of life to the severely/profoundly handicapped.

COSTS OF INSTITUTIONAL CARE

The provision of even minimal care within an institutional setting on a budget of only $11 per day per patient [the average amount available to state residential facilities in 1970 (Dunn, 1973)] costs substantially more than provisions for care within the family setting.

It is important to remember that such care is a lifelong necessity for the severely handicapped individual who receives no educational programming; in fact, requirements for attendant and medical care may increase greatly as the resident grows older.

LIFELONG EXPENSES IF NO TRAINING PROVIDED

But—without provision of a program to provide even minimal self-help or housekeeping skills, the severely handicapped individual must always be provided for; he can never assume responsibilities for himself.

Thus, he represents a lifelong financial drain upon society, and is never able to return such investments with services at any level. By providing the severely handicapped individual with even the most rudimentary life skills, we subtract from total care needs and costs.

MORE OPTIONS AVAILABLE TO TRAINED INDIVIDUAL

Individuals who become independent in simple self-care tasks and housekeeping skills are often able to reside in settings other than institutional ones.

COST–BENEFITS FOR ALTERNATIVES TO INSTITUTIONS

Costs of placement within alternative living arrangements are notably less than those for institutional care.

The cost of minimal services within a group home in the state of Washington, for instance, is about half that of similar care provided in an institution.

FUTURE DIRECTIONS

It is traditional that an outgoing president is permitted to offer reflections on the proper course of future events; and, if it were possible for me to influence any single aspect of our work with the severely/profoundly handicapped, it would be the *measurement* aspect.

Without precise measures of what we have done, we will, in all probability, be unable to show that we have done anything. However, the precise documentation and interpretation of the development and growth of severely handicapped children, at least under present educational systems, may present a difficult problem. Studies of the learning capabilities and methods to facilitate and evaluate behavior change in the severely and profoundly handicapped have been conducted in many research laboratories and classrooms. Although researchers have certainly demonstrated the effectiveness of the general techniques of applied behavior analysis in work with the severely/profoundly handicapped, and have, in fact, repeatedly shown that these individuals are capable of benefiting from training, the classroom teacher, when confronted with this population, still faces immense problems in both the selection and evaluation of appropriate programs, tools, and techniques. In order to make appropriate program selections, modifications, and revisions, concerned professionals need a precise measurement tool capable of giving daily descriptions of the growth and progress of pupils for whom a program is provided.

A second aspect I would like to influence is that of *longitudinal studies*. If we are to demonstrate the effectiveness of immediate educational strategies and, ultimately, the benefits of providing education to this population, we must track the progress of pupils receiving progress from year to year.

A crucial issue to be considered here, too, is the location in which educational programs are to take place. Some (Sontag, Burke, and York, 1973) have suggested that the proximity of programs for severely handicapped to those for other students may substantially affect acceptance of this population.

Educational intervention has been criticized as having little long-term effect, as in the quotation above. Anyone who understands the nature of behavior should expect responses which are not reinforced to drop out of a repertoire.

The effectiveness of educational programs being implemented today for severely/profoundly handicapped individuals will depend not only upon these specific procedures, programs, and curricula applied, but also upon the attitudes of the society in which these individuals must function. Without continuing programs which *keep on* reinforcing appropriate responses—and without a social commitment to funding such programs—we can expect that today's gains will "wash out" in time. Indeed, we could expect nothing else.

CONCLUSION

The future directions we've been pointing to here are only the beginnings. I can't hope to raise and settle every question concerning the severely/profoundly handicapped—in fact, this conference is designed to allow all of *you* to raise questions and to begin to seek answers. That is its purpose: Any one of us alone could not hope to do what we can accomplish as we work together.

I couldn't resist using this forum to present what I consider to be major issues in the education of the severely/profoundly handicapped, but the task forces in which we participate will no doubt sharpen and refine many of these and other issues in the next days and months.

II

Specific Remedial or Training Programs

Barbara Swetlik and
Lou Brown

A

Teaching Severely Handicapped Students to Express Selected First, Second, and Third Person Singular Pronoun Responses in Answer to "Who-doing" Questions

Impaired language and communication skills constitute major impediments to the social, emotional, and vocational adjustment of retarded citizens (Schiefelbusch, Copeland, and Smith, 1967). In fact, deficits in language probably define developmental retardation more than any other aspect of behavior (Bricker and Bricker, 1972). More specifically, the language of retarded children has been characterized as "not being developed beyond stereotyped patterns of speech," and "delayed in the development of such conceptual linguistic functions as generalization, association, discrimination, and the manipulation of verbal concepts" (Schlanger, 1967, p. 137). Keane (1972, p. 5) concludes, "The one undisputed fact that has been well documented is that there is a higher than normal incidence of communication (speech, language, and hearing) disorders found in the mentally retarded collectively."

This paper was supported in part by Grant No. OEG-0-73-6137 to the University of Wisconsin-Madison from the Department of HEW, Bureau of Education for the Handicapped, Division of Training Programs, Washington, D.C. This paper is an approximate version of that presented in L. Brown, W. Williams, and T. Crowner (eds), A Collection of Papers and Programs Related to Public School Services for Severely Handicapped Students, Volume IV, Madison Public Schools, Madison, Wis., August, 1974.

If retarded citizens, particularly severely handicapped citizens, are to function with some degree of success in the mainstream of our society, they must be taught the language skills necessary to communicate effectively in a variety of social, recreational, and occupational settings (Sontag, Burke, and York, 1973). If language training is not effective, the probability of ultimate adjustment to a public living environment is low. Recent studies have suggested, however, that language training can be effective. Bricker and Bricker (1971); McLean, Yoder, and Schiefelbusch (1972); and Schiefelbusch, Copeland, and Smith (1967) have reported programs demonstrating that severely handicapped children can benefit from language training if instructional efforts are structured, precisely sequenced, and used simultaneously with appropriate reinforcement principles.

One important communication skill which is often deficient in retarded children is the ability to ask and answer questions appropriately. Questions are an indispensable part of most linguistic transactions. Of crucial importance are skills related to "wh" questions (i.e., questions introduced by an interrogative word such as what, where, who, when, and why). Unfortunately, these skills appear difficult for severely handicapped students to acquire. This apparent difficulty may be a function of the specific semantic and syntactic constraints associated with responses to "wh" questions. For example, a "who" question must be answered semantically by a response that refers to a person and syntactically by a noun phrase or a pronoun.

The classroom teacher who developed this program observed that her students often did not answer "wh" questions correctly—neither in response to questions asked about the content of stories in preprimer reading books nor in oral communication situations. In order to develop the students' abilities to answer questions about the content of reading material, it seemed essential that the students first learn to answer "wh" questions in oral communication. Thus, teaching the students to respond correctly to at least "who" questions becomes one major objective of this program.

In addition to skills related to "who" questions, the pronoun system is another aspect of language which is often deficient in language-delayed children (Waryas, 1973). In order to use pronouns correctly, students must learn what pronouns mean (i.e., what words they refer to), which pronoun to select for use in a particular situation, and when not to use pronouns at all. It was determined that the students rarely used pronouns, either in response to direct questions or in less structured communications. The teacher also noticed that although the students were taught to label pronouns contained in their preprimer reading books, they had difficulty delineating the persons to whom the pronouns referred. Thus, in addition to teaching students to respond correctly to "who" questions, a second major objective is to teach students to use singular subject pronouns in a semantically and syntactically acceptable manner.

In summary, this program is an attempt to organize and teach several basic language and communication skills, and to provide an instructional model for the development of selected pronoun usage skills of severely handicapped students. In order to communicate the relevant components of the instructional program, as well as to delineate the specific skills required, a detailed task analysis follows:

PHASE I

Teaching students to, or verifying that students could, imitate selected one, two, and three-word verbal responses.

> *Part 1*—Teaching students to, or verifying that students could, imitate one-word verbal responses (e.g., "I").
>
> *Part 2*—Teaching students to, or verifying that students could, imitate two-word verbal responses (e.g., "I am").
>
> *Part 3*—Teaching students to, or verifying that students could, imitate three-word verbal responses (e.g., "I am standing.").

PHASE II

Teaching students to perform actions in response to verbal cues, to visually discriminate actions, and to label actions.

> *Part 1*—Teaching students to perform actions in response to verbal cues (e.g., "Show me standing.").
>
> *Part 2*—Teaching students to visually discriminate actions (e.g., "Touch someone standing.").
>
> *Part 3*—Teaching students to label actions (e.g., "What is John doing?").

PHASE III

Teaching students to visually discriminate themselves, the teacher, and classmates in response to name cues.

> *Part 1*—Teaching students to visually discriminate themselves in response to a name cue (e.g., "John, touch John.").
>
> *Part 2*—Teaching students to visually discriminate the teacher in response to a name cue (e.g., "John, touch Ms. Swetlik.").
>
> *Part 3*—Teaching students to visually discriminate classmates in response to name cues (e.g., "John, touch Peggy.").
>
> *Part 4*—Teaching students to visually discriminate themselves, the teacher, and classmates in response to name cues (e.g., "John, touch John, Ms. Swetlik, and Peggy.").

PHASE IV

Teaching students to visually discriminate males and females in response to third person singular subject pronoun cues.

> *Part 1*—Teaching students to visually discriminate males in response to the third person singular subject pronoun cue "he" (i.e., "Touch a *he*.").
>
> *Part 2*—Teaching students to visually discriminate females in response to the third person singular subject pronoun cue "she" (i.e., "Touch a *she*.").
>
> *Part 3*—Teaching students to visually discriminate males and females in response to the third person singular subject pronoun cues "he" and "she" (i.e., "Touch a *he*.", "Touch a *she*.").

PHASE V

Teaching students to make proper name responses to "who" questions containing first, second, and third person singular subject pronouns.

> *Part 1*—Teaching students to label the teacher in response to "who" questions containing the first person singular subject pronoun "I" (i.e., "Who am *I*?").
>
> *Part 2*—Teaching students to label themselves in response to "who" questions containing the second person singular subject pronoun "you" (i.e., "Who are *you*?").
>
> *Part 3*—Teaching students to label the teacher and themselves in response to "who" questions containing the first and second person singular subject pronouns "I" and "you" (i.e., "Who am *I*?", "Who are *you*?").
>
> *Part 4*—Teaching students to label male classmates in response to "who" questions containing the third person singular subject pronoun "he" (i.e., "Who is *he*?").
>
> *Part 5*—Teaching students to label female classmates in response to "who" questions containing the third person singular subject pronoun "she" (i.e., "Who is *she*?").
>
> *Part 6*—Teaching students to label male and female classmates in response to "who" questions containing the third person singular subject pronouns "he" and "she" (i.e., "Who is *he*?", "Who is *she*?").
>
> *Part 7*—Teaching students to label themselves, the teacher, and male and female classmates in response to "who" questions containing first, second, and third person singular subject pronouns (i.e., "Who am *I*?", "Who are *you*", "Who is *he/she*?").

PHASE VI

Teaching students to respond to "who-doing" questions with the first person singular subject pronoun and present progressive verbs (e.g., Q: "Who is standing?" A: "*I* am standing.").

PHASE VII

Teaching students to respond to "who-doing" questions with the second person singular subject pronoun and present progressive verbs (e.g., Q: "Who is standing?" A: "*You* are standing.").

PHASE VIII

Teaching students to respond to "who-doing" questions with the first and second person singular subject pronouns and present progressive verbs (e.g., Q: "Who is standing?" A: "*I* am standing." Q: "Who is standing?" A: "*You* are standing.").

PHASE IX

Teaching students to respond to "who-doing" questions with third person singular subject pronouns and present progressive verbs.

> *Part 1*—Teaching students to respond to "who-doing" questions with the third person singular subject pronoun "he" (e.g., Q: "Who is standing?" A: "*He* is standing.").
>
> *Part 2*—Teaching students to respond to "who-doing" questions with the third person singular subject pronoun "she" (e.g., Q: "Who is standing?" A: "*She* is standing.").
>
> *Part 3*—Teaching students to respond to "who-doing" questions with the third person singular subject pronouns "he" and "she" (e.g., Q: "Who is standing?" A: "*He/She* is standing.").

PHASE X

Teaching students to respond to "who-doing" questions with first, second, and third person singular subject pronouns and present progressive verbs (e.g., Q: "Who is standing?" A: "*I* am standing." Q: "Who is standing?" A: "*You* are standing." Q: "Who is standing?" A: "*He/she* is standing.").

Examination of the task analysis should make several program parameters salient:

1. "Who" questions were used rather than other "wh" question forms. "Who" questions were selected because of the following considerations: (a) The students had demonstrated the skills necessary to answer many "yes-no," "what + be," "what + do," and "what kind"

questions, and did so frequently in classroom situations. Thus, "who" questions seemed a logical choice, according to the postulated developmental sequence of question acquisition skills presented by Yoder (1972). (b) Beginning reading and pictorial material, because of the emphasis on characters and conversation, is replete with content appropriate for "who" questions. It was intended that acquiring skills required to answer "who" questions would better prepare students for development of more complex reading comprehension skills.

2. The students were required to answer "who" questions with pronoun responses. Pronoun responses were required because: (a) the students rarely used pronouns in their speech; (b) understanding and correct usage of pronouns are skills which many severely handicapped students must be systematically taught; and (c) acquiring skills in pronoun usage would probably facilitate the correct delineation of persons to which pronouns referred in reading materials.

3. The students were required to make complete three-word sentence responses containing a pronoun and a present progressive verb (e.g., "I am standing."). This response form was required because: (a) The students had exhibited the ability to use three-word verbal chains, but did not normally use them in unstructured classroom settings. (b) According to Dale (1972), the present progressive is the first verb inflection to be acquired in normal language developmental sequence. (c) Repeated practice with the sentence forms "I am _____", "You are _____", "He is _____", and "She is _____" might contribute to the development of a strategy for generating complete sentence responses to "wh" questions which contain other verbs in other situations.

4. The students seemed most interested in discussions about persons in the immediate classroom environment. Because of this already established interest, it was decided to ask "who" questions about the students and the teacher before substituting pictures or printed material.

5. The skills necessary to complete each component of the program were empirically verified through criterion measurement.

METHOD

Students (Ss)

The eight Ss involved were enrolled in a public school program for trainable level retarded students. Ss ranged in chronological age from 6 years 10 months to 11 years 11 months ($\overline{X}$ = 8.9), and in MA from 3 years 8 months to 5 years 5 months ($\overline{X}$ = 4.4).

Psychological reports indicated that Ss had obtained I.Q. scores on the Stanford-Binet that ranged from 37 to 56 ($\overline{X}$ = 49.13). Years in public school, as of September 1973, ranged from 1 to 4 ($\overline{X}$ = 2.7).

The eight Ss were divided into two instructional groups of four (Groups A and B). All instruction was conducted as a regular class activity. Each group participated in the program for at least 20 min per day, 4 days per week. While Group A (Ss 1, 2, 3 and 4) was seated with the teacher (T) on one side of the classroom, Group B (Ss 5, 6, 7, and 8) received phonics instruction from a university practicum student, and vice versa.

Instructional Setting

PHASES I, III, AND V

Ss were seated in chairs arranged in a semicircle. T also sat in a chair facing Ss.

PHASES II AND VI—X

T designated a part of the classroom as the action corner. This corner consisted of a chair and a table upon which were placed a scissors, comb, zipping board, preprimer reading book, and piece of construction paper. Additional chairs were arranged facing the action corner and T and Ss sat in them.

PHASE IV

Two additional Ss (one male and one female) were secured. These Ss did not receive direct instruction, but they were used to form the two male–female pairs needed for the required gender discriminations. Ss and T were seated facing the action corner. Two chairs were placed in the action corner, and the table was removed.

Materials

PHASES I, III, IV, AND V

The materials used in these phases included chairs for T and each S and mimeographed grid type data sheets.[2]

PHASES II AND VI–X

In addition to the materials listed above, the materials used in these phases included a table and chair, scissors, comb, zipping board, preprimer reading book, and pieces of construction paper.

[2]Examples of data sheets are presented in Appendix A.

Graphs and Tangible Consequences

Individual graphs were constructed for each S. These graphs depicted the number of correct responses across trials for each part of each phase of the program. Social praise was dispersed immediately after each correct response. In addition, each S was presented with a consumable (M & M, pretzel, peanut butter, cereal, etc.) if he or she responded correctly to the first cue provided by T in each part of each phase.

TEACHING DESIGN AND PROCEDURES

Phase I: Teaching Ss to, or verifying that Ss could, imitate selected one, two, and three-word verbal responses.

In Phases VI-X, Ss would required to articulate appropriate pronouns and present progressive verbs in order to answer "who-doing" questions correctly. Thus, it was decided to verify that Ss could make the required three-component responses prior to Phase VI.

Phase I was divided into three parts. The objectives of parts 1, 2, and 3 respectively were to teach Ss to imitate selected one, two, and three-word verbal responses. Baseline measures of the skills required in all three parts were obtained before teaching of part 1 was initiated.

The imitative cues used in part 3 were grouped into four sets of six, and each set was taught separately. When Ss reached criterion on the four individual sets, the sets were combined. The instructional program for Phase I was organized as follows: (a) baseline parts 1, 2, and 3; (b) teach part 1; (c) teach part 2; (d) teach part 3, Set I; (e) teach part 3, Set II; (f) teach part 3, Set III; (g) teach part 3, Set IV; (h) rebaseline part 3, Sets I, II, III, and IV.

BASELINE PROCEDURES—PARTS 1, 2, AND 3

Baseline measures of the ability of Ss to perform the tasks required in part 1 were obtained in the following manner: Ss were seated facing T. T looked at S_1 and said, "S_1, say this word. Say 'I.' " Regardless of S_1's response, T said, "Thank you." T recorded a "+" on the data sheet for a correct response and a "−" for an incorrect response or no response. T then presented a different imitative cue to S_2, etc. Ss were given two opportunities to respond to each of the 13 imitative cues.

Baseline procedures as described for Part 1 were also used to determine each S's ability to respond to the verbal cues contained in parts 2 and 3.

TEACHING PROCEDURES

*Part 1: Teaching Ss to, or verifying that Ss
could, imitate one-word verbal responses
(e.g., "I").*

If baseline measures suggested that Ss could not imitate one-word responses, the following procedures were implemented:

>*Step 1*—Ss were seated facing T. T looked at S_1 and said, "S_1, say this word. Say 'I.' " If S_1 correctly matched the behavior modeled by saying "I," T smiled, said, "Good," delivered a consumable consequence, recorded a correct response, and proceeded to implement the same procedures with S_2, etc.
>
>*Step 2*—If S_1 did not imitate "I" (within 5 sec), T said, "No," and repeated the cue, "S_1, say this word. Say 'I.' " If S_1 correctly imitated T's verbal model, T said, "Good," recorded "M_2" (second model), and proceeded to S_2, etc.
>
>*Step 3*—If S_1 still did not correctly imitate the verbal model, T said, "No! I wanted you to say 'I,' " recorded an incorrect response, and terminated teaching for this trial. T then proceeded to S_2.
>
>When necessary, T proceeded through step 3 with S_1 before proceeding to step 1 with S_2. However, it should be noted that: (a) steps 2 and 3 were implemented only once before T proceeded to S_2, and (b) on subsequent trials, instruction with S_1 began on step 1. These procedures were followed until each S correctly imitated the 13 words in part 1 under the conditions set forth in step 1 on three consecutive occasions.

*Part 2: Teaching Ss to, or verifying that Ss
could, imitate two-word verbal responses
(e.g., "I am").*

Steps 1 and 2 were identical to the first two steps in part 1 except that a two-word response was required.

>*Step 3*—If S_1 did not correctly imitate the verbal response, T modeled the components of the response, then repeated the cue, "S_1, say 'I am.' " If S_1 matched the 2 component response correctly, T said, "Good," recorded "M_3", and proceeded to step 1 with S_2.
>
>*Step 4*—If S_1 said the two words separately but did not say them together, a partial prompt was used in an attempt to have S_1

[3]The ability to imitate single word verbal responses was a prerequisite for this program. If baseline data revealed Ss who were not able to do so, those Ss would have been placed in an imitative speech program designed to develop verbal imitation skills.

chain the words together. That is, T would say, "S_1, say these words. Say 'I am.' " If S_1 responded with "I" only, T then provided a prompt in the form of "a-a-a." If S_1 said "am," T said, "Good," and recorded "P" (prompt) on the data sheet. S_1 was then asked to say "I am."

Step 5—If S_1 still did not correctly imitate the verbal model, T said, "No! I wanted you to say 'I am,' " recorded an incorrect response, and terminated teaching for this trial. T then proceeded to step 1 with S_2.

These procedures were followed until each S correctly imitated each of the two-word responses in part 2 on three consecutive occasions without assistance from T.

Part 3: Teaching Ss to, or verifying that Ss could, imitate three-word verbal responses (e.g., "I am standing.").

The procedures were identical to those used in part 2, except that a three-word verbal response was required. These procedures were followed until each S imitated each of the three-word responses in each set on three consecutive occasions without assistance from T.

Phase II: Teaching Ss to perform actions in response to verbal cues, to visually discriminate actions, and to label actions.

Phase II was designed to develop skills related to the performance of overt motor actions. Six actions (standing, waving, cutting, combing, reading, and zipping) were selected. The reasons for choosing these actions were: (a) they are relatively discrete; (b) they are actions frequently performed in classrooms and/or elsewhere in schools; and (c) Ss could perform these actions and answer questions simultaneously.

In part 1, Ss were taught to perform actions in response to verbal cues (e.g., "Show me standing.") The present participle (e.g., standing) was used because that verb form would be required in order to answer questions in Phases VI–X correctly.

In part 2, Ss were taught to visually discriminate a classmate who was performing one of the six actions. Finally, in part 3, Ss were taught to label actions being performed by their classmates using the present participle.

The instructional program for Phase II progressed as follows: (a) baseline parts 1, 2, and 3; (b) teach part 1; (c) teach part 2; (d) teach part 3.

BASELINE PROCEDURES—PARTS 1, 2, AND 3

Prior to instruction, baseline measures of the ability of Ss to perform the tasks required in Phase II, parts 1, 2, and 3 were obtained in the following manner:

Part 1—Ss were seated in their chairs facing the action corner. T looked at S_1 and said, "S_1, sit in the action corner," while pointing to the appropriate place. If S_1 did not respond, T physically guided S_1 until he/she was sitting in the chair located in the action corner. When S_1 was seated in the action corner, T said, "S_1, show me standing." Regardless of S_1's response, T said, "Thank you," and instructed S_1 to return to the group and sit down. T recorded a "+" on the data sheet for a correct response and a "−" for an incorrect response or no response. T then instructed S_2 to sit in the action corner and presented a different cue to S_2. Each S was given two opportunities to respond to the six verbal cues (i.e., "Show me standing, waving, cutting, combing, reading, and zipping.").

Part 2—Ss and T were seated facing the action corner. T looked at S_1 and S_2 and said, "S_1 and S_2, go and sit in the action corner." When Ss 1 and 2 were seated in the two chairs in the action corner, T went to the action corner and whispered, "Show me standing," into the ear of S_1 and, "Show me waving," into the ear of S_2.

While S_1 was standing and S_2 was waving, T walked over to S_3 and said, "Touch someone standing." Regardless of S_3's response, T said, "Thank you," and instructed S_3 to return to the group and sit down. Each S was given two opportunities to respond to each of the six different actions.

Part 3—Ss and T were seated facing the action corner. T looked at S_1 and said, "S_1, go and sit in the action corner." When S_1 was seated appropriately, T went to the action corner and whispered, "Show me standing," into the ear of S_1. When S_1 was standing, T looked at S_2 and said, "What is S_1 doing?" Regardless of S_2's response, T said, "Thank you." Each S was given two opportunities to label the six different actions as they were being performed by their classmates.

TEACHING PROCEDURES

Part 1: Teaching Ss to perform actions in response to verbal cues (e.g., "Show me standing.").

Step 1—Ss and T were seated facing the action corner. T looked at S_1 and said, "S_1, sit in the action corner," while pointing to the appropriate place. When S_1 was seated in the action corner, T said, "S_1, show me standing." If S_1 responded correctly by standing, T said, "Good," recorded a correct response, presented a consumable consequence, and instructed S_1 to return to the group and sit down. T then instructed S_2 to sit in the action corner, etc.

Step 2—If S_1 did not stand, T said, "Show me standing," and modeled the correct response. T then repeated the cue, "S_1, show me standing." If S_1 stood, T said, "Good," recorded "M" (S matched the modeled response), and instructed S_2 to perform a different action, etc.

Step 3—If S_1 still did not stand, T went to S_1 and said, "S_1, show me standing," and physically guided the sitting student to a standing position. T said, "This is standing." T then told S_1 to return to the group, recorded "P" (prime) on the data sheet, and initiated step 1 with S_2.

These procedures were followed until each S performed the six actions (i.e., standing, waving, cutting, combing, reading, and zipping) in response to verbal cues on three consecutive occasions without the assistance of modeling or priming cues.

Part 2: Teaching Ss to visually discriminate actions (e.g., "Touch someone standing.").

Step 1—Prior to instruction on Part 2, an additional chair was placed in the action corner. Ss and T were seated facing the action corner. T looked at S_1 and S_2 and said, "S_1 and S_2, go and sit in the action corner." After Ss 1 and 2 were seated in the two chairs in the action corner, T whispered, "Show me standing," into the ear of S_1 and, "Show me waving," into the ear of S_2. While S_1 was standing and S_2 was waving, T walked over to S_3 and said, "Touch someone standing." If S_3 responded correctly by touching S_1, T smiled, said, "Good," recorded a correct response, and delivered a consumable consequence.

Step 2—If S_3 did not respond correctly, T said, "No," repeated the cue, and modeled the correct response. T then repeated the cue, "S_3, touch someone standing." If S_3 responded correctly, T said, "Good," and recorded "M" on the data sheet.

Step 3—If S_3 did not respond correctly to the modeling cues provided by T, he/she was primed through the correct response, and "P" was recorded on the data sheet.

These procedures were followed until all priming and modeling cues were faded, and Ss responded correctly to the three pairs of actions on three consecutive occasions (i.e., standing–

waving, cutting–combing, and reading–zipping). It should be noted that each S was required to discriminate six different actions.

Part 3: Teaching Ss to label actions (e.g., "What is John doing?").

Step 1—Ss and T were seated facing the action corner. T looked at S_1 and said, "S_1, go and sit in the action corner." When S_1 was seated appropriately, T went to the action corner and whispered, "Show me standing," into the ear of S_1. When S_1 was standing, T looked at S_2 and said, "What is S_1 doing?" If S_2 responded correctly by saying "Standing," T said, "Good," recorded a correct response, delivered a consumable consequence, and presented a different action cue to S_3, etc.[4]

Step 2—If S_2 did not respond correctly, T said, "No," repeated the cue, "What is S_1 doing?", and verbally modeled the correct response by saying, "Standing." T repeated the cue, "S_2, what is S_1 doing?" If S_2 responded correctly, T smiled, said, "Good," recorded "M_1", and presented a different action cue to S_3, etc.

Step 3—If S_2 made no response or did not correctly imitate the verbal model, T said, "No," repeated the cue, "S_2, what is S_1 doing? Say 'standing.'" If S_2 responded correctly, T provided only social consequences and recorded "M_2". S_3 was then given a different action cue, etc.

Step 4—If S_2 made no response or an incorrect response, T said, "No! S_1 is standing," recorded an incorrect response, and terminated teaching for that trial. S_3 was then given a different action cue, etc.

These procedures were followed until each S labeled the six different actions as they were performed by classmates on three consecutive occasions (i.e., standing, waving, cutting, combing, reading, and zipping).

Phase III: Teaching Ss to visually discriminate themselves, the teacher, and classmates in response to name cues.

The purpose of Phase III was to teach Ss to recognize the names of themselves, their classmates, and T by touching different persons in response to name cues. In Phase IV, Ss would have to choose from their classmates those who could be referred to as a "he" and those who could be referred to as a "she." Since a pronoun may function as a noun

---

[4]It should be noted that "S_1 is standing.," "S_1 standing," and "Standing" were all considered acceptable responses.

substitute, it was decided to first teach the proper names for which the pronouns would later substitute. Phase III was divided into 4 parts. In part 1, Ss were required to touch themselves in response to their own name cues. In part 2, Ss were asked to touch T, and in part 3, their classmates. In part 4, Ss were required to touch themselves, T, and their classmates in response to name cues.

The instructional program for Phase III progressed as follows: (a) baseline parts 1, 2, 3, and 4; (b) teach part 1; (c) teach part 2; (d) teach part 3; (e) teach part 4.

BASELINE PROCEDURES—PARTS 1, 2, 3, AND 4

> *Part 1*—The baseline measures for part 1 were obtained as follows: Ss were seated facing T. T looked at S_1 and said, "S_1, touch S_1." Regardless of S_1's response, T said, "Thank you." T recorded a "$+$" for a correct response (i.e., S_1 touched himself) and a "$-$" for an incorrect response (e.g., S_1 touched S_2) or no response. T then presented a different cue to S_2 (i.e., "S_2, touch S_2."). These procedures were followed until Ss were given two opportunities to touch themselves in response to the appropriate name cues.

> Baseline procedures as described for part 1 were also used to determine each S's ability to respond to the verbal cues contained in parts 2–4.

TEACHING PROCEDURES

> *Part 1: Teaching Ss to visually discriminate*
> *themselves in response to a name cue (e.g.,*
> *"John, touch John.").*

> > *Step 1*—Ss were seated facing T. T looked at S_1 and said, "S_1, touch S_1." If S_1 responded correctly by touching himself, T smiled, said, "Good," presented a consumable consequence, recorded a correct response, and looked at S_2, etc.

> > *Step 2*—If S_1 did not respond correctly, T said, "No," repeated the cue, and modeled the correct response by touching S_1. T then repeated the cue, "S_1, touch S_1." If S_1 touched himself, T smiled, said, "Good," recorded "M" on the data sheet, and presented S_2's name cue to S_2, etc.

> > *Step 3*—If S_1 did not imitate T, T said, "No," repeated the cue, "S_1, touch S_1," and primed the response by physically guiding S_1 through the touching response. T said, "Good," recorded "P" on the data sheet, looked at S_2, etc. On each subsequent trial, T decreased the amount of physical prompting until S_1 responded

to the imitative cue provided by T. Subsequently, imitative cues were faded.

The procedures described for part 1 were used to teach Ss to respond correctly to the verbal cues contained in parts 2–4. In each part, instruction continued until each S responded correctly to each name cue on three consecutive occasions.

Phase IV: Teaching Ss to visually discriminate males and females in response to third person singular subject pronoun cues.

The objective of Phase IV was to teach Ss to touch a male classmate in response to the cue "Touch a he," and to touch a female classmate in response to the cue "Touch a she." The other two pronouns, "I" and "you," are relative to a given situation (speaker and listener), and could not be taught in quite as straightforward a manner.

Phase IV was divided into three parts. In part 1, Ss were required to touch a male classmate in response to the cue "Touch a he" when presented with two different male-female pairs. Aftsr Ss reached criterion on part 1, they were required to touch a female classmate in part 2 when T said, "Touch a she." Finally, in part 3, T presented the two cues in an alternating fashion and Ss were required to touch either a "he" or a "she."

In this phase T attempted to develop the general rule: "If someone is a boy (man), I call him a *he*. If someone is a girl (woman), I call her a *she*."

The design for Phase IV was as follows: (a) baseline parts 1, 2, and 3; (b) teach part 1; (c) teach part 2; (d) teach part 3.

BASELINE PROCEDURES—PARTS 1, 2, AND 3

> *Part 1*—The baseline measures for Phase IV, part 1, were obtained as follows: Six Ss and T were seated in their chairs facing the action corner.[5] T looked at S_1 and S_2 and said, "S_1 and S_2, go and sit in the action corner." When S_1 and S_2 were seated in the two chairs in the action corner, T walked over to S_3 and said, "Touch a he." Regardless of S_3's response, T said, "Thank you." T then initiated the same procedure with S_4, using a different male–female pair. Each S was given two opportunities to respond to the cue "Touch a he" when presented with two different male–female pairs.[6]

[5]Before baseline measures were obtained in Phase IV, two students (one male and one female) were added to the group. These Ss did not receive direct instruction, but were used to form the two male–female pairs needed for the gender discriminations required in this phase.

[6]Males: S_1, S_3, S_5　Females: S_2, S_4, S_6

Baseline measures for parts 2 and 3 were obtained in the same manner as part 1, except that in part 2, each S was told to "Touch a she," while in part 3 each S was told to first "Touch a he" and then to "Touch a she."

TEACHING PROCEDURES

*Part 1: Teaching Ss to visually discriminate
males in response to the third person
singular subject pronoun cue "he" (i.e.,
"Touch a he.").*

Step 1—Ss and T were seated in their chairs facing the action corner. T looked at S_1 and S_2 and said, "S_1 and S_2, go and sit in the action corner." After Ss 1 and 2 were seated in the two chairs in the action corner, T walked over to S_3 and said, "Touch a he." If S_3 responded correctly, T smiled, said, "Good," recorded a correct response, and delivered a consumable consequence.

Step 2—If S_3 did not respond correctly, T said, "No," repeated the cue, "Touch a he," and modeled the correct response by going to the action corner and touching S_1. While modeling the response, T said, "This is S_1. S_1 is a boy. Listen, I can say it another way. *He* is a boy. If he is a boy, I can call him a *he*. This is a *he*. S_3, is this a he?" If S_3 responded correctly, T said, "Good," and repeated the cue, "S_3, touch a he." If S_3 responded correctly by touching S_1, T said, "Good," recorded "M" on the data sheet, and told S_3 to return to his seat. T initiated step 1 with S_4, using a different male–female pair.

Step 3—If S_3 did not respond correctly to the modeled cues provided by T, he was primed through the correct response and "P" was recorded on the data sheet.

The procedures described for part 1 were used to teach Ss to respond correctly to the verbal cues contained in part 2 and 3. These procedures continued until all priming and modeling cues were faded and each S responded correctly to the cues in parts 1, 2, and 3 when presented with two different male–female pairs on three consecutive occasions.

**Phase V: Teaching Ss to make proper name
responses to "who," questions containing
first, second, and third person singular subject
pronouns.**

In Phase V, Ss were required to respond to "who" questions with the proper names of T, themselves, and male and female classmates. That is,

T asked one of the following questions: "Who am I?"; "Who are you?"; "Who is he?"; or "Who is she?" Ss were required to answer by giving the first name or first and last names of the person referred to. Complete sentence responses (e.g., "I am John.") were not required but were considered correct if they contained the appropriate names.

There were two reasons for including Phase V in this program. First, in Phases VI–X, Ss would be required to refer to themselves, T, and their classmates using the pronouns "I," "you," "he," and "she," respectively. Phase V was included to verify that Ss could give the proper names for which the pronouns would later stand.

Second, the proper use of "I" and "you" can be confusing to children, because these pronouns can be substitutes for a variety of proper nouns, depending on who is speaking. For example, a child, in referring to himself would say, "I am here today." But if T would refer to that same child, she would say, "Are *you* here today?" In Phase V, Ss gave their own names in response to the question "Who are you?", and gave Ts name in response to the question "Who am I?" Conversely, in Phases VI, VII, and VIII, Ss would use the pronoun "I" in reference to themselves and the pronoun "you" in reference to T. Thus, Ss were required to differentially respond to "I" and "you."

Phase V was divided into seven parts. In part 1, Ss were taught to label T in response to the question "Who am I?" In part 2, they were taught to give their own names in response to the question "Who are you?" In part 3, T alternately asked Ss to label either T or themselves. In the same manner Ss were taught to label their males classmates in part 4 when asked, "Who is he?" and their female classmates in part 5 when asked, "Who is she?" In part 6, T alternately asked, "Who is he?" or "Who is she?" Finally, in part 7, Ss were required to label T, themselves, and their male and female classmates when asked appropriate questions.

The design for Phase V was as follows: (a) baseline parts 1–7; (b) teach part 1; (c) teach part 2; (d) teach part 3; (e) teach part 4; (f) teach part 5; (g) teach part 6; (h) teach part 7.

BASELINE PROCEDURES—PARTS 1–7

> *Part 1*—The baseline measures for part 1 were obtained as follows: Ss were seated in their chairs facing T. T looked at S_1 and said, "Who am I?" Regardless of S_1's response, T said, "Thank you." T then presented the same cue to S_2. Ss were given two opportunities to label T in response to the cue "Who am I?"
>
> *Part 2*—Baseline measures for Phase V, part 2, were obtained in the same manner as part 1 except that each S was given two opportunities to label himself in response to the cue "Who are you?"
>
> *Part 3*—Baseline measures for Phase V, part 3, were obtained in

the same manner as part 1 except that each S was given two opportunities to label T and himself in response to the cues "Who am I?" and "Who are you?"

Part 4—The baseline measures for part 4 were obtained as follows: Ss were seated in their chairs facing T. T looked at S_1 and said, "Show me standing." When S_1 was standing, T looked at S_2 and said, "S_2, who is he?", pointing in the direction of S_1. Regardless of S_2's response, T said, "Thank you." T then told a different male S to stand and presented the same verbal cue to S_3. Ss were given two opportunities to respond to the cue "Who is he?" when presented with two different male classmates.

Part 5—Baseline measures for Phase V, part 5, were obtained in the same manner as part 4 except that each S was presented with a female classmate and asked, "Who is she?"

Part 6—Baseline measures for Phase V, part 6, were obtained in the same manner as parts 4 and 5, except that each S was given two opportunities to label two male and female classmates in response to the cues "Who is he?" and "Who is she?"

Part 7—Lastly, baseline measures of the ability of Ss to perform the tasks required by Phase V, part 7, were obtained in the following manner: Ss were seated in their chairs facing T. T looked at S_1 and said, "Who am I?" Regardless of S_1's response, T said, "Thank you." T then presented a different cue to S_2 (e.g., "Who are you?"). Ss were given two opportunities to label T, themselves, and two male and female classmates in response to the following cues: "Who am I?"; "Who are you?"; "Who is he?"; and "Who is she?"

TEACHING PROCEDURES

Part 1: Teaching Ss to label the teacher in response to "who" questions containing the first person singular subject pronoun "I" (i.e., "Who am I?").

Step 1—Ss were seated in their chairs facing T. T looked at S_1 and said, "S_1, who am I?" If S_1 responded correctly by saying "Ms. Swetlik," T smiled, said, "Good," presented a consumable consequence, and recorded a correct response.[7]

Step 2—If S_1 did not respond correctly, T said, "No," repeated the cue, "Who am I?", and modeled the correct response by saying,

---

[7]Any one of the following responses was considered correct: "Swetlik"; "Ms. Swetlik"; "You 'Ms.' Swetlik"; or "You are (Ms.) Swetlik."

"Ms. Swetlik. I am Ms. Swetlik." T also touched herself to emphasize the word "I." T then repeated the cue, "S_1, who am I?" If S_1 imitated T and said "Ms. Swetlik," T smiled, said, "Good," recorded "M_1" on the data sheet, and presented the same cue to S_2.

Step 3—If S_1 did not imitate T, T said, "No," repeated the cue, "S_1, who am I? Say 'Ms. Swetlik' (or 'Swetlik')." If S_1 responded correctly, T said, "Good," recorded "M_2" on the data sheet, and presented the same cue to S_2.

Step 4—If S_1 still made no response or an incorrect response, T said, "No! I am Ms. Swetlik," recorded an incorrect response, and terminated the teaching of S_1 for that trial. S_2 was then given the same cue.

The procedures described for part 1 were used to teach Ss to respond correctly to the verbal cues contained in parts 2–7. These procedures continued until all modeling cues were faded and each S labeled T, himself, and two male and female classmates in three consecutive trials in response to the following cues: "Who am I?"; "Who are you?"; "Who is he?"; and "Who is she?"

Phase VI: Teaching Ss to respond to "who-doing" questions with the first person singular subject pronoun and present progressive verbs.

In Phase VI, Ss were required to perform selected actions. T then asked Ss questions using "who" and verbs in the present progressive tense (e.g., "Who is standing?"). Ss were required to respond with the pronoun "I" and the correct present progressive verb (e.g., "I am standing."). Thus, in order to make the responses required in this phase, Ss had to select an appropriate pronoun, label the action they were performing in the present progressive tense, and combine those two responses to form a complete sentence.

Phase VI was designed to include a test of generalization to a new set of verbs. Ss learned to label six actions in Phase II. In Phase VI, those actions were divided into two sets, with three actions in each set. First, T obtained a baseline measure of each S's ability to respond to the "who-doing" questions in Sets I and II. Then Ss were taught to respond to the verbal cues in Set 1. Next, T rebaselined the skills required in Sets I and II.

The design for Phase VI was as follows: (a) baseline Sets I and II; (b) teach Set I; (c) rebaseline Sets I and II; (d) teach Set II, if necessary; (e) rebaseline Sets I and II.

BASELINE PROCEDURES—SETS I AND II

Baseline measures of the responses required in Phases VI, VII, and IX were obtained before Phases I–V. This procedure was used in an attempt to minimize the occurrence of incidental learning during the baselines of Phases I–V that might distort performance on the initial baselines of Phases VI, VII, and IX. Also, the terminal behaviors for this program were found in the Phase VI–IX tasks, and any S who responded correctly to all of the cues in those phases would be removed from the instruction group.

The baseline measures for Phase VI were obtained as follows: Ss and T were seated in their chairs facing the action corner. T looked at S_1 and said, "Sit in the action corner," while pointing to the appropriate place. When S_1 was seated in the chair in the action corner, T said, "Show me standing."

While S_1 was standing, T said to S_1, "Who is standing?" If S_1 responded correctly by saying, "I am standing," T said, "Thank you," recorded a correct response, and presented a different cue to S_2, etc. It should be noted that the only responses recorded as correct were present progressive verbs preceded by "I am."

If S_1 said nothing, responded incorrectly, or gave an incomplete response, T said, "Thank you," recorded the response, and presented a different cue to S_2, etc.

If S_1 gave a response containing his own proper name, T attempted to obtain a pronoun response by saying, "Say it another way." T then said, "Thank you," recorded the response, and presented a different cue to S_2, etc. Ss were given two opportunities to respond to each of the cues in Sets I and II (i.e., "Who is standing, waving, cutting, combing, reading, and zipping?").

TEACHING PROCEDURES

Step 1—Ss and T were seated in their chairs facing the action corner. T looked at S_1 and said, "Sit in the action corner," while pointing to the appropriate place. When S_1 was seated in the chair in the action corner, T said, "Show me standing." When S_1 was standing, T looked at S_1 and said, "Who is standing?" If S_1 responded correctly by saying "I am standing," T said, "Good," recorded a correct response, presented a consumable consequence, and instructed S_1 to return to the group and sit down. T then told S_2 to sit in the action corner, etc.

Step 2—If S_1 responded incorrectly, T followed one of the following procedures:

a. If S_1 used his own proper name instead of "I," T recorded S_1's first response, said, "O.K., now say it another way," and repeated the cue, "Who is standing?" If S_1 responded correctly, T said, "Good," recorded "+ C_2" (correct response —second cue), and initiated step 1 with S_2, etc.

b. If S_1 gave an incomplete response (e.g., "I," "I standing," "am standing"), T recorded S_1's first response and said, "O.K., now say the whole sentence." T then repeated the cue, "Who is standing?" If S_1 gave the correct response, T said, "Good," recorded "+ C_2" (correct response—second cue), and initiated step 1 with S_2, etc.

c. If S_1 gave an incorrect response (e.g., "I am waving."), T recorded S_1's first response, said, "No," repeated the cue, "Who is standing?", and modeled the correct response, "Say 'I am standing.' " T then repeated the cue. If S_1 correctly imitated T's verbal model, T said, "Good," recorded "M_1," and initiated step 1 with S_2, etc.

Step 3—If S_1 responded incorrectly in step 2, T followed one of the following procedures:

a. If S_1 again used his own proper name instead of "I" (see step 2a), T said, "No," repeated the cue, "Who is standing?," and modeled the correct response, "Say it another way. Say 'I am standing.' " T then repeated the cue, "Who is standing?" If S_1 correctly imitated T's verbal model, T said, "Good," recorded "M_1," and initiated step 1 with S_2, etc.

b. If S_1 again gave an incomplete response (see step 2b), T said, "No," repeated the cue, "Who is standing?," and modeled the correct response, "Say the whole sentence. Say 'I am standing.' " T then repeated the cue, "Who is standing?" If S_1 correctly imitated T's verbal model, T said, "Good," recorded "M_1," and initiated step 1 with S_2, etc.

c. If S_1 did not correctly imitate T's model (see step 2c), T said, "No," repeated the cue, "Who is standing?," and modeled the correct response, "Say the whole sentence. Say 'I am standing.' " T then repeated the cue, "Who is standing?" If S_1 correctly imitated T's verbal model, T said, "Good," recorded "M_2", and initiated step 1 with S_2, etc.

Step 4—If S_1 responded incorrectly in step 3, T followed one of the following procedures:

a. If S_1 used his own proper name instead of "I," T followed the procedures used in step 3a. If S_1 correctly imitated T's second verbal model, T said, "Good," recorded "M_2", and initiated step 1 with S_2, etc.

   b. If S_1 gave an incomplete response, T followed the procedures
      used in step 3b. If S_1 correctly imitated T's second verbal
      model, T said, "Good," recorded "M_2", and initiated step 1
      with S_2, etc.
   c. If S_1 gave an incorrect response, T said, "No! I wanted you
      to say 'I am standing,' " recorded an incorrect response, and
      terminated teaching for this trial. T then proceeded to step 1
      with S_2, etc.

Step 5—If S_1 responded incorrectly in step 4 (a or b), T said, "No!
I wanted you to say 'I am standing,' " recorded an incorrect
response, and terminated teaching for this trial. T then proceeded to step 1 with S_2, etc. When necessary, T proceeded
through step 5 with S_1 before proceeding to step 1 with S_2. However, it should be noted that: (a) steps 2–5 were implemented
only once before T proceeded to S_2, and (b) on subsequent trials,
instruction with S_1 began on step 1. These procedures were followed until each S responded correctly to each of the cues in Sets
I and II under the conditions set forth in step 1 in three consecutive trials.

Phase VII: Teaching Ss to respond to "who-doing" questions with the second person singular pronoun and present progressive verbs.

The objective of Phase VII was to teach Ss to answer questions with
the pronoun "you." That is, T performed an action. S was then asked a
"who-doing" question and was required to respond with the pronoun
"you" and the appropriate present progressive verb. In Phase VI, Ss
were taught to use the pronoun "I" as another way of talking about
themselves. In Phase VII, Ss were taught to use the pronoun "you" when
referring to T, who was asking questions.

The design for Phase VII was as follows: (a) baseline Sets I and II; (b)
teach Set I; (c) rebaseline Sets I and II; (d) teach Set II, if necessary; (e)
rebaseline Sets I and II.

BASELINE PROCEDURES—SETS I AND II

Baseline measures of the tasks in Phase VII were obtained after
Phase VI baselines, but before Phases I–V.

The baseline measures for Phase VII were obtained as follows: Ss
and T were seated in their chairs facing the action corner. T went to the
action corner and performed an action (e.g., standing). While standing, T

said to S_1, "S_1, who is standing?" If S_1 responded correctly by saying "You are standing," T said, "Thank you," recorded a correct response, and presented a different cue to S_2, etc. It should be noted that the only responses recorded as correct were present progressive verbs preceded by "You are."

If S_1 said nothing, responded incorrectly, or gave an incomplete response, T said, "Thank you," recorded the response, and gave a different action and verbal cue to S_2, etc.

If S_1 gave a response containing T's proper name, T attempted to obtain a pronoun response by saying, "Say it another way." T then said, "Thank you," recorded the response, and presented a different action and verbal cue to S_2, etc. Ss were given two opportunities to respond to each of the cues in Sets I and II (i.e., "Who is standing, waving, cutting, combing, reading, and zipping?").

TEACHING PROCEDURES

The procedures described for Phase VI were used to teach Ss to respond correctly to the questions asked in Phase VII. These procedures were followed until each S responded correctly to each of the three cues in Sets I and II in three consecutive trials.

Phase VIII: Teaching Ss to respond to "who-doing" questions with the first and second person singular subject pronouns and present progressive verbs.

In Phase VIII, T presented in an alternating fashion the "who-doing" questions used in Phases VI and VII. That is, either T or S performed an action. S was then asked a "who-doing" question and was required to respond with the appropriate pronoun (either "I" or "you") and the correct present progressive verb.

As stated previously, "I" and "you" appear more difficult to teach than "he" and "she," because the rules for using them cannot be stated simply, and because their use depends on, and varies across, situations. For these reasons, it seemed important to include a phase where the pronouns "I" and "you" were clearly contrasted. By alternately having either T or S perform an action, particular attention was drawn to the differences in the "I" and "you" pronoun responses required.

The design for Phase VIII was as follows: (a) baseline Sets I and II; (b) teach Set I; (c) rebaseline Sets I and II; (d) teach Set II if necessary; (e) rebaseline Sets I and II.

BASELINE PROCEDURES—SETS I AND II

The baseline measures for Phase VIII were obtained as follows: Ss and T were seated in their chairs facing the action corner. T looked at S_1 and said, "Sit in the action corner," while pointing to the appropriate place. When S_1 was seated in the chair, T said, "Show me standing."

While S_1 was standing, T said to S_1, "Who is standing?" T recorded S_1's response, said, "Thank you," and proceeded exactly as described in the baseline procedures for Phase VI. When S_1 had returned to his seat, T went to the action corner and performed an action (e.g., waving). While waving, T said to S_2, "S_2, who is waving?" T recorded S_2's response and proceeded exactly as described in the baseline procedures for Phase VII.

When T returned to her seat, she presented a different cue to S_3, etc. In an alternating fashion, T either performed an action herself or directed an S to do it. Ss were given two opportunities to respond to each of the cues in Sets I and II as performed by themselves and T (i.e., "Who is standing, waving, cutting, combing, reading, and zipping?").

TEACHING PROCEDURES

Step 1—Ss and T were seated in their chairs facing the action corner. T looked at S_1 and said, "Sit in the action corner." When S_1 was seated, T said, "Show me standing." When S_1 was standing, T looked at S_1 and said, "Who is standing?" If S_1 responded correctly by saying "I am standing," T said "Good," recorded a correct response, presented a consumable consequence, and instructed S_1 to return to the group and sit down. T then went to the action corner and gave a different action and verbal cue to S_2, etc.

Steps 2–5—If S_1 responded incorrectly to an action he/she performed, T followed the procedures used in steps 2–5 of Phase VI. If S_1 responded incorrectly to an action performed by T, T followed the procedures used in steps 2–5 of Phase VII.

These procedures were followed until each S responded correctly to each of the action and verbal cues in Sets I and II in three consecutive trials.

Phase IX: Teaching Ss to respond to "who-doing" questions with third person singular subject pronouns and present progressive verbs.

The objective of Phase IX was to teach Ss to use the pronouns "he" and "she" correctly with present progressive verbs in answer to "who-doing" questions. This phase was divided into three parts. In part 1, S s were taught to respond to "who-doing" questions concerning a male classmate performing an action with the singular subject pronoun "he." In part 2, S s were taught to respond to the same "who-doing" questions asked about a female classmate with the singular subject pronoun "she." In part 3, T presented in an alternating fashion the questions used in parts 1 and 2. That is, either a male or female classmate performed an action. S s were then asked "who-doing" questions and were required to respond with the appropriate pronoun ("he" or "she") and the correct present progressive verbs.

The design for Phase IX was as follows: (a) baseline part 3, Sets I and II; (b) teach part 1, Set I; (c) teach part 2, Set I; (d) rebaseline part 3, Sets I and II; (e) teach part 3, Set I; (f) rebaseline part 3, Sets I and II; (g) teach part 3, Set II if necessary; (h) rebaseline part 3, Sets I and II.

BASELINE PROCEDURES—PART 3, SETS I AND II

The baseline measures for Phase IX, part 3, were obtained as follows:[8] S s and T were seated in their chairs facing the action corner. T looked at S_1 and said, "S_1, sit in the action corner," while pointing to the appropriate place. When S_1 was seated in the chair in the action corner, T walked to S_1 and whispered, "Show me standing," into his ear. While S_1 was standing, T walked over to S_2 and said, "Who is standing?" If S_2 responded correctly by saying "He/she is standing," T said, "Thank you," recorded a correct response, and presented a different cue to S_3. It should be noted that the only responses recorded as correct were present progressive verbs preceded by "He/She is."

If S_2 said nothing, responded incorrectly, or gave an incomplete response, T said, "Thank you," recorded the response, and presented a different cue to S_3, etc. If S_2 gave a response containing S_1's proper name, T attempted to obtain a pronoun response by saying, "Say it another way." T then said, "Thank you," recorded S_2's second response, and presented a different cue to S_3, etc. S s were given two opportunities to respond to each of the cues in Sets I and II as performed by two male and two female classmates (i.e., male/female standing, waving, cutting, combing, reading, and zipping).

TEACHING PROCEDURES

The procedures described for Phase VI were used to teach S s to respond correctly to the questions asked in Phase IX, Parts 1, 2, and 3, except that the correct response was "He is standing" in part 1, "She is

[8]Baseline measures of Phase IX, parts 1 and 2 were judged unnecessary.

standing" in part 2, and "He/She is standing" in part 3. These procedures were followed until each S responded correctly to each of the cues in parts 1, 2, and 3 in three consecutive trials.

Phase X: Teaching Ss to respond to "who-doing" questions with first, second, and third person singular subject pronouns and present progressive verbs.

The responses "I am," "You are," and "He/She is" were taught separately in Phases VI, VII, and IX. For this reason, Phase X was included to determine if the Ss could respond with appropriate pronoun responses when the action and verbal cues used in Phases VI–IX were randomly presented. That is, either T, S, or a male or female classmate performed an action. S was then asked a "who-doing" question and was required to respond with the appropriate pronoun and the correct present progressive verb.

One minor change was made in the procedures used for this phase as compared with Phases VI–IX. That is, instead of asking Ss only one question in a single turn, each S was asked four questions. For example, in one turn an S was required to answer "I am standing.," "You are waving.," "He is cutting.," and "She is reading.," in response to appropriate action and verbal cues.

The design for Phase X was as follows: (a) baseline Sets I and II; (b) teach Set I; (c) rebaseline Sets I and II; (d) teach Set II, if necessary; (e) rebaseline Sets I and II.

BASELINE PROCEDURES—SETS I AND II

Ss and T were seated in their chairs facing the action corner. T looked at S_1 and said, "Sit in the action corner." When S_1 was seated in the chair in the action corner, T walked to S_1 and whispered, "Show me standing," into his ear. While S_1 was standing, T said to S_1, "Who is standing?" If S_1 responded correctly by saying "I am standing," T said, "Thank you," recorded a correct response, and presented a different action and verbal cue to S_1. It should be noted that the only responses recorded as correct were present progressive verbs preceded by "I am," "You are," or "He/She is." If S_1 said nothing, responded incorrectly, or gave an incomplete response, T said, "Thank you," recorded the response, and presented a different cue to S_1, etc. If S_1 gave a response containing his own proper name, T attempted to obtain a pronoun response by saying, "Say it another way." T then said, "Thank you," recorded the response, and presented a different cue to S_1. Each S was given two opportunities to respond to each of the cues in Sets I and II as performed by themselves, T, and a male and a female classmate (i.e., "Who is standing, waving, cutting, combing, reading, and zipping?").

TEACHING PROCEDURES

Step 1—Ss and T were seated in their chairs facing the action corner. T looked at S_1 and said, "Sit in the action corner," while pointing to the appropriate place. When S_1 was seated in the action corner, T said, "Show me standing." When S_1 was standing, T looked at S_1 and said, "Who is standing?" If S_1 responded correctly by saying "I am standing," T said, "Good," recorded a correct response, and presented a consumable consequence to S_1. T then went to the action corner and gave a different action and verbal cue to S_1 (e.g., "Who is waving?"), etc. T presented S_1 with four different action and verbal cues before proceeding to S_2.

Steps 2–5—If S_1 responded incorrectly, T followed one of the following procedures:

a. If S_1 responded incorrectly to an action he performed, T followed the procedures used in steps 2–5 of Phase VI.

b. If S_1 responded incorrectly to an action performed by T, T followed the procedures used in steps 2–5 of Phase VII.

c. If S_1 responded incorrectly to an action S_3 (a male) performed, T followed the procedures used in steps 2–5 of Phase IX, part 1.

d. If S_1 responded incorrectly to an action S_2 (a female) performed, T followed the procedures used in steps 2–5 of Phase IX, part 2.

These procedures were followed until each S responded correctly to each of the cues in Sets I and II under the conditions set forth in step 1 in three consecutive trials. In each trial, S was required to respond to questions asked about himself, T, a male classmate, and a female classmate performing each of the actions.

RESULTS

Group A

Ss 1, 2, 3, and 4 (Group A) advanced through the program by attaining a defined criterion performance on each part of each phase. It should be noted that actually two different criterion levels were established. During baseline trials, criterion performance was defined as two consecutive errorless trials on any part of any phase. During teaching trials, criterion performance was defined as three consecutive errorless trials on any part of any phase.[9]

BASELINE MEASURES

Prior to instruction on the tasks required in Phases I–X, baseline measures of each S's ability to perform the tasks required in Phases VI, VII, and IX were obtained. In Phase VI, each S could make from 0 to 3 correct responses to the cues in Sets I and II. In the two baseline trials of Phase VI, Ss 1, 2, 3, and 4 averaged 2.5, 0, 0, and 0 correct responses to the cues in Set 1; and 2, 0, 0, and 0 correct responses in Set II, respectively. In the baseline trials of Phase VII, each S could make from 0 to 3 correct responses in Sets I and II. Ss 1, 2, 3, and 4 averaged 0 correct responses in Sets I and II, respectively. In Phase IX, part 3, each S could make from 0 to 12 correct responses to the cues in Sets I and II. Ss 1, 2, 3, and 4 averaged 0 correct responses to the cues in Sets I and II, respectively.

As can be discerned from the baseline performance, except for S_1, who averaged 2.5 and 2.0 correct responses in Phase VI, Ss made no correct responses during the baseline trials of Phases VI, VII, and IX. In other words, Ss did not answer the "who-doing" questions correctly with "I," "you," "he," or "she" and correct present progressive verbs.

Teaching trials

Table I in Appendix B depicts the number of teaching trials each S required to attain criterion performance in Phases I through X. It should be noted that Ss performed at criterion on selected parts during baseline trials, making instruction on those parts unnecessary.

Phase I

It can be discerned from Table I in Appendix B that during the baseline trials of parts 1, 2, and 3, it was verified that Group A could imitate the required one, two, and three-word verbal responses. Since no incorrect responses were made, teaching trials were unnecessary.

Phase II

Group A made no incorrect responses in the baseline trials of parts 1, 2, and 3. Thus, it was verified that Ss could perform the selected actions in response to verbal cues in part 1, visually discriminate those actions in

---

[9]A graphic depiction of the performance of each S in each phase is available, but it will not be presented here. The reader interested in a graphic presentation of the performance of Ss can write the first author at the Department of Specialized Educational Services, Madison Public Schools, 545 W. Dayton Street, Madison, Wis. 53704.

part 2, and label those actions, using the present progressive verb form in part 3. Since Ss responded correctly to the cues used in parts 1, 2, and 3 in two consecutive trials, instruction was unnecessary.

Phase III

During the two baseline trials of parts 1, 2, 3, and 4, Group A again responded correctly to the cues in all four parts. Thus, it was verified that Ss could visually discriminate by touching: themselves in part 1, T in part 2, their classmates in part 3, and all of the above in part 4 in response to name cues. Since no incorrect responses were made in the baseline trials, instruction was unnecessary.

Phase IV

In the baseline trials of parts 1, 2, and 3, no S manifested criterion performance. In parts 1 and 2, each S could make from 0 to 2 correct responses. Ss 1, 2, 3, and 4 all averaged 0.5 correct responses to the cues in part 1 and 0 correct responses to the cues in part 2. In part 3, each S could make from 0 to 4 correct responses. Ss 1, 2, 3, and 4 averaged 0 correct responses to the cues in part 3.

In part 1, S_1 and S_3 were taught to "Touch a he" and attained criterion performance after only three teaching trials. These two Ss made no incorrect responses after the baseline trials. It appeared that observing T teach the correct response to another S was sufficient to induce correct responding when the cue "Touch a he" was presented. S_2 and S_4 required more teaching trials in order to reach criterion performance (four and five trials, respectively).

In part 2, Ss were taught to visually discriminate a female classmate in response to the cue "Touch a she." As can be discerned from Table I, criterion performance was attained after three teaching trials. It appeared that acquiring the skills necessary to touch a "he" facilitated the performance of the skills necessary to touch a "she."

In part 3, the cues "Touch a he" and "Touch a she" were alternately presented. S_1, S_2, and S_3 responded correctly to the cues when they were alternated. However, six teaching trials were necessary to teach S_4 to visually discriminate male and female classmates when the cues "Touch a he" and "Touch a she" were presented in an alternating manner.

Phase V

Group A made no incorrect responses in the baseline trials of parts 1–7. Thus, it was verified that Ss could make proper name responses to "who" questions containing first, second and third person singular subject pronouns. Since Ss responded correctly to the cues used in parts 1 through 7 in two consecutive baseline trials, instruction was unnecessary.

Phase VI

Baseline measures of Phases VI, VII, and IX were obtained at the start of the program. As noted earlier, S_2, S_3, and S_4 made no correct responses in the baseline trials of Phase VI, Sets I and II. S_1, however, averaged 2.5 of a possible three correct responses in Set I and 2.0 of a possible three correct responses in Set II.

S_1, S_2, S_3, and S_4 received instruction regarding responding to "who-doing" questions with the first person singular subject pronoun and the present progressive verbs in Set I. It can be discerned from Table I that criterion performance was reached after four, six, four, and five teaching trials respectively.

After Ss reached criterion on Set I, baseline measures of Sets I and II were again obtained. Ss maintained correct responding to Set I and made a remarkable three of three correct responses to the questions in Set II. In other words, all four Ss attained criterion performance on Set II without direct instruction.

Because of correct responding on Set II, instruction was unnecessary. The factors that account for improved performance on Set II without teaching cannot be determined. However, it appears that Ss acquired skills related to generalizing responses to "who-doing" questions using the first person singular subject pronoun across different actions.

It should be noted that none of the Ss in Group A responded with incomplete sentences to the questions asked in Phases VI–X. Errors occurred only in Ss using proper names instead of pronouns, selecting the wrong pronouns, or labeling the actions incorrectly. It appeared that requiring Ss to imitate three-word verbal responses in Phase I facilitated the production of those responses in Phases VI–X.

Phase VII

In baseline trials of Phase VII, S_1, S_2, S_3, and S_4 made zero out of three possible correct responses to the questions in Sets I and II, respectively.

S_1, S_2, S_3, and S_4 received instruction regarding responding to "who-doing," questions with the second person singular subject pronoun and the present progressive verbs in Set I. Teaching was unnecessary for S_1 (except for consequation) in that S_1 reached criterion on Set I after three teaching trials. As can be discerned from Table I, S_2, S_3, and S_4 reached criterion after seven, four, and four teaching trials, respectively.

After Ss reached criterion on Set I, baseline measures of Sets I and II were again obtained. Ss maintained correct responding to Set I and made three out of three correct responses to the questions in Set II. As in Phase VI, Ss reached criterion on Set II without direct instruction.

Phase VIII

The baseline measures of Phase VIII were obtained after Ss reached criterion on Sets I and II in Phase VII. It can be discerned from Table 1 that, during the baseline trials of Sets I and II, S_1, S_3, and S_4 made no incorrect responses. Thus, it was verified that three Ss could respond correctly to "who-doing" questions with the first and second person singular subject pronouns "I" and "you" and present progressive verbs. S_2, however, averaged 4.0 of six possible correct responses in Set I and 3.5 of a six possible correct responses in Set II, respectively.

Instruction on Set I was initiated with S_2, and five teaching trials were required before S_2 reached criterion.

In rebaseline trials, S_2 averaged six out of six correct responses to the questions in Sets I and II. In other words, it was necessary to teach S_1 to respond appropriately only to the questions in Set I.

Phase IX

Baseline measures of Phases IX, part 3, were obtained at the start of the program. As noted earlier, Ss made no correct responses in the baseline trials of part 3, Sets I and II. It was deemed unnecessary to baseline parts 1 and 2 since the responses required in parts 1 and 2 were required in part 3.

In part 1, Set I, S_1, S_2, S_3, and S_4 were taught to respond to "who-doing" questions with the third person singular subject pronoun "he" and present progressive verbs. Each S attained criterion performance after four teaching trials.

After Ss reached criterion on part 1, Set I, instruction began on part 2, Set I. In part 2, Ss were taught to respond to "who-doing" questions with the third person singular subject pronoun "she" and present progressive verbs. Only three teaching trials were required before S_1, S_2, and S_3 reached criterion performance. S_4 achieved criterion after five teaching trials.

After Ss reached criterion on Set I of parts 1 and 2, baseline measures of part 3, Sets I and II, were obtained. The number of correct responses increased from 0 of a possible 12 for each S in trials 1 and 2 to 12 of 12 in Sets I and II for S_1, S_2, and S_3. Thus, it was verified that S_1, S_2, and S_3 could respond correctly to "who-doing," questions with the third person singular subject pronouns "he" and "she" and present progressive verbs. S_4, however, averaged 7.5 of a possible 12 correct responses in Set I and 5.5 of a possible 12 correct responses in Set II. Instruction was initiated with S_4 and a total of four teaching trials were required before S_4 achieved criterion on Set I.

In the final rebaseline trials, criterion responding was maintained by
S_4 in response to the questions in both Sets I and II of part 3. In other
words, S_4 reached criterion on Set II without direct instruction.

Phase X

Phase X combined all of the skills required in Phases I–IX. Baseline
measures of Phase X were not obtained until Ss reached criterion in Phase
IX, part 3. As can be discerned from Table I, Ss responded correctly to all
12 action and verbal cues in Sets I and II, respectively.

Thus, it was established that Group A could respond to selected
"who-doing" questions with the first, second, and third person singular
subject pronouns "I," "you," "he," and "she" and present progressive
verbs.

Group B

Ss 5, 6, 7, and 8 (Group B) advanced through the program by attaining a defined criterion performance on each part of each phase. As with
Group A, two different criterion levels were established. During baseline
trials, criterion performance was defined as two consecutive errorless
trials on any part of any phase. During teaching trials, criterion performance was defined as three consecutive errorless trials on any part of any
phase.

BASELINE MEASURES

Prior to instruction on the tasks required in Phases I–X, baseline
measures of each S's ability to perform the tasks required in Phases VI,
VII, and IX were obtained. Neither S_5, S_6, S_7, nor S_8 made a correct
response during the initial baseline trials of Phases VI, VII, and IX. In
other words, Ss did not answer the "who-doing" questions correctly with
"I," "you," "he," or "she" and correct present progressive verbs.

Teaching trials

Table II in Appendix B depicts the number of teaching trials each S
required to attain criterion performance in Phases I–X. It should be noted
that Ss performed at criterion on selected parts during baseline trials,
making instruction on those parts unnecessary.

Phase I

It can be discerned from Table II that during the baseline trials of
parts 1, 2, and 3, it was verified that Group B could imitate the required
one and two-word verbal responses. Since Ss responded correctly to the

cues used in parts 1 and 2, instruction was unnecessary. In the baseline trials of part 3, each S could make from 0 to 6 correct responses to the cues in Sets I–IV. Ss 5, 6, 7, and 8 averaged 6, 6, 5.5, and 3.0 correct responses in Set I; 4.5, 6, 3.0, and 3.0 correct responses in Set II; 2.5, 5.5, 4.5, and 2.0 correct responses in Set III; and 4.0, 6, 3.5, and 1.5 correct responses in Set IV, respectively. As can be discerned from the baseline measures, the teaching of Sets I, II, and IV in part 3 was unnecessary for S_6.

S_5, S_7, and S_8 were taught to imitate the six three-word verbal responses containing the pronoun "I" in part 3, Set I. S_5 attained criterion performance after six teaching trials, while S_7 and S_8 required eight teaching trials.

S_5, S_7, and S_8 achieved criterion imitating the six three-word verbal responses containing the pronoun "you" in part 3, Set II, after seven, nine, and six teaching trials, respectively.

S_5, S_6, S_7, and S_8 were taught to imitate the six three-word verbal responses containing the pronoun "he" in part 3, Set III. Criterion performance was attained after five, four, five, and five teaching trials, respectively.

After Ss completed instruction on part 3, Set IV, baseline measures were again obtained of Ss' responses to the cues in Sets I–IV on two occasions. Group B maintained criterion responding to the cues in all four sets.

Phase II

As can be discerned from Table II, Group B made no incorrect responses in the baseline trials of parts 1 and 2. Thus, it was verified that Ss could perform the selected actions in response to verbal cues in part 1 and visually discriminate those actions in part 2. However, S_6 was the only S who responded correctly to the cues in part 3 in two baseline trials. S_5, S_7, and S_8 averaged 5.5, 5.5, and 0.5 of a possible six correct responses, respectively.

S_5, S_7, and S_8 were taught to label six actions using the present progressive verb form. Criterion performance was attained after three, three, and four teaching trials, respectively.

Phase III

During the two baseline trials of parts 1, 2, 3, and 4, Group B responded correctly to the cues in all four parts. Thus, it was verified that Ss could visually discriminate by touching themselves in part 1, T in part 2, their classmates in part 3, and all of the above in part 4 in response to name cues. Since no incorrect responses were made in the baseline trials, instruction was unnecessary.

Phase IV

In the baseline trials of parts 1, 2, and 3, no S manifested criterion performance. In parts 1 and 2, each S could make from 0 to 2 correct responses. Ss 5, 6, 7, and 8 averaged 1.0, 1.5, 1.0, and 0 correct responses in part 1; and 0, 0.5, 0.5, and 1.5 correct responses in part 2, respectively. In part 3, each S could make from 0 to 4 correct responses. Ss 5, 6, 7, and 8 averaged 2.0, 1.0, 1.5, and 1.5 correct responses, respectively, to the cues in part 3.

In part 1, S_6 was taught to "Touch a he" and attained criterion performance after only three teaching trials. S_6 made no incorrect responses after the baseline trials. It appeared that observing T teach the correct response to another S was sufficient to induce correct responding when the cue "Touch a he" was presented. S_5, S_7, and S_8 required more teaching trials in order to reach criterion performance (four, five, and four trials, respectively).

In part 2, Ss were taught to visually discriminate a female classmate in response to the cue "Touch a she." As can be discerned from Table II, S_5, and S_8 reached criterion performance after three teaching trials. For these Ss, it appeared that acquiring the skills necessary to touch a "he" facilitated the performance of the skills necessary to touch a "she." S_6 and S_7 required more teaching trials in order to reach criterion performance (five and eight trials respectively).

In part 3, the cues "Touch a he" and "Touch a she" were alternately presented. S_5 and S_6 responded correctly to the cues when they were alternated. However, five and four teaching trials, respectively, were necessary to teach S_7 and S_8 to visually discriminate male and female classmates when the cues "Touch a he" and "Touch a she" were presented in an alternating manner.

Phase V

Group B made no incorrect responses in the baseline trials of parts 1–7. Thus, it was verified that Ss could make proper name responses to "who" questions containing first, second, and third person singular subject pronouns. Since Ss responded correctly to the cues used in parts 1–7 in two consecutive baseline trials, instruction was unnecessary.

Phase VI

Baseline measures of Phases VI, VII, and IX were obtained at the start of the program. As noted earlier, Group B made no correct responses in the baseline trials of Phase VI, Sets I and II.

S_5, S_6, S_7, and S_8 received instruction regarding responding to "who-doing" questions with the first person singular subject pronoun and the present progressive verbs in Set I. It can be discerned from Table II that criterion performance was reached after five, five, six, and five teaching trials, respectively.

After S s reached criterion on Set I, baseline measures of Sets I and II were again obtained. S s maintained correct responding to Set I and made a remarkable three out of three correct responses to the questions in Set II. In other words, all four S s attained criterion performance on Set II without direct instruction.

Because of correct responding on Set II, instruction was unnecessary. The factors that account for improved performance on Set II without teaching cannot be determined. However, it appears that like Group A, Group B acquired skills related to generalizing responses to "who-doing" questions using the first person singular subject pronoun across different actions.

It should be noted that Group B responded with only complete sentences to the questions asked in Phases VI–X. It appears that requiring S s to imitate three-word verbal responses in Phase I facilitated the production of those responses in Phases VI–X.

Phase VII

In baseline trials of Phase VII, S_5, S_6, S_7, and S_8 made zero out of three possible correct responses to the questions in Sets I and II respectively. S_5, S_6, S_7, and S_8 received instruction regarding responding to "who-doing" questions with the second person singular pronoun and the present progressive verbs in Set I. As can be discerned from Table 2, S_5, S_6, S_7, and S_8 reached criterion after four, six, six, and four teaching trials, respectively.

After S s reached criterion on Set I, baseline measures of Sets I and II were again obtained. S s maintained correct responding to Set I and made three out of three correct responses to the questions in Set II. As in Phase VI, S s reached criterion on Set II without direct instruction.

Phase VIII

The baseline measures of Phase VIII were obtained after S s reached criterion on Sets I and II in Phase VII. It can be discerned from Table 2 that during the baseline trials of Sets I and II, S_5 made no incorrect responses. Thus, it was verified that S_5 could respond correctly to "who-doing" questions with the first and second person singular subject pronouns "I" and "you" and present progressive verbs. S_6, S_7, and S_8, however, averaged 5.5, 3.0, and 3.0 of a possible six correct responses in Set I and 4.5, 5.5, and 3.0 of a possible six correct responses in Set II, respectively.

Instruction on Set I was initiated with S_6 and four teaching trials were required before S_6 reached criterion. S_7 and S_8 reached criterion performance after five and seven trials, respectively.

In rebaseline trials, S_6, S_7, and S_8 averaged six out of six correct responses to the questions in Sets I and II. In other words, it was necessary to teach S_6, S_7, and S_8 to respond appropriately only to the questions in Set I.

Phase IX

Baseline measures of Phase IX, part 3, were obtained at the start of the program. As noted earlier, Ss made no correct responses in the baseline trials of part 3, Sets I and II. It was deemed unnecessary to baseline parts 1 and 2 since the responses required in parts 1 and 2 were required in part 3.

In part 1, Set I, S_5, S_6, S_7, and S_8 were taught to respond to "who-doing" questions with the third person singular subject pronoun "he" and present progressive verbs. Each S attained criterion performance after four teaching trials.

After S reached criterion on part 1, Set I, instruction began on part 2, Set I. In part 2, S were taught to respond to "who-doing" questions with the third person singular subject pronoun "she" and present progressive verbs. Only three teaching trials were required before S_6 reached criterion performance. S_5, S_7, and S_8 achieved criterion after four, four, and five teaching trials, respectively.

After Ss reached criterion on Set I of parts 1 and 2, baseline measures of part 3, Sets I and II were obtained. The number of correct responses increased from 0 of a possible 12 for each S in trials 1 and 2 to 12 of 12 in Sets I and II for S_5, S_6, and S_7. Thus, it was verified that S_5, S_6, and S_7 could respond correctly to "who-doing" questions with the third person singular subject pronouns "he" and "she" and present progressive verbs. S_8, however, averaged 6 of a possible 12 correct responses in Sets I and II. S_8 responded to all the cues in part 3 with the pronoun "she," whether a male or female classmate had performed the action. In this and other instances when responses taught separately were combined, S_8 tended to respond with the most recently learned responses. In this case, those were the responses containing the pronoun "she" and present progressive verbs. Instruction was initiated with S_8 and a total of four teaching trials were required before S_8 achieved criterion on Set I.

In the final rebaseline trials, criterion responding was maintained by S_8 in response to the questions in both Sets I and II of part 3. In other words, S_8 reached criterion on Set II without direct instruction.

Phase X

Phase X combined all of the skills required in Phases I–IX. Baseline measures of Phase X were not obtained until Ss reached criterion in Phase IX, part 3. As can be discerned from Table II, S_5 responded correctly to all

12 action and verbal cues in Sets I and II, respectively. S_6, S_7, and S_8, however, averaged only 8.5, six, and six correct responses in Set I; and eight, six, and six correct responses in Set II, respectively. As in Phase IX, Ss seemed to be responding with the most recently learned responses ("he" and "she").

S_6, S_7, and S_8 were taught to respond to "who-doing" questions with first, second, and third person singular subject pronouns and the present progressive verbs in Set I. Criterion performance was reached after three, six, and four teaching trials, respectively.

When Group B reached criterion on Set I, baseline measures of Sets I and II were again obtained. Ss maintained correct responding to Set I, and made 12 of a possible 12 correct responses to the questions in Set II.

Thus, it was established that Group B could respond to selected "who-doing" questions with the first, second, and third person singular subject pronouns "I," "you," "he," and "she" and present progressive verbs.

DISCUSSION

The performance of the students in Groups A and B as reported above strongly suggests that the two major objectives of the program were realized in that: (a) the students responded correctly to the "who" questions presented; and (b) they used semantically and syntactically acceptable first, second, and third person singular pronoun responses.

While the skills acquired certainly do not solve all the developmental communication problems of the students, they do provide them access to communication vehicles heretofore unavailable. That is, they now have a reasonable probability of understanding pronouns presented in reading material, and have a higher probability of social acceptance in that their speech patterns are more similar to their nonhandicapped age peers.

In addition to the empirical data presented above, there were other notable changes in the communication repertoires of the students. While observations of these changes can only be considered anecdotal, they are nevertheless worthy of presentation here. First, it appeared that longer verbal response chains were emitted by the students as they progressed through the final phases. For example, students frequently answered "who-doing" questions with responses such as: "She is reading a book."; "He is cutting paper with a scissors." These responses are in marked contrast to the single-word responses typically observed prior to the program.

Second, the students often generalized pronouns appropriately across classroom activities. For example, during the baseline trials of another program concerned with the development of preposition usage skills, the teacher asked each student where he or she was standing. Several students reported their positions by saying, "I am standing in front of Marge."

Third, it appeared that some degree of generalization also occurred in the student's ability to visually discriminate between males and females. After the students had reached criterion in Phase IV, using male and female classmates, the teacher used herself, the student teacher, and the principal in various male–female combinations. All of the students responded correctly to the cues "Touch a he" and "Touch a she" the first time they were requested to do so.

Inasmuch as the students are in need of other communication skills, it seems that the teacher can now entertain several programmatic options, which include: requiring longer, more embellished responses; requiring responses to "who" questions, using other verbs and a different teacher; developing similar responses using the pronouns "it," "we," and "they"; and developing similar responses to other "wh" question forms.

Finally, now that the skills taught here have been developed in oral communication situations, they will be applied to reading materials in some of the following ways: (1) Students will be asked to answer "who" questions about pictures of characters in their reading books. (2) Students will be asked to read a sentence (e.g., He is standing.) and select the picture that illustrates it. (3) Students will be asked to read a story and answer "who-doing" questions about the characters.

ADDENDUM

An attempt was made to investigate whether the skills acquired would be performed during other classroom activities in response to "who-doing" questions other than those taught. Four activities were chosen (reading, math, printing, and self-help), and two questions were asked during each activity (e.g., "Who is tying the shoe?", "Who is counting the pennies?"). Either the teacher, the student himself, or a male or female classmate performed an action. The student was then asked a "who-doing" question and his/her response was recorded by the teacher without indicating accuracy. All four of the students in Group A responded correctly to both questions in each of the four activities the first time they were requested to do so.

Thus, it would appear that if environmental demands are made on the students that require them to use pronouns in answer to "who" questions, they are capable of meeting such demands. Unfortunately, the school year ended before this program supplement could be initiated with Group B.

REFERENCES

Bricker DD, Bricker WA: Toddler Research and Intervention Project: Year I. IMRID Behavioral Science Monograph No. 20, Institute on Mental Retardation and Intellectual Development, George Peabody College, Nashville, Tenn., 1971

Bricker WA, Bricker DD: Assessment and modification of verbal imitation with low-functioning retarded children. J Speech Hearing Res 15(4):690–698, 1972

Keane VE: The incidence of speech and language problems in the mentally retarded. Ment Retard 10:3–8, 1972

McLean J, Yoder D, Schiefelbusch R: Language Intervention with the Retarded. Baltimore, Md., University Park Press, 1972

Schiefelbusch R, Copeland R, Smith JO: Language and Mental Retardation. New York, Holt, Rinehart and Winston, 1967

Schlanger B: Issues for speech and language training of the mentally retarded, in Schiefelbusch R, Copeland R, Smith JO (eds): Language and Mental Retardation. New York, Holt, Rinehart and Winston, 1967

Sontag E, Burke P, York R: Considerations for serving the severely handicapped in the public schools. Educ Train Ment Retard 8:20–26, 1973

Waryas CL: Psycholinguistic research in language intervention programming: The pronoun system. J Psycholing Res 2:221–237, 1973

Yoder D: Wh-Questions. Unpublished material, University of Wisconsin, Madison, Wis., 1972

APPENDIX A: SAMPLE DATA SHEETS

Date _____   Phase I   Part 1   Trial _____

Name	I	you	he	she	am	are	is	stand-ing	wav-ing	cut-ting	comb-ing	read-ing	zip-ping	

(Total)

Cue: "S_1, say 'I'."
1. If S immediately imitates the verbal model, record (+).
2. If S imitates model as in Step 2, record (M_2).
3. If S does not imitate the model as in Step 3, record (−).

Date _____   Phase II   Part 1   Trial _____

Name	standing	waving	cutting	combing	reading	zipping	

(Total)

Cue: "Show me _____."
1. If S immediately follows T's verbal cue, record (+)
2. If S follows verbal cue after T models response as in Step 2, record (M).
3. If S follows verbal cue with physical guidance from T as in Step 3, record (P).

Date _____   <u>Phase II</u>   Part 2   Trial _____

Cue: "Touch someone _____."

	S_1	S_2	S_3	S_4
standing - waving				
standing - *waving*				
cutting - combing				
cutting - *combing*				
reading - zipping				
reading - *zipping*				

1. If S immediately follows verbal cue, record (+).
2. If S follows cue after T models correct response as in Step 2, record (M).
3. If S follows verbal cue with physical guidance from T as in Step 3, record (P).

Date _____   <u>Phase II</u>   Part 3   Trial _____

Name	standing	waving	cutting	combing	reading	zipping	

(Total)

Cue: "What is S_1 doing?"

1. If S immediately labels action, record (+).
2. If S labels action after modeled by T as in Step 2, record (M).
3. If S labels action after second model by T as in Step 3, record (M$_2$).
4. If S does not label action as in Step 4, record (−).

Date_____   Phase III   Part 4   Trial _____

Name	S_1	S_2	S_3	S_4	T	

(Total)

Cue: "S_1, touch S_1" (S_2, S_3, S_4 and T)

1. If S immediately follows verbal cue, record (+).
2. If S follows cue after T models correct response as in Step 2, record (M).
3. If S follows verbal cue with physical guidance from T as in Step 3, record (P).

Date _____   Phase IV   Part 3   Trial_____

Males (S_1, S_3, S_5)   Females (S_2, S_4, S_6)

Name	S_1 & S_2	S_1 & S_2	S_3 & S_4	S_3 & S_4	S_5 & S_6	S_5 & S_6	
S_1							
S_2							
S_3							
S_4							

(Total)

Cue: "Touch a he; Touch a she."

1. If S immediately follows verbal cue, record (+).
2. If S follows verbal cue after modeled by T as in Step 2, record (M).
3. If S follows verbal cue with physical guidance from T as in Step 3, record (P).

Date _____   Phase V   Part 7   Trial_____

Cues: "Who am I?; Who are you?;
Who is he?; Who is she?"

Name	T	S_1	S_2	S_3	S_4	S_5	S_6	
S_1			.					
S_2								
S_3								
S_4								

(Total)

1. If S immediately responds to verbal cue, record (+).
2. If S responds to verbal cue after first model by T as in Step 2, record (M_1).
3. If S responds to verbal cue after second model by T as in Step 3, record (M_2).
4. If S does not respond correctly to T's verbal cue in Step 4, record (−).

Baseline—Phases VI, VII, IX

Date _____   Phase _____   Trial _____

Name	(+) or (−)	Response (1)	Response (2)

Correct response _____
Cue: "Who is _____?"

1. If S says the correct response, record (+).
2. If S says anything else, or nothing, record (−) and write response under Response (1).
3. If S includes proper name in 1st response, record first response (1). Then say, "Say it another way." Record 2nd response under Response (2).

Teaching and Rebaseline—Phases VI–X

Date _____ Phase _____ Part _____ Trial _____

Name	1st response	record

Correct response _____
Cue: "Who is _____?"

Step 1: Correct response: "I am _____" (record +)

Step 2: If S responds correctly to the cues in Step 2, record S's first response and:

(a)	(b)	(c)
Proper name R	Incomplete R	Incorrect R
+ C_2 (a)	+ C_2 (b)	M_1
(correct R—2nd cue)	(correct R—2nd cue)	

Step 3: If S responds correctly to the cues in Step 3, record S's first response and:

| M_1 | M_1 | M_2 |

Step 4: If S responds correctly to the cues in Step 4 (a or b) record S's first response and: If S does not imitate the 2nd model, record:

| M_2 | M_2 | $(-)$ |

Step 5: If S does not imitate the 2nd model as in Step 5 (a or b) record first response and:

| $(-)$ | $(-)$ |

Table I
Teaching Trials to Criteriom: Group A

Group A Name	Phase I Part 1	Part 2	Part 3 Set I	Set II	Set III	Set IV	Phase II Part 1	Part 2	Part 3	Phase III Part 1	Part 2	Part 3	Part 4	Phase IV Part 1	Part 2	Part 3
S_1	0	0	0	0	0	0	0	0	0	0	0	0	0	3	3	3
S_2	0	0	0	0	0	0	0	0	0	0	0	0	0	4	3	3
S_3	0	0	0	0	0	0	0	0	0	0	0	0	0	3	3	3
S_4	0	0	0	0	0	0	0	0	0	0	0	0	0	5	3	6

Group A Name	Phase V Part 1	Part 2	Part 3	Part 4	Part 5	Part 6	Part 7	Phase VI Set I	Set II	Phase VII Set I	Set II	Phase VIII Set I	Set II
S_1	0	0	0	0	0	0	0	4	0	3	0	0	0
S_2	0	0	0	0	0	0	0	6	0	7	0	5	0
S_3	0	0	0	0	0	0	0	4	0	4	0	0	0
S_4	0	0	0	0	0	0	0	5	0	4	0	0	0

Group A	Phase IX						Phase X	
	Part 1		Part 2		Part 3			
Name	Set I	Set II	Set I	Set II	Set I	Set II	Set I	Set II
S_1	4	0	3	0	0	0	0	0
S_2	4	0	3	0	0	0	0	0
S_3	4	0	3	0	0	0	0	0
S_4	4	0	5	0	4	0	0	0

Criterion was set at 3 consecutive correct trials without teacher assistance. "0" refers to the fact that criterion was reached during the 2 baseline trials. "3" refers to the fact that criterion was reached after the first 3 teaching trials.

Table II
Teaching Trials to Criterion Group B

Group B Name	Phase I Part 1	Phase I Part 2	Phase I Part 3 Set I	Phase I Part 3 Set II	Phase I Part 3 Set III	Phase I Part 3 Set IV	Phase II Part 1	Phase II Part 2	Phase II Part 3	Phase III Part 1	Phase III Part 2	Phase III Part 3	Phase III Part 4	Phase IV Part 1	Phase IV Part 2	Phase IV Part 3
S_5	0	0	6	7	5	6	0	0	3	0	0	0	0	4	3	3
S_6	0	0	0	0	4	0	0	0	0	0	0	0	0	3	5	3
S_7	0	0	8	9	5	5	0	0	3	0	0	0	0	5	8	5
S_8	0	0	8	6	5	5	0	0	4	0	0	0	0	4	3	4

Group B Name	Phase V Part 1	Phase V Part 2	Phase V Part 3	Phase V Part 4	Phase V Part 5	Phase V Part 6	Phase V Part 7	Phase VI Set I	Phase VI Set II	Phase VII Set I	Phase VII Set II	Phase VIII Set I	Phase VIII Set II
S_5	0	0	0	0	0	0	0	5	0	4	0	0	0
S_6	0	0	0	0	0	0	0	5	0	6	0	4	0
S_7	0	0	0	0	0	0	0	6	0	6	0	4	0
S_8	0	0	0	0	0	0	0	5	0	4	0	7	0

Group B	Phase IX						Phase X	
	Part 1		Part 2		Part 3			
Name	Set I	Set II	Set I	Set II	Set I	Set II	Set I	Set II
S_5	4	0	4	0	0	0	0	0
S_6	4	0	3	0	0	0	3	0
S_7	4	0	4	0	0	0	6	0
S_8	4	0	5	0	4	0	4	0

Criterion was set at 3 consecutive correct trials without teacher assistance. "0" refers to the fact that criterion was reached during the 2 baseline trials. "3" refers to the fact that criterion was reached after the first 3 teaching trials.

Weston Williams, Peggy Coyne,
Fran Johnson, Nancy Scheuerman,
Barbara Swetlik, and Robert York

B

Skill Sequences and Curriculum Development: Application of a Rudimentary Developmental Math Skill Sequence in the Instruction and Evaluation of Severely Handicapped Students[1,2]

PURPOSE OF THE SEQUENCE AND HOW TO USE IT

Educational objectives for severely handicapped students should encompass skills which will enhance their ability to effectively interact with objects, events, and people across environments. Teaching students to functionally use skills related to the concepts of sets, one–many, one-to-one correspondence, equivalence, more and less, counting, addition, subtraction, money, time-telling and calendar should enhance students' abilities to effectively interact with their environment. This paper will attempt to communicate the current thinking of several classroom teachers of severely handicapped students regarding the components of a functional math skill sequence (i.e., math skills with utility across environments) from zero skills through rudimentary addition.

[1]The development and dissemination of this paper was supported in part by Madison Public Schools, Federal Contract No. OEC-0-74-7993, and in part by Grant No. OEG-0-73-6137 to the University of Wisconsin-Madison, from the Department of HEW, Bureau for Education of the Handicapped, Division of Training Programs, Washington, D.C.

[2]Extensive revision of "A Rudimentary Developmental Math Skill Sequence for Severely Handicapped Students," W. Williams, P. Coyne, F. Johnson, N. Scheuerman, J. Stepner, and B. Swetlik, August, 1974.

The sequence delineated should not be viewed as a recipe or a prescription, but rather as an illustration. This sequence is dynamic; that is, it is in a continuous process of refinement and revision based upon the students' performance within it. Thus, what is depicted here is a selected snapshot of a continuously developing sequence. In short, a math skills sequence with a sampling of activities teachers may use to supplement their daily planning is delineated.

At least three factors necessitate the development and delineation of empirically verified math skill sequences or curricula for severely handicapped individuals. (1) Sequential programming of mathematical skills provides teachers with basic notions of what math skills to teach and when to teach them. That is, a skill sequence delineates starting points, terminal objectives, and enhances the possibility that essential component skills will not be neglected. (2) Potentially there are many math skill sequences which may be used in the instruction of severely handicapped students. However, it is advantageous for students to progress through one flexible sequence rather then components of several potentially incompatible sequences. Developmental skill sequences should minimize the potentially deleterious effects of changes in teachers and administrators on the long-term programming of severely handicapped students. (3) Most existing math skill curricula are not directly applicable to severely handicapped students. They are not applicable for at least four reasons: (a) they do not allow for sufficient practice or instruction of skills; (b) they are locked into instructional procedures (e.g., large group instruction, worksheets) which are often not appropriate for individual severely handicapped students; (c) they teach the skills through relatively nonfunctional tasks, and thus the skills taught are often nonfunctional for severely handicapped students (e.g., they may teach one-to-one correspondence by requiring the students to match circles to squares, while a more functional task might require students to match straws to cups); (d) they require that the students process relatively high-level receptive and expressive language repertoires.

The applicability of many of the components of the skill sequence articulated below has been empirically verified for severely handicapped students. However, at this point, no severely handicapped student has progressed through the entire sequence of skills. Thus, although the efficacy of individual components has been empirically verified, the entire sequence has not.

SEQUENCE RATIONALE

The underlying rationale for the sequence evolved from the notion that there are basic concepts and operations which may be utilized in the solution of most math problems. In the sequence articulated here, the fundamental concepts encompass sets, counting, and equivalence.

The first step in the sequence (See the Scope and Sequence Chart) involves teaching students to sort objects into sets (i.e., place objects that vary along at least one dimension into separate units of space

(e.g., $\begin{smallmatrix} \bigcirc\bigcirc\triangle \\ \triangle\bigcirc\triangle \end{smallmatrix} \rightarrow \begin{smallmatrix} \triangle & \bigcirc \\ \triangle\triangle & \bigcirc\bigcirc \end{smallmatrix}$). Next, students are taught to match the members of sets in one-to-one correspondence

(e.g., $\begin{smallmatrix} & \bigcirc & & \triangle \\ \bigcirc & \bigcirc & & \triangle \\ & \bigcirc & & \triangle \end{smallmatrix} \rightarrow \begin{smallmatrix} \bigcirc & & \triangle \\ \bigcirc & \bigcirc & \triangle \\ \bigcirc & & \triangle \end{smallmatrix} \rightarrow \begin{smallmatrix} \bigcirc & \triangle \\ \bigcirc & \triangle \\ \bigcirc & \bigcirc & \triangle \end{smallmatrix}$).[3] When students demonstrate that they can use the operation of one-to-one correspondence to match sets on the basis of quantity, they are taught equivalence. That is, students are taught to utilize the operation of one-to-one correspondence to determine if sets are equivalent and to separate equivalent sets by an equals sign (e.g. ☐ ☐ → ☐+☐ → ☐ = ☐).

Subsequent to equivalence, the students are taught addition. Addition as conceptualized in this program involves the student joining two sets of objects to form a new set (e.g., a set of circles and/plus a set of triangles is/equals a set of circles and triangles or $\bigcirc\bigcirc + \triangle\triangle = \bigcirc\bigcirc\triangle\triangle$ Addition also entails the students using the operation of one-to-one correspondence and/or rational counting to determine if the sets on both sides of the equals sign contain the same quantity (e.g., $\bigcirc\bigcirc + \triangle\triangle = \bigcirc\bigcirc\triangle\triangle$

Concurrent to teaching the concepts of sets, one-to-one correspondence, equivalence and rudimentary addition, the concepts of one-many and more/less are taught. It may be helpful to translate the rationale into more concrete examples from the math skill sequence. In the following paragraphs, we will briefly describe selected components of the skill sequence and how they relate to each other.

Sets

The sets component of the skill sequence teaches students to sort objects along specified dimensions (e.g., form, color, size). Concurrent with learning to sort objects along selected dimensions, students learn the names of the object dimensions (e.g., object names, color, size). Objec-

---

[3]The lines indicate the student's performance of the one-to-one correspondence operation.

tive 8 of the sets component teaches students to join sets of objects to make a new set (e.g., make a set of blocks and/plus bears). Joining sets is the basis of addition.

One—Many

In the one–many component of the skill sequence students are taught to discriminate between one and many objects. In later components (one-to-one correspondence, more/less, counting), this skill is elaborated to teach students to discriminate between one and two objects, eight and ten objects, etc.

One–to–One Correspondence

In the one-to-one correspondence component, students are taught to align the members of two sets in one-to-one correspondence. The students learn to solve three basic problems through aligning members of sets in one-to-one correspondence: (1) equivalence—the sets to be aligned in one-to-one correspondence have the same number of members; (2) addition—the sets to be aligned in one-to-one correspondence are not equivalent ($: \neq :$) and the students learn to determine and indicate there are "not enough" members of one set, and they have to add/plus more objects to one set to make the sets equal. For instance, although students do not know the concept of 2 or 4, they learn to use one-to-one correspondence to add 2 more objects to the set of 2 to make it equivalent to the set of 4. This problem is a concrete form of the more abstract problem 2 + ____ = 4. In later components of the skill sequence, students will learn the concepts of 2, 4, etc., that 2 is less than 4, and to solve problems presented in the abstract form of 2 + ____ = 4; (3) subtraction—the sets to be aligned in one-to-one correspondence are not equivalent, and the students learn to use one-to-one correspondence to determine and indicate that one set has "too many" objects, and they have to "take away"/"subtract" members from one set to make the sets equal. For example, although students do not know the concept of 3 or 2, they learn to use one-to-one correspondence to take one number away from the set of 3 objects to make the sets equal. This is a concrete form of the more abstract problem 3 − ____ = 2.

Equivalence

Equivalence is an extension of one-to-one correspondence. In the equivalence component of the skills sequence, students learn the terms "equal," "not equal" and the equals sign "=" which correspond to the terms "enough" and "not enough" they learned through one-to-one correspondence. Equivalence problems may be solved by two methods: (1) counting the objects in two sets and indicating that 3 equals 3; and (2) aligning the members of each set in one-to-one correspondence to determine set equivalence. Students who use the first method are taught a self-regulation procedure for detecting and correcting their own errors. That is, if a student incorrectly or correctly indicates that 3 equals 3, the teacher asks, "How can you tell?" Then the student aligns the members of the sets in one-to-one correspondence to check and, if necessary, correct the answer. Throughout the remaining components of skill sequence, similar self-regulation procedures are delineated to teach students to detect and correct their own mistakes.

More and Less

In the more and less component of the skill sequence, students learn to use one-to-one correspondence to determine which sets have more or less members. At this point in the sequence, students have not learned that 4 is more than 3 or 8 is less than 10, etc. Thus, they determine more and less by aligning members of sets in one-to-one correspondence, and designating the set with at least one member left over as the set with more. Conservation of number is introduced in the more and less component of the skill sequence. That is, students are taught to determine the equivalence of sets, even when the sets are not aligned in one-to-one correspondence (e.g., $..\overset{....}{\overset{||}{..}}.$ or $.\overset{...}{\overset{||}{..}}.$ or $.\overset{\bullet\;\bullet}{\overset{||}{.}}.$), or the arrangement of the members of one set is significantly changed after equivalence has been determined (e.g., $..\overset{..\;..}{\overset{||}{..}}.. \rightarrow ..\overset{..\;..}{\overset{||}{..}}..$). Subsequent to more and less, in the ordering numerals and ordering quantities components of the skill sequence, students learn that 2 is less than 4 and 8 is more than 7, etc., and then they no longer have to rely solely on one-to-one correspondence to determine which set is more or less.

Counting Forward

As delineated above, addition problems can be solved through one-to-one correspondence. Addition problems may also be solved through counting the number of additional objects needed to make 2 sets equal (: + ＿＿ = ⋮). In the counting forward component of the skill sequence, students learn to rationally count (count objects), rote count (count without object referents), count from a number to a number (e.g., count from 3 to 9), match a numeral to a quantity (e.g., $\boxed{.}\ \overset{/3}{\boxed{:}}\ \boxed{:}$), match a quantity to a numeral (e.g., $2\ \overset{\boxed{\cdots}}{\diagdown}3$), order numerals (e.g., 2 3 4 6 5 1 → 1 2 3 4 5 6), order quantities (e.g., ⬚ ⬚ ⬚ → ⬚ ⬚ ⬚),   which numbers are more and less than other numbers, and which numbers come before and after other numbers.

Addition

In the addition component of the skill sequence, students learn to join two sets of objects to make a third set of objects with more members than either of the two sets joined. Joining sets was also taught in objective eight of the sets component of the skills sequence. As delineated above, concrete addition is taught in the one-to-one corresponding component. The addition component of the sequence elaborates on the skills taught in objective eight of sets and one-to-one correspondence through teaching students to use the skills of rational counting, rote counting, matching numerals to quantities, matching quantities to numerals, more, less, equivalence, and ordering numerals to more efficiently solve addition problems.

SCOPE AND SEQUENCE

Listed below are the major components of the math skills sequence and their prerequisites. The chart which follows the listing of each major component and its prerequisite is a depiction of this listing (the program scope and sequence) in a chart format.

A. PREREQUISITES

1. Imitation
2. Functional object use

B. SETS

a. Motor imitation

C. ONE–MANY

a. Sorting objects which differ along at least one dimension (B. sets, objective 2)

D. ONE–TO–ONE CORRESPONDENCE

a. Sorting objects which differ along at least one dimension (B. sets, objective 2)

E. EQUIVALENCE

a. Discriminating one from many (C. one–many, objective 1)
b. Arranging objects in a configuration which manifests one-to-one correspondence (D. one-to-one correspondence, objective 1)

F. MORE AND LESS
1. More
a. Discriminating one from many (C. one–many, objective 1)
b. Arranging objects in a configuration which manifests one-to-one correspondence (D. one-to-one correspondence, objective 1)
c. Rational count to 10 (G. counting, 1. rational, objective 3)
d. Discriminate equivalence (E. equivalence, objective 2)
2. Less
a. Discriminate more (F. more and less, 1. more)
3. More/Less
a. Discriminate more and less (F. more and less, 1. more and 2. less)
4. Conservation of number
a. Discriminate more from less (F. more and less, 3. more/less)

G. COUNTING FORWARD
1. Rational
a. Verbal imitation and/or signing
b. Sorting objects which vary along at least one dimension (B. sets, objective 2)
2. Rote
a. Rational count to 10 (G. counting, 1. rational, objective 3)
3. Numeral recognition
a. Rational count to 10 (G. counting, 1. rational, objective 3)
4. Matching numerals to quantities
a. Rational count to 10 (G. counting, 1. rational, objective 3)
b. Discriminate numerals 1 through 10 (G. counting, 3. numeral recognition, objective 1)
5. Matching quantities to numerals
a. Rational count to 10 (G. counting, 1. rational, objective 3)
b. Discriminate numerals 1 through 10 (G. counting, 3. numeral recognition, objective 1)
6. Ordering numerals
a. Rational count to 10 (G. counting, 1. rational, objective 3)
b. Rote count to 10 (G. counting, 2. rote, objective 2)
c. Discriminate numerals 1 through 10 (G. counting, 3. Numeral recognition, objective 1)
7. Ordering quantities
a. Discriminate more from less (F. more and less)
b. Order numerals from 1 to 10 (G. counting, 6. ordering numerals)

H. ADDITION
1. Addition with objects ($\square + \square = \square$).
a. Join sets of unlike objects (B. sets, objective 8)

b. Rational count to 10 (G. counting, 1. rational, objective 3)
c. Equivalence (E. equivalence, objective 2)
2. Numerals and objects (⊡ + ⊡ = ⊡).
               1   2   3
   a. Discriminate numerals 1 through 10 (G. counting, 3. Numeral recognition, objective 1)
   b. Match numerals 1 through 10 to a quantity (G. counting, 4. matching numerals to quantities, objective 1)
   c. Match quantities 1 to 10 to a numeral (G. counting, 5. matching numerals to quantities, objective 1)
   d. Join sets of objects and tell how many (H. addition, 1. objects)
3. Numerals and lines (⊡ + ⊡ = ⊡).
              1   2   3

   a. Ability to draw lines
   b. Add objects using numerals to denote the number (H. addition, 2. numerals and objects, objective 1)
4. Numerals (1 + 2 = 3)

   a. Add using numerals and lines to denote number (H. addition, 3. numerals and lines, objective 1)
5. Fingers (2 + 2 = ____ and 2 + ____ = 4)
   a. Rote count from a number to a number from 1 to 10 (G. counting, 2. rote, objective 3)
6. Facts
   a. Rote count from a number to a number from 1 to 10 (G. counting, 2. rote, objective 3)
   b. Add using numerals and lines (H. addition, 4. numerals, objective 1) and/or add using fingers (H. addition, 5. fingers, objective 1)

I. STORY PROBLEMS

1. One-to-one correspondence
   a. Motor imitation
   b. Sorting objects which differ along at least one dimension (B. sets, objective 2)
   c. Rational count to five (G. counting, 1. rational, objective 2)
2. X + Y = ____
   a. Add using numerals and lines (H. addition, 4. numerals, objective 1) and/or add using fingers (H. addition, 5. fingers, objective 2)
3. X + ____ = Y
   a. Add using fingers (H. addition, 5. fingers, objective 4)

Scope and Sequence Chart

Objectives

Skill	1	2	3	4	5	6	7	8	9	10	11	12	13	14	15	16	17	18
A. Prerequisites																		
1. Imitation	1																	
2. Functional Object Use	1																	
B. Sets	1	2	3	4	5	6	7	8	9									
C. One-Many			1	2	3													
D. One-to-One Correspondence			1															
E. Equivalence				1	2													
F. More and Less																		
1. More							1											
2. Less								1	2									
3. More/Less										1	2							
4. Conservation of Number												1	2	3	4	5	6	
G. Counting Forward																		
1. Rational				1	2	3	4	5	6	7								
2. Rote								1	2	3								
3. Numeral Recognition								1										
4. Matching Numerals to Quantities								1										
5. Matching Quantities to Numerals								1										
6. Ordering Numerals									1	2	3	4	5	6	7	8	9	
7. Ordering Quantities																		1
H. Addition (Equation)																		
1. Objects								1	2									
2. Numerals and Objects									1									
3. Numerals and Lines										1								
4. Numerals											1							
5. Fingers												1	2	3	4			
6. Facts										1	2	3	4	5	6			
I. Story Problems																		
1. One-to-One Correspondence						1												
2. X + Y = __											1							
3. X + __ = Y															1			

All the skills taught in the sequence are listed vertically (functional object use, imitation, sets, etc.). The objectives for each skill are listed horizontally. As can be discerned from the chart, the objectives of various skills may often be taught concurrently. For instance, a student could be learning objectives 3, 4, 5 of sets concurrently with objectives 1, 2, 3 of one-many.

ADAPTING THE MATH SKILLS SEQUENCE

A skill sequence is a task analysis, and involves the precise delineation of the skills to be taught broken into their component parts and sequenced from simple to complex. According to Resnick, Wang, and Kaplan (1974) task analysis involves:

> (the) develop(ment of) hierarchies of learning objectives such that mastery of objectives lower in the hierarchy (simpler tasks) facilitates learning of higher objectives (more complex tasks) . . . . This involves a process of task analysis in which specific behavioral components are identified and prerequisites for each of these determined. (p. 680)

A skills sequence or task analysis of a curriculum area is delineated to provide an organized set of learning objectives around which instructional programs of many types may be organized. A skills sequence is not a statement of how a task is to be taught or assessed, but rather a prerequisite to the delineation of specific instructional and measurement procedures.

The underlying assumption of a skill sequence is that most students learn skills in the same order. However, a skills sequence should be adapted to individual student needs (e.g., motor handicaps, blindness, deafness, muteness). In adapting a skill sequence to individual students, the basic presentation order of skills may be constant across students. However, when needed, the sequence may be modified or broken into smaller steps. A skills sequence may be adapted to individual students through: (a) adapting instructional procedures; (b) adapting tasks and materials; and (c) adapting response requirements.

Adapting Instructional Procedures

Many instructional procedures may be used to teach the same skill (e.g., play activities, highly structured drills, group instruction, individual instruction, combinations of group, and individual instruction), and procedures which are most effective with students of concern should be used. However, whatever instructional procedures are used, the teacher can use the skill sequence to monitor student progress.

After delineating how to adapt the tasks and responses to be used in the math skills sequence, a basic instructional procedure we have found to be relatively successful with severely handicapped students is articulated and its adaption to the sequence illustrated.

Adapting Tasks and Materials

A skill may be taught through many tasks and materials. The tasks and materials selected to teach a skill should be chosen on the basis of their: (a) functional use to the individual student; (b) accessibility or frequency of occurrence across the environment of the individual student; (c) reinforcement value to the individual student; (d) facilitation of discrimination learning; (e) applicability to repeated practice during skill acquisition; (f) facilitation of later skill development; and (g) facilitation of skill maintenance.

Selecting tasks on the basis of functional use involves selecting tasks students can potentially use outside a controlled instructional setting. For example, the operation of sorting (concept of sets) can be taught through teaching students to sort circles and squares into separate sets in the classroom, pennies and nickels into separate sets in the classroom, glasses and silverware into separate sets while the students are doing the dishes, and food and nonfood items into sets while the students are preparing a snack. In the above example, sorting dishes and food items are more functional tasks that may be utilized when teaching sorting than sorting circles and squares.

Choosing tasks based upon the criterion of accessibility or frequency of occurrence involves teaching students skills through tasks which they may encounter in environments they frequently inhabit. For instance, setting the table is a functional task through which the operation of one-to-one correspondence may be taught. However, for students who live in an environment in which they are not, and probably will not, be required to set the table, the task is relatively inappropriate.

Choosing tasks on the basis of their reinforcement value to individual students involves selecting materials students readily interact with, preferably in a free-play situation (a situation where the material is available, but the student is not prompted to interact with it or externally reinforced for interactions). Reinforcing materials may be structured into reinforcing tasks; that is, tasks that are fun for both the student and teacher. In many instances, this will involve teaching skills through toys, games, music, and songs. For instance, math facts may be taught through dull flashcard drills or through a math fact game (e.g., races in which students compete to answer math fact problems faster than other students or the teacher). Some potential instructional advantages of using tasks with reinforcement value to students are: (1) correct responses may be reinforced by allowing students to continue to perform the task and/or to interact with the task, materials instead of relying on external reinforcers such as M & Ms; and (2) students are more likely to interact with the task materials and perform the skills taught through them outside of the instructional situation.

The criteria that tasks be chosen on the basis of their functionality, frequency of occurrence, and reinforcement value to the students presents a major problem in programming for many severely handicapped students. That is, many severely handicapped students live in environments, such as institutions, where they are not expected to or required to perform functional tasks. Also, for many severely handicapped students, there appear to be few appropriate materials or tasks which have reinforcement value to them.

Some criteria for selecting potentially reinforcing tasks are: (a) tasks should be novel or offer results that are not always predictable; (b) tasks should be matched to students' functioning levels. Tasks which are either too easy or too sophisticated are not appropriate. However, tasks, just above current functioning level, should hold interest and pace development; and (c) tasks should allow active engagement and manifest cause and effect relationships.

Selecting tasks on the basis of facilitation of discrimination learning involves teaching skills through tasks or events to which students can readily differentially respond. For instance, one-to-one correspondence could be taught through teaching students to align forks and spoons in an arrangement which manifests one-to-one correspondence. Obviously, students who could differentially respond to forks and spoons (e.g., sort them) at the initiation of instruction would learn to perform the one-to-one correspondence operation through this task more readily than students who could not initially differentiate between them. Before selecting tasks to teach skills or concepts, the discriminations which must be taught should be identified. For instance, if an objective is to teach numeral recognition, then the basic discriminations to be taught are numeral forms (e.g., 2, 3). Tasks which facilitate discrimination learning should be selected and devised. The fundamental discrimination learning rule when selecting tasks to teach a concept is to choose tasks which will insure that the students' responding is controlled only by the essential characteristics of the concept. For instance, in teaching numeral recognition, tasks should be selected which will insure that the students' responding is controlled by the form of the numerals and not their size, color, texture, or spatial position. Becker, Engelmann, and Thomas (1971) suggest that to insure that the essential characteristics control the students' responding instructional tasks should be chosen which allow the teacher to:

1. Teach the concept through a set of instances and not instances of the concept (e.g., instances of the numeral 2 and not instances of the numeral 2).

2. Construct instances of the concept such that they all have essen-

tial concept characteristics and construct not instances such that they have none or some of the essential characteristics.

3. Frequently vary the nonessential characteristics of the instances, and not instances to insure that the students learn to respond only to essential characteristics (e.g., in teaching the numeral 2 the size, color, texture, and position of instances, and not instances of the numeral should be varied.

Functional and frequently occurring tasks often do not meet the optimum discrimination learning requirements specified above necessitating that skills be taught through a combination of functional and relatively nonfunctional tasks.

Selecting tasks that have continued applicability to repeated practice during skill acquisition involves choosing tasks through which the student can be presented many opportunities to respond. This selection criterion is based on the notion that frequent opportunities to respond typically results in more efficient learning than less frequent opportunities. One problem with many of the more functional tasks is that they do not permit the student to respond frequently. For instance, passing out cookies at juice time is a relatively functional task for teaching one-to-one correspondence, but it typically permits only one response opportunity for one student per day. Thus, in most instances it will be necessary to teach a skill through both functional tasks that permit few response opportunities and several relatively nonfunctional tasks (e.g., giving each bear a block) that permit numerous response opportunities.

Choosing tasks on the basis of their facilitation of later skill development involves teaching of tasks that will become a component of a higher level skill in more advanced stages of the sequence. For instance, teaching students to count their fingers may not have great utility at the time rational counting is taught, but it will have such during the teaching of addition.

Selecting tasks which facilitate the maintenance of math skills involves utilizing tasks which will enhance the probability that students will retain and utilize the math skills after initial acquisition. Generally, maintenance of skills can be insured through students' repeated practice or use of the skills. Teaching skills through functional tasks which frequently occur in the environments the students inhabit should enhance skill maintenance. Skill maintenance may also be enhanced through devising games which require that students utilize particular skills, and in making these games a regular component of their academic program and free time activities. Some of the game formats we use include: races between individuals or teams of students which require the students to utilize math skills (e.g., the students race to label numerals and the teacher tallies the

score $\dfrac{\text{Student 1} \quad | \quad ////}{\text{Student 2} \quad | \quad //}$); board games, similar to "Chutes

and Ladders," which require use of math skills (e.g.,

| start | 2 or ⊙⊙ 5 | count to 5 | etc. | finish |

. The students compete to win a board game and may have to spin a spinner, turn over a number card, or shake dice and rationally count the correct number of squares. Then, to stay on a square, a student must perform a math skill represented on the square, such as sort objects into sets; and grab bag, which involves the students drawing an object or card from a bag, and in order to keep the object or card, the student must perform a skill related to it (e.g., label an object, label a numeral, count to 5). The teacher may arrange the games in a way that the same individuals or teams do not consistently win or lose. It is sometimes advantageous to set up the games so that the students are competing with the teacher and/or their previous best score.

It is unlikely that one task which fulfills all the criteria delineated above may be devised. Thus, in teaching a skill, it will often be necessary to teach it through many tasks which, when combined, fulfill the criteria. Use of these three basic tasks should fulfill the task selection criterion: (a) functional tasks; (b) games; and (c) repeated practice tasks.

A. FUNCTIONAL TASKS

As discussed above, selecting tasks on the basis of functional use involves teaching skills through functional tasks students frequently encounter. For example, the operation of sorting glasses and silverware can be taught through teaching students to sort glasses and silverware into separate sets at a worktable in the classroom, or sorting glasses and silverware into separate sets while putting away the dishes after lunch.

B. GAMES

Tasks which facilitate the maintenance and generalization of skills should be selected. Skill maintenance can be insured through students' repeated use of skills. Teaching skills through tasks which frequently occur in environments the students inhabit should enhance skill maintenance. Skill maintenance may also be enhanced through devising games or fun activities (e.g., songs, play) which require that students use particular skills, and making these games and fun activities a regular component of students' daily programs and free-time activities. In addition, games and fun activities have potential reinforcement value to students, and thus students are more likely to play the game and use the skills outside of the instructional setting.

C. REPEATED PRACTICE TASKS

A problem with some functional tasks and games is that they only provide infrequent response opportunities (practice) or do not facilitate discrimination learning. Selecting tasks with continued applicability to repeated practice, and which facilitate discrimination learning involves choosing tasks which may be presented under controlled conditions and through which the student can be presented many opportunities to respond. In some cases, repeated practice tasks may have to be used in conjunction with functional tasks and games.

C. Adapting Responses

Through a task, students may learn at least concepts and operations. That is, in teaching a task, students may learn to discriminate a ball from nonballs or to discriminate many balls differing in dimensions of size, color, and composition (the concept balls) from nonballs. Operations are concepts which are general response classes or general procedures (e.g., touching, placing, labeling) the student may use to demonstrate knowledge of skills. Concepts which are taught early in the sequence may be used as operations in the acquisition of later skills. For example, in the math sequence, one-to-one correspondence is taught as a concept which the student later uses as an operation to solve equivalence problems.

It should be noted that tasks are taught, not concepts or operations. It is inferred that students know concepts and operations on the basis of their performance over a number of tasks. For instance, through tasks students could be taught to differentially respond to balls. After students differentially respond across a range of balls using a variety of operations, it is inferred that the students have learned a concept of ball. Similarly, after students have been taught to "touch" across a number of tasks requiring them to touch different items, it is inferred that the students know the operation "touch."

Most skill sequences or curricula require students to use verbal operations (e.g., speech) to demonstrate knowledge of tasks, and are therefore inappropriate for nonverbal and many severely handicapped students. What is delineated here is a sequence of math skills through rudimentary addition which may be adapted to either verbal or nonverbal students. Both nonverbal and verbal operations that students can use to demonstrate knowledge of the skills are provided.

The nonverbal and verbal operations delineated for each skill in the sequence are only meant to be illustrative. There are at least two criteria that may be used in selecting verbal and nonverbal operations. One, select nonverbal operations which allow the student to interact with the task (e.g., take, show me). Two, select only operations which are appropriate to the individual student's level of language production. That is, nonverbal students should be expected to use nonverbal operations (e.g., touching, signing). Likewise, students who use one-word utterances should be expected to respond with one-word utterances, and students who use four-word utterances should be expected to respond with four word utterances. In short, a skill sequence can be adapted to students with specific motor and expressive language problems through allowing students to learn and demonstrate skill mastery through responses they are capable of performing. Whenever possible, students should be taught to use a variety of appropriate verbal and nonverbal operations to demonstrate knowledge of the same skill.

Facilitating Performance of Skills Across Environments in Which They Are Functional

The success of a program should be assessed on at least two criteria: (1) student acquisition of new skills, and (2) student performance of skills across environmental configurations.[4]

Typically, it is the aim of instructional programs for students to appropriately perform skills acquired in one teaching environment in other environments where those skills are functional. However, neither systematic programming nor accurate measurement of skill performance across environments usually occurs. For instance, a program may teach a student the one-to-one correspondence operation (skill) through nonfunctional tasks (e.g., aligning blocks and bears in one-to-one correspondence) and then suggest that the teacher take advantage of every opportunity to require students to use the skill across functional tasks and environments (e.g., having the students use the one-to-one correspondence operation to give each of his classmates a cup of juice at snack time.).

However, if the success of a program is to be assessed in terms of a student's performance of skills across environmental configurations, then the objective for each major skill taught in a program should include a student's performance of skills across selected environmental configurations. For example, the instructional objective for the one-to-one correspondence skill might be: Given the response cues "Give each _____ a _____ " or "Give every _____ a _____ " by at least three different control figures (e.g., teacher, mother, peer) across at least three settings (e.g., classroom, playground, home) and across at least three functional

---

[4]As used here, environmental configurations include cues to respond, physical settings, control figures, and functional tasks.

tasks (e.g., setting the table, passing out cookies, musical chairs), the student should appropriately demonstrate use of the one-to-one correspondence operation.

Potentially, there are many instructional strategies which could be employed to insure that students master the objective. Some selected strategies are:

1. Instruct the students on several functional tasks in one teaching environment with one teacher and test and then if necessary, teach the student to perform the skill across varied cues to respond, functional tasks, control figures, and settings.

2. Instruct the student on several nonfunctional tasks in one teaching environment with one control figure and take advantage of every opportunity to require the student to use the skill on functional tasks across settings, control figures, and cues to respond. Then test and, if necessary, teach the student to perform the skill across functional tasks, control figures, settings, and cues to respond.

3. Instruct the student on several functional and nonfunctional tasks across several settings, control figures, and cues to respond. Then test to assess if the student can perform the skill on untaught tasks with new control figures in new settings.

The third option may be the most viable. If students are to perform the skills across functional tasks, then teach the skill through a combination of functional tasks and repeated practice tasks which fulfill the task selection requirements previously delineated. For instance, teach the students one-to-one correspondence through such tasks as passing out juice cups and giving each bear a block. If the students are to perform the skills across settings, then it may be advantageous to teach the skills in several settings. For instance, teaching might occur in the gym, on the playground, in the hall, in the bathroom, and in a kitchen area, using tasks appropriate to those areas. If it is necessary that students perform skills under the direction of several control figures, these may be used in instruction. If the students are likely to encounter varied cues to respond, then instruction should include cues to respond which frequently occur. For instance, students might be taught to use the one-to-one correspondence operation in response to the following cues: "Give *every* (_____) a (_____)," "Give *each* (_____) a (_____)," "Give *one* (_____) to each (_____)," "Put the (_____) in each (_____)," etc.

Many educational programs are evaluated in terms of how quickly they advance students vertically from "lower" level skills to "higher" level skills (e.g., from one-to-one correspondence, to equivalence, to addition). However, the effectiveness of a program should be evaluated in terms of whether it teaches students skills and whether they can perform the skills across functional tasks, control figures, cues to respond, and settings. This emphasis requires that both rate of skill acquisition and utility of the skill be assessed in determining the efficacy of a program.

Summary

A basic task analysis or skill sequence of math skills ranging from zero skills through rudimentary addition will be discussed. The skill sequence may be adapted to specific students and situations through:

1. Teaching the skills through instructional procedures which are the most effective for individual students.

2. Choosing the tasks and materials to teach skills on the basis of their functional use to individual students, accessibility or frequency of occurrence across settings individual students inhabit, reinforcement value to individual students, facilitation of discrimination learning, facilitation of repeated practice, enhancement of later skill development, and facilitation of skill maintenance.

3. Requiring students to use operations (e.g., touching, signing, speech) which are appropriate to their level of language functioning.

In implementing the sequence to facilitate the performance of skills across environments in which they are functional, the skills should be taught: (1) through tasks and materials the student readily interacts with, preferably in a free play situation; (2) through a wide range of functional tasks; (3) across a number of control figures; (4) across a number of environmental settings; (5) across a number of frequently occurring cues to respond.

PROCEDURES

A basic instructional and measurement procedure we have found to be relatively successful with severely handicapped students is articulated below. Following a description of this basic procedure, selected variants which may make it more effective for specific students and situations are delineated.

In the basic instructional procedure, the teaching and measurement procedures are incorporated into test-teach designs. That is, the teacher presents a cue; if students respond correctly, they are rewarded; if they respond incorrectly, they are taught the correct response through either a modeling procedure (the teacher models the response and requires the student to imitate it) or a priming procedure (the teacher physically guides the student through the correct response). For students who initially err, the modeling cues and prompts are faded until the correct response occurs in response to verbal cues (models are faded by gradually modeling less of the correct response—prompts are faded by gradually withdrawing physical support until the student performs the response without teacher asisstance).

Acquisition and Proficiency Criterion

Acquisition criterion levels may be set in terms of trials. That is, when teaching numeral recognition, the numerals can be taught in sets of one, two, three, etc., depending on the abilities of the student. The responses a student makes to a complete set is considered a trial: e.g., for a set of one, one response equals a trial, for a set of two, two responses equals a trial, etc. A commonly employed acquisition criterion is three consecutive correct trials. A sample data sheet should further clarify the notions of trials and criterion.

Sample Data Sheet*

Date _____ Behavior Objective _No. Rec._____ Set _1, 2, 3_____

Name	Trial	No. 1	No. 2	No. 3	Tot. Correct
Student No. 1	1	P	P	M	0
	2	+	+	+	3
	3	+	M	+	2
	4	+	+	+	3
	5	+	+	+	3 †
	6	+	+	+	3

*In the data system utilized: +, a correct response; M, a correct response after a model, and P, a correct response after a prime.

†Criterion met three consecutive correct trials.

If students have acquired a skill and performed it correctly on three consecutive trials, it does not indicate that they can proficiently use the skill. As used here, proficiency means that the students can correctly perform a skill and perform it correctly at a selected rate criterion. For instance, students should be able to correctly rationally count objects and count them quickly before they can be considered proficient at rational counting.

There are at least two reasons for setting proficiency criterion in terms of rates of correct responding. One is, if the students are to be tolerated by and compete with other individuals in the community, they will have to perform skills quickly and correctly. For example, slow but correct coin counters cannot readily compete for many clerk jobs. Two, if skill "A" is necessary for acquisition and performance of skill "B," then a slow rate of performance on skill "A" may impede the acquisition and performance on skill "B." This concept may be illustrated through several examples. For instance, a teacher's objective is to teach students to imitate motor gestures such as patting knees and clapping hands. If the students do not have proficient eye–hand coordination on motor patterns similar to those they are to imitate, then the students will have trouble getting their hands to go where they should, impeding their ability to imitate a model. However, if students have mastered eye–hand coordination on motor patterns similar to those they are to imitate, then they should be ready to learn the task of imitating the model's gestures. Thus, as Bruner (1973) points out, preliminary motor-skill proficiency provides the basis for utilizing modeling and for carrying out imitation. Similarly, in the math-skill sequence, rational counting is one of the component (prerequisite) skills involved in addition. Rapid and correct rational counting should facilitate the acquisition of addition tasks. Since developmental skills sequences are cumulative (new skills involve previously acquired skills), students should be approaching proficiency in the component (prerequisite) skills of an unfamiliar task before being presented instruction on the task.[5] Once students have acquired a skill, they may attain proficiency through additional practice of the skill which requires correct and rapid responding. Games and races similar to those described in an earlier section (adapting tasks) are excellent vehicles for giving students additional practice on a skill.

Basic Instructional and Measurement Procedure

1. Secure the attention of the student(s) to the teacher or the task.
2. Present materials.
3. Present a cue for the student(s) to attend to the instructional materials.
4. Present a cue for the student(s) to respond.
5. Evaluate student's response.

    a. Correct response: Immediately consequate the student's response with verbal praise (e.g., the teacher says, "Good," and describes why it was good—"Good, there are enough," or "Good, they are the same"), a smile and, if necessary, some tangible reward (food, toy, to-

---

[5]Skill proficiency levels may be estimated by calculating adult rates of correct performance of a skill and then dividing this rate by two. Obviously, special adjustments in proficiency rates have to be made to accommodate individuals with motor impairments.

ken). Record the correct response on a data sheet and begin the next trial, go to the next student, etc. If the student performs correctly in three consecutive trials, place an emphasis on the rate of correct responding.

b. Incorrect response: Say "No," and tell the student why it was wrong (e.g., "No, not enough" or "No, not the same"), then go to step six.

6. Secure the attention of the student and provide a model of the correct response. Then present a cue to respond.

7. Evaluate the student's response.

a. Correct response: Immediately consequate the student's response with verbal praise (e.g., the teacher says, "Good," and describes why the response was good—"Good, there are enough," or "Good, they are the same"), a smile and if necessary some tangible reward. Record that the response was performed correctly after a model was provided (M), and on subsequent trials gradually fade out the model.

b. Incorrect response: Say "No," and tell why it was wrong (e.g., "No, not enough" or "No, not the same"), then proceed to step eight.

8. Secure the attention of the student, present the cue to respond and prime the correct response by physically guiding the student in its performance. Consequate the response with verbal praise and describe why it was correct (e.g., "Good, there are enough"), smile and if necessary, provide some tangible consequence. Record that the response was primed (P), and on subsequent trials fade out the prime.

9. Follow the procedures until the student performs correctly in three consecutive trials.

C. Adapting the Instructional Procedure to Behavioral Objectives

The basic procedures presented above may be adapted to each behavioral objective. An illustration of an adaption to a selected objective is described below.

ADAPTATION TO AN EQUIVALENCE OBJECTIVE

Behavioral Objective 1—Instructional Sequence Step b:
When the teacher places a selected number of items (from 1 to 10) in a set and says, "Make your set equal to my set," the student should use the operation of one-to-one correspondence to make his/her set equal and then place an equals sign between the two sets, (i.e., the student should match members of his/her set with the teacher's until there are no unmatched members).

Teacher | Student   Teacher | Student
. | . | .
. | =   . | .
. | |
.   . | ≠
        | |

Adaptation of Teaching Method:
1. The teacher says, "Look," and secures the attention of the students to the task.
2. The teacher puts a set of items in his/her set in a vertical array.

Teacher | Student
. | .
                 | .   .
. | .
                 |

3. The teacher selects one student and says, "Joe, look at this," while he/she points to the materials.
4. The teacher says, "Make your set equal to my set."
5. The teacher evaluates the student's response.
   a. Correct response: If the student utilizes the operation of one-to-one correspondence to put the same number of objects on his/her half of the sheet and places an equal sign between the sets, he is immediately consequated with verbal praise (e.g., "Good, there are enough" or "equal"), a smile and, if necessary, a consumable. The data sheet is marked with a "+." If the student has three consecutive correct trials, place an emphasis on the rate of correct responding.
   b. Incorrect response: If the student does not utilize the operation of one-to-one correspondence and/or puts out the wrong number of items, the teacher says, "No, not equal," "too many," or "not enough," and goes to step six.
6. The teacher secures student attention and models the correct response (including the one-to-one correspondence operation) and then presents the cue to respond (See step four).
7. The teacher evaluates the student's response.
   a. Correct response: If the student uses the operation of one-to-one correspondence to place the same number of objects in his set and places an equal sign between the sets, he is immediately consequated with verbal praise (e.g., "Good, there are enough" or "equal") and a smile and the teacher marks an "M" on the data sheet.
   b. Incorrect response: If the student does not use the operation of one-to-one correspondence and/or puts out the wrong number of items, the teacher says, "No, not equal," "too many," or "not enough," and goes to step eight.

8. The teacher secures the student's attention, presents the response cue, and primes the correct response by physically guiding the student through it. The teacher consequates a correct response with verbal priase (e.g., "Good, there are enough," or "equal") and a smile and marks the data sheet with a "P."

9. Follow these procedures until the student performs correctly in three consecutive trials.

Sample Data Sheet

Date_____	Behavior Objective		_Equivalence 1_	Array	_Vertical___
Name	Trial	Task 1	Task 2	Task 3	Tot. Correct
Student 1	1	+	M	+	2
	2	+	P	M	1
	3	+	M	+	2
	4	+	+	+	3
	5	+	+	+	3
	6	+	+	+	3

D. Variants on the Basic Instructional Procedures

Potentially, there are a great number of variations that can be made on the basic instructional procedure illustrated. Only a few selected variants will be discussed. The introductory sections on adapting the skills sequence to individual students through adapting the tasks (materials), adapting cues to respond and facilitating performance across environments illustrated many of the basic variants on the instructional procedure. Briefly, these variants included: (1) varying the task and task materials; (2) presenting the task in fun format, such as through a game, a race, toys, a song, etc.; (3) varying the cues to respond and responses the students are expected to emit (e.g., motor responses, verbal responses, motor and verbal responses, written responses); (4) varying the control figure and/or setting.

Some other variants which may enhance student interest (attention) or performance on almost any task are:

1. Varying the intensity (loudness) of task presentation so that the students at times have to strain to hear and at other times are mildly startled by the loudness of a response cue.

2. Varying the responses expected of the students over a range of responses they have mastered or are learning, so that the students have to closely listen and watch to emit correct responses (e.g., "Give me more," "Touch more," "Is this more?"). This can be a game where the teacher

says, "Listen carefully, I'll try to fool you," and then varies the response requirement slightly. Typically, it becomes quite difficult to fool the students.

3. Vary the intensity of the response expected from the students from whispers to shouts. As in 2, this can be made into a game.

4. Varying the pace of task presentation from fast to slow, in such a way that the students must closely attend to determine when cues to respond and potential reinforcers are going to be delivered. As in 2, this can be made into a "I bet I can fool or trick you" game.

5. Vary calling on the group to respond (e.g., "Everyone, is this more?") and a calling on individuals (e.g., "Tom, is this more?"), so that students must attend closely in order not to miss their turns. This too can be made into a game.

Many skills can be taught and practiced through group response procedures, with the teacher systematically calling on individual students to assess whether they can perform the skills without assistance. Through such procedures, students learn to imitate the teacher and other students to learn skills.

6. Utilize procedures which reduce error responding. Once some students have learned to associate a wrong response to a response cue, it is often difficult to teach them to associate a correct response with that response cue. Thus, it is often advantageous to prevent error responses from occurring. There are several variants on group and individual responding procedure that may be employed to attempt to prevent errors. One is a rehearsal procedure and the other a modeling procedure.

In the rehearsal procedure, the teacher calls upon the group or an individual to respond and then makes the response along with them. Then the teacher gradually fades out her demonstration until the group or individual can make the response without teacher assistance.

In the modeling procedure, the teacher models the entire response chain (cue and response) before calling on the group or an individual to respond, and then uses the rehearsal procedure. Next, the teacher fades out the model when the students can respond to the rehearsal procedure alone. Finally, the rehearsal procedure is faded out.

Across all procedures, if at any point students start to initiate an error response, they should be stopped and the correct response should be immediately demonstrated through either the modeling or rehearsal procedure.

The effectiveness of these variants and combinations of these variants on the basic instructional procedure is generally dependent upon the characteristics of individual students. We recommend systematically experimenting with various formats to determine which formats individual students enjoy and learn from most effectively.

The following paragraphs delineate several potentially viable instructional models.

INITIAL INSTRUCTION

An instructional program should teach students to perform functional skills across tasks, materials, verbal language cues, people, and settings that the students will frequently encounter. However, one could conjecture that teaching a student to perform a skill across several language cues, people, settings, tasks, and materials concurrently might impede the student's acquisition of a skill. Thus, initially it may be efficient to concentrate on instructing students on one task, given one verbal language cue in one setting with one teacher. However, take advantage of every opportunity to require the students to use the skill across functional tasks, settings, people, and verbal language cues to respond.

SKILL MASTERY INSTRUCTION

When students have correctly performed a skill on one task, given one verbal language cue in one setting, with one teacher, concentrate on teaching students to use the skill across several functional tasks, settings, people, and verbal language cues to respond concurrently.

A skill may be taught through many tasks. The tasks selected to teach a skill should be chosen on the basis of their: (a) functional use to the individual student; (b) accessability or frequency of occurrence across the environment of the individual student; (c) reinforcement value to the individual student; (d) facilitation of discrimination; (e) applicability to repeated practice during skill acquisition; (f) facilitation of later skill development; and (g) facilitation of skill maintenance.

As noted earlier, it is unlikely that one task which fulfills all the criteria delineated above may be devised. However, three basic tasks, functional tasks, games and repeated practice tasks should meet the task selection criterion. In many instances, you may be able to devise tasks applicable to repeated practice which are functional and which are games. However, in describing the model, we will separate the three basic tasks.

The first step in developing an instructional model should be to describe functional tasks, games, and repeated practice tasks for the skill of concern. For example, some potential sorting (sets) tasks are:

Potential Functional Tasks: List potential functional tasks. Systematically require each student to use sorting on functional tasks several times a day. Continually look for additional functional tasks the students can use the skill on.

1. Sort food items at snack time (e.g., put the milk on the shelf and cookies on the table).

2. Sort objects when setting up or cleaning up an activity (e.g., put the puzzles on the shelf and the balls in the box; put the plates on the shelf and the spoons in the drawer; put the crayons in the box and paint in the cupboard).

3. Join (add) sets when cleaning up or setting up an activity (e.g., put the paint and the crayons on the table; put the paper and scissors on the floor.

Potential Games: List potential games. Each day during free time or during instructional time, encourage students to play games involving the sorting skill. Games are excellent repeated practice and skill-maintenance tasks. Continually devise new games or variations of existing games.

1. Card games similar to "Old Maid," which require the student to sort and match cards on the basis of form, size, and/or color.

2. Sorting boxes, puzzles, or peg boards, which require objects to be sorted on the basis of form, size, and/or color.

3. Art activities which require the student to differentially operate on items which differ along dimensions of form, size, and color (e.g., color the house red and balls blue, paste the eyes on the head and paste the hands on the arms).

4. Board games (e.g., | start | · | ▢ | ⌂ | 𝗣 | · | ⌂ |) which require the students to draw a card and move their marker to the next square on the board which matches the card. Verbal students could be required to label the card (e.g., red, house, spoon) before advancing on the board.

5. Grab bag, which requires students to draw an object from a bag and then label it.

Potential Tasks Which Are Applicable to Repeated Practice:

1. Sort or make sets of objects (e.g., block and bears, forks and cup, straws and cups) at the classroom worktable.

2. Sort or make sets of flannel items.

3. Sort or make sets of pictures.

For repeated practice tasks, develop a procedure for systematically varying the tasks, materials, settings, instructors and language cues. A rotation procedure may be effective (Fig. 1). For instance, on day 1 teacher "A" teaches sets with one set of language cues and materials in setting A. Teacher "B" teaches one-to-one correspondence and teacher "C" teaches numeral recognition. On day 2, teacher "B" teaches sets with a different set of language cues and materials in setting B. Teacher

Figure 1
Sample Rotation Procedure

	Day 1		*Day 2*
	Teacher 'B'		Teacher 'B'
	1-to-1 cor.		sets

Teacher 'A'
rec.

Teacher 'A'	Teacher 'C'
sets	# rec.

Teacher 'C'
1-to-1 cor.

"A" teaches numeral recognition and teacher "C" teaches one-to-one correspondence, etc. Obviously, many variations of the rotation procedure are possible.

To insure that students learn to perform a skill across tasks, language cues, settings, and people, students should be systematically required to use the skills throughout the day. The following is a sample daily routine for teaching and requiring students to use the skills of one–many and one-to-one correspondence.

Opening: 8:30–9:00
One-to-One Correspondence Activities:
a. Attendance: The bulletin board is divided into a present and absent section. Each student has a name card, and there should be one name card in the present section of the bulletin board for each student present. To teach one-to-one correspondence, ask a student to take role (or you take role) by giving one name card to each students. If there are too many name cards, someone is absent. In this instance, reading and naming classmates are being taught concurrently with one-to-one correspondence.

b. Another section of the bulletin board is devoted to a job board with pictures of the various jobs (e.g., watering plants, feeding fish). A check is placed next to each job if it has been completed. During opening, students can ascertain if all jobs have been completed by determining if each job has a check. In this case, home-living skills (jobs) and cooperating (everyone has a job), are being taught concurrently with one-to-one correspondence.

One–Many Activities:
a. During attendance, the students can be asked if one or many students are present or absent.

b. Students may be asked to bring one or many crayons, pieces of paper, etc. to opening with them for a special activity.

Math Class: 9:00–9:30

During math class, repeated practice tasks are presented. For example:

One-to-One Correspondence Activities:

a. Students are requested to give each flannel circle a flannel star.

b. Students are requested to give each cup a saucer.

c. Students are requested to give each paintbox a brush.

d. Students are asked to give each piece of candy a penny.

One–Many:

a. A set of one apple and a set of many apples is presented the students, and they are requested to touch, point to, take the set with one or many.

b. Pictures of sets of one comb and many combs are presented the students, and they are requested to point to the set with one or many.

c. The teacher points to a set of objects and asks students if the set has one or many objects.

Language: 9:30–10:00

In language, the students may be learning the functional use of objects (drink from cup, eat with spoon, stir with spoon, eat from bowl) to demonstrate nonverbal comprehension of object labels (presented with objects and the cue "Take a spoon," the student takes a spoon), and to label objects (asked "What is this?" or "What do you want?," students state the object name). These language skills may be taught through such tasks as tea party play. During the course of the tea party, the students are requested to demonstrate functional object use, to demonstrate receptive comprehension of object labels, and to label objects. Students can also be requested to give each classmate a cup to demonstrate one-to-one correspondence and receptive comprehension of the label "cup," go to the counter and bring back one or many spoons to demonstrate receptive knowledge of the label "spoons" and "one–many," etc.

Snack Time: 10:00–10:15

Snack time is a variation on the tea party activities of the language period. Students are asked: to give each classmate a napkin, to bring one or many cartons of milk from the kitchen, to state if they want one or many pieces of cookie, etc.

Recess: 10:15–10:30

One–Many

a. Students can be asked to take one or many balls, jump ropes, etc., outside.

One-to-One Correspondence

a. Games such as musical chairs should be played.

Prereading:10:30–11:00

One-to-One Correspondence

a. While looking at pictures, students can be asked if each person in the picture has a hat on, if every bear has feet, etc.

b. Students can be requested to give each classmate a book, worksheet, etc.

One–Many

a. Students can be requested to bring 1 or many pencils, crayons, pieces of paper to reading class.

b. While looking at pictures, students can be asked if there are one or many dogs, cats, policemen, etc., in the picture.

The skills of one-to-one correspondence and one-many can be used throughout all other daily activities (art, lunch, gym, music, etc.). It is hoped that these limited examples illustrate that skills should not be taught in isolation, but should be taught in relation to other skills (language, reading, recreation, social) if they are to be functional, maintain, and generalize.

E. Variants on the Basic Measurement Procedure

The basic measurement procedure illustrated utilized a discrete trial format. That is, the teacher presented the student with a cue to respond, the student emitted a response, and the teacher scored the accuracy of each response. This is a direct and continuous measurement system which is extremely sensitive in that it accounts for all student responses, making it possible for the teacher to be relatively precise in determining the efficacy of an instructional procedure and in pinpointing exactly when a student reaches criterion on a selected skill. However, it is difficult, if not impossible, to continuously measure and record behavior when some of the variants illustrated above are employed as components of the instructional procedure. Alternatives to continuous measurement and recording of student behavior are pretest, post-test measures and/or periodic probes of the student's skills. Generally, the more frequent the measurement, the more accurate is the assessment of an individual student's progress within a program and the evaluation of the effectiveness of that program.

It has been our experience that it is necessary for teachers to initially use the basic instructional measurement procedure described above. The basic procedure requires the teacher to precisely specify tasks, materials, language cues, student responses (correct and error), and teacher consequences for each student response. The use of such a highly structured instructional and measurement procedure continually provides the teacher with the relevant dimensions of the instructional task, relevant dimensions of student performance, and direct and continuous measures of student skill acquisition. However, teachers may initially feel that use of the highly structured instructional and measurement procedure results in unnatural, stilted, and choppy task presentations. Fortunately, with practice, task presentations become natural and fluid. With sufficient practice, teachers should learn to set up tasks, select materials, appropriately respond to student responses, and assess student skill acquisition without referring to the basic instructional and measurement procedure. Thus, the basic instructional and measurement procedure is a training device.

Once teachers can successfully use the basic procedure, they may vary the basic instructional procedure (see the suggested variations above) and employ different measurement systems. When this occurs, teachers may cease continuously recording each student response and switch to periodically recording each response. It should be noted that every time a student emits a response, the teacher obtains a potentially relevant assessment of a student's skills. Periodic recorded assessments should be performed to test the validity of unrecorded assessments of student skill acquisition. We will refer to the periodic recorded assessment as probes.

We suggest that student skill acquisition should be probed at least once a week on Tuesday, Wednesday, or Thursday. Mondays and Fridays are less likely to be representative of general student skill performance. The probes should follow the format of the basic instructional and measurement procedure.

The record system of the basic instructional and measurement procedure helps all individuals who are teaching a student (e.g., master teacher, student teachers, methods students, aides) keep track of where each student is in the skill sequence, and what tasks, materials and language cues are instructionally relevant for each student. If the basic instructional and measurement procedure is not used, an alternative system for keeping track of student programs should be employed. We suggest that the following system may be viable (Table 1).

For each student, devise a summary grid which includes all the relevant instructional objectives of the math program. A sample summary grid is depicted below. Each student's summary grid should be readily accessible in the classroom, so that at any time any individual can determine what skills the student should be currently receiving instruction on and which skills the student has already mastered.

For each objective in the skill sequence, the summary grid indicates instruction is in progress; there should also be an adjunct grid. The adjunct grid should indicate which tasks and cues the student has mastered

Table 1.

Student John

Summary Grid

I = Instruction in Progress
M = Skill Acquired

A. Prerequisite		H. Conservation		H. Addition		
Motor imitation	M	of number		1. Objects		
Verbal imitation		Obj. 1		Obj. 1		
Whole word	I	Obj. 2		Obj. 2		
Isolated sounds	I	Obj. 3		2. Numerals		
		Obj. 5		and Obj.		
B. Functional Obj. Use	M	Obj. 5		Obj. 1		
		Obj. 6		3. Numerals		
C. Sets				and lines		
Obj. 1		M H. Counting forward		Obj. 1		
Obj. 2		M	1. Rational	4. Numerals		
Obj. 3		M	Obj. 1	Obj. 1		
Obj. 4		M	Obj. 2	5. Fingers		
Obj. 5		M	Obj. 3	Obj. 1		
Obj. 6		M	Obj. 4	Obj. 2		
Obj. 7		M	Obj. 5	Obj. 3		
Obj. 8	I		Obj. 6	Obj. 4		
Obj. 9			Obj. 7	6. Facts		
			2. Rote	Obj. 1		
D. One-to-one			Obj. 1	Obj. 2		
correspondence			Obj. 2	Obj. 3		
Obj. 1	M		Obj. 3	Obj. 4		
			3. Numeral	Obj. 5		
E. One–many			Recognition	Obj. 6		
Obj. 1	M		Obj. 1			
Obj. 2	M		4. Match No. to	I. Story problems		
Obj. 3	M		quantities	1. One-to-one		
			Obj. 1	correspondence		
F. Equivalence			5. Match Quantities	Obj. 1		
Obj. 1	I		to No.	2. X + Y = __		
Obj. 2			Obj. 1	Obj. 1		
			6. Ordering	3. X + __ = Y		
G. More and less			numerals	Obj. 1		
1. More			Obj. 1			
Obj. 1			Obj. 2			
2. Less			Obj. 3			
Obj. 1			Obj. 4			
Obj. 2			Obj. 5			
3. More/less			Obj. 6			
Obj. 1			Obj. 7			
Obj. 2			Obj. 8			
			Obj. 9			
			7. Ordering			
			quantities			
			Obj. 1			

within the objective, and on which tasks and cues instruction is in progress. Probe assessment should be used to determine when students have mastered specific tasks and language cues within an objective. A sample objective grid for equivalence is depicted below (Table 2).

Placing the Student

Utilization of skill sequences and task analyses facilitates individualization of instruction. Within the task analysis model, students' mastery of various objectives can be assessed before instruction, and they may only be instructed on objectives on which they failed and for which they have mastered the prerequisites. Students can be permitted to proceed through the sequence at their own pace, taking longer on trouble spots and skipping steps on which they demonstrate mastery. The level of a student's entrance into the sequence and mastery of behavioral objectives is assessed through administering baseline tests composed of a sampling of items from selected behavioral objectives.

Typically, one baseline measure (test) is given for each selected behavioral objective and basically consists of implementing steps one through four of the basic teaching procedure. For example, the baseline measure for the equivalence behavior objective could be administered as follows:

1. The teacher says, "Look," and secures eye contact with the materials.

2. The teacher puts a set of items on his/her half of the paper in one of the specified arrays.

3. The teacher selects one student and says, "S, look at this," while he/she points to the materials and says, "Make your side equal to my side." If S looks, the teacher goes on to step four. If S does not look, the teacher physically primes S to look and then goes on to step four.

4. The teacher marks a "$+$" for a correct response and a "$-$" for an error response.

Obviously, it would be inefficient to test the students on every behavioral objective of the math skill sequence before beginning instruction. Typically, students are only tested on skills for which they have demonstrated the requisite behaviors. For instance, a student who did not demonstrate mastery of rational counting or equivalence and matching quantities to numerals would not be tested on an addition objective. Similarly, students are not initially tested on every objective of a math skill. They may be initially tested on the highest numbered objectives, and only if they fail these objectives would they be tested on lower numbered objectives. For example, in testing knowledge of "sets," the students might

Table 2.

Student　John

Equivalence–Objective 1

M = Skill Acquired
I = Instruction in Progress

Tasks:
  Functional
    Passing out cups at juice time　　　　　　　I
    Giving each classmate a pencil　　　　　　I
    Giving each classmate a crayon during art　I
    Etc.

  Games
    Musical Chairs　　　　　　　　　　　　I
    Etc.

  Repeated practice
    Give each bear a block　　　　　　　　I
    Put a straw in each cup　　　　　　　　I
    Give each tree a bird　　　　　　　　　I
    Etc.

Object Arrays
  Vertical　　　　　M
  Horizontal　　　　M
  Varied　　　　　　I
  Linear　　　　　　I

Set equivalence
  Enough　　　　　M
  Not Enough　　　M
  Too Many　　　　M

Language cues
  Make your set equal　M
  Are the sets equal　　I
  Are there enough　　I
  Are there too many　I
  Etc.

Scope and sequence chart.　All the skills taught in the sequence are listed vertically (functional object use, imitation, sets, etc.) The objectives for each skill are listed horizontally. As can be discerned from the chart, the objectives of various skills may often be taught concurrently. For instance, a student could be learning objectives 3, 4, 5 of sets concurrently with objectives 1, 2, 3, of one–many.

initially be tested on objective 9; and only if they failed objective 9 would they be tested on objective 8, 7, 6, 5, etc. If there are a potentially large number of objectives to be tested, the teacher may systematically test various objectives (e.g., 8, then 3, then 5, then 6) until the appropriate instructional objective is determined.

In evaluating the student's entry level, a checklist or grid may be devised which will reflect baseline test results. Below are grids on which several possible testing outcomes are depicted (Tables 3–5).

PREREQUISITES

There are two prerequisites students should meet before being programmed through the math skills sequence: (1) the students should be imitative; and (2) the students should readily interact with the objects and task materials they will encounter during instruction of the math skills sequence.

A. Imitation

Prompting and modeling are two general instructional procedures which may be utilized to teach most tasks. Prompting is a procedure, which involves physically guiding students through a response or response sequence. For instance, to teach students a one-to-one correspondence operation, the students could be physically guided through the chain of responses required to align sets in a configuration manifesting one-to-one correspondence. The prompts could then be eliminated by gradually withdrawing the physical guidance until the students performed the responses on their own. Modeling is an instructional procedure which involves demonstrating (modeling) a response or chain of responses to the students and directing the students to immediately imitate the demonstration. Models can be eliminated by gradually presenting a less demonstrative model until the students perform the responses on their own.

Modeling is a more efficient instructional procedure than prompting, but the students have to be imitative before it may be used. Briefly, the general procedure for teaching students to imitate is for the teacher to say "Do this," present a model (such as clapping her hands), and then physically guide students through the response. The prompting is gradually faded until the students consistently make the response without assistance. When the students consistently imitate a wide range of object manipulations (e.g., roll ball, stacking blocks) and body gestures (e.g., stamping feet, standing up), they may be considered imitative.

Table 3.
Student: Mary

Skills	Tests 1 2 3	
Imitation		
Motor	+ + +	+ = meets criterion
Verbal		
Isolated sounds	+ + +	
Whole words	− − −	− = does not meet criterion
Functional object use	+ + +	
		She made approximations
Sets	+ + +	
One–Many		
One-to-one correspondence	− − −	
Equivalence	− − −	
More/less		
More		
Less		
More/less		
Conservation of number		
Counting forward		
Rational		
Rote		
Numeral recognition		
Matching numerals to quantities		
Matching quantities to numerals		
Ordering numerals		
Ordering quantities		
Addition		
Objects		
Numerals and objects		
Numerals and lines		
Numerals		
Fingers		
Facts		
Story problems		
One-to-one correspondence		
$X + Y = \_\_$		
$X + \_\_ = Y$		

Comments: This evaluation indicates that the student has met the imitation criteria for motor and verbal behaviors. Verbal operations would be given emphasis in this student's program.

Table 4
Student: Larry

Skills	Tests 1 2 3	
Imitation		
Motor	+ + +	+ = meets criterion
Verbal		
Isolated sounds	− + −	
Whole words	− + −	− = does not meet criterion
Functional Object Use	+ + +	
Sets	− − −	
One–many		
One-to-one correspondence	− − −	
Equivalence		
More/Less		
More		
Less		
More/Less		
Conservation of number		
Counting Forward		
Rational		
Rote		
Numeral recognition		
Matching numerals to quantities		
Matching quantities to numerals		
Ordering numerals		
Ordering quantities		
Addition		
Objects		
Numerals and Objects		
Numerals and Lines		
Numerals		
Fingers		
Facts		
Story problems		
One-to-one correspondence		
X + Y = __		
X + __ = Y		

Comments: This evaluation indicates that the student has the prerequisite motor imitation and functional object use skills to enter the program at the level of sets. Verbal operations would be emphasized after the student has mastered the sound imitation criteria.

Table 5.
Student: Mike

Skills	Tests 1 2 3	
Imitation		
Motor	− − −	+ = meets criterion
Verbal		
Isolated sounds	− − −	
Whole words	− − −	− = does not meet criterion
Functional object use	− − −	
Sets	− − −	
One–many		
One-to-one correspondence		
Equivalence		
More/less		
More		
Less		
More/less		
Conservation of number		
Counting forward		
Rational		
Rote		
Numeral recognition		
Matching numerals to quantities		
Matching quantities to numerals		
Ordering numerals		
Ordering quantities		
Addition		
Objects		
Numerals and objects		
Numerals and lines		
Numerals		
Fingers		
Facts		
Story problems		
One-to-one correspondence		
X + Y = __		
X + __ = Y		

Comments: This evaluation indicates that the student does not have the requisite imitation skills to be included in the math program. When he meets criterion in the motor imitation and functional object use programs, he can begin the math program.

B. Functional Object Use

The prerequisite that the students readily interact with the objects and tasks they will encounter during instruction of the math sequence relates to the criteria for selection of tasks to teach a skill through. That is, if some of the criteria for selecting tasks are that they be functional, frequently occur across environments, and have reinforcement value for individual students, then it would appear to be advantageous for the students to be functionally using the objects or interacting with them (e.g., drink from cup, stir with spoon) before they are utilized in instructional tasks.

A deficit frequently exhibited by many severely handicapped students is that they do not readily interact with objects and/or people. Before implementing the math skills sequence, students' interaction with various objects should be assessed, and, if necessary, they should be taught to functionally use the objects and materials to be used in tasks in the math skills sequence.

BEHAVIORAL OBJECTIVES

While specific tasks, materials, and cues to respond are illustrated for each objective, students should demonstrate knowledge of the concept or ability to use an operation across a wide range of materials, tasks, and cues to respond. It is important to use only materials students have demonstrated they can discriminate (such as in objective 2 of the sets program). For example, students should be able to discriminate the objects they are to match in one-to-one correspondence before the objects are used in the one-to-one correspondence program. Note: Do not follow this skills sequence as if it is a curriculum. Use the notions and criterion articulated above to adapt the skills sequence to individual students. It is expected that many components of the sequence will have to be broken into smaller steps for some students.

A. Prerequisites

1. IMITATION:

The student should be able to imitate responses which may be required of him/her in the math skill sequence. The responses may include:

Motor imitation: Given the cue, "Do this," and a selected motor gesture, the student should imitate the gesture.

Subobjective: The student should imitate at least the following motor gestures: (a) touching an object; and (b) moving or manipulating selected objects.

Verbal imitation: (Note: Students do not have to imitate verbal behaviors to progress through the skill sequence.) The student should be able to imitate (make gross approximations of) isolated sounds or whole words.

2. FUNCTIONAL OBJECT USE:

Presented with objects to be used in tasks of the skill sequence, the student should be able to demonstrate at least one appropriate functional use of the object (e.g., spoon—stir; cup—drink).

B. Sets

EXAMPLE OF POTENTIAL TASKS:

Potential Functional Tasks:
   1. Sort food items at snack time (e.g., put the milk on the shelf and cookies on the table).
   2. Sort objects when setting up or cleaning up an activity (e.g., put the puzzles on the shelf and the balls in the box; put the plates on the shelf and the spoons in the drawer; put the crayons in the box and paint in the cupboard).
   3. Join (add) sets when cleaning up or setting up an activity (e.g., put the paint and the crayons on the table; put the paper and scissors on the floor).

Potential Games:
   1. Card games similar to "Old Maid," which require the student to sort and match cards on the basis of form, size, and/or color.
   2. Sorting boxes, puzzles, or peg boards which require objects to be sorted on the basis of form, size, and/or color.
   3. Art activities which require the student to differentially operate on items which differ along dimensions of form, size, and color (e.g., color the house red and balls blue, paste the eyes on the head and paste the hands on the arms).
   4. Board games (e.g., | start | · | □ | ⌂ | ⌂ | · | ⌂ |) which require the students to draw a card and move their marker to the next square on the board which matches the card. Verbal students could

be required to label the card (e.g., red, house, spoon) before advancing on the board.

Potential Tasks Which Are Applicable to Repeated Practice:
   1. Sort or make sets of objects (e.g., block and bears, forks and cup, straws and cups) in instructional settings.
   2. Sort or make sets of flannel items.
   3. Sort or make sets of pictures.

BEHAVIORAL PREREQUISITES:

Motor Imitation.

BEHAVIORAL OBJECTIVE 1

Given a group of objects whose members differ along at least one dimension (e.g., forks and spoons) with one member of each set separated out to serve as a match cue, the student should sort the objects into separate sets when the teacher points and says, "Make a set of (spoons) and a set of (forks), put the (spoons) here and the (forks) here.

Match △   △ ○ △
                               △ ○ ○ Group to be sorted
Cues ○   ○ △

Instructional sequence: The student should be able to sort into separate sets at least: (a) groups of objects of different colors, (b) groups of objects of like color.

Verbal operation: The same procedure as in objective 1 is followed. After the student correctly sorts the objects the teacher points and says, "This is a set of (spoons/forks). What is this set?" and the student should label the set (e.g., "spoons" or "forks").

BEHAVIORAL OBJECTIVE 2

Given a group of objects whose members differ along at least one dimension, the student should sort the objects into separate sets when the teacher points and says, "Make a set of (cups) and a set of (plates). Put the (cups) here and the (plates) here."

Instructional sequence: The student should be able to sort into separate sets: (a) objects, (b) flannel items.

Verbal operation: The same procedure as in objective 2 is followed. After the student correctly sorts the objects, the teacher points and says,

"What is this set?" and the student should label the set (e.g., "blocks," or "bears").

BEHAVIORAL OBJECTIVE 3

Given three sets (e.g., Set 1, blocks; Set 2, bears; Set 3, pennies) of objects composed of from one to five members, and when the teacher touches one set of objects and says, "This is a set of (blocks/bears/pennies). Take the set of (blocks/bears/pennies)," the student should take the correct set.

Instructional sequence: The student should take the correct set when presented: (a) two unlike sets with one object in each set; (b) three unlike sets with one object in each set; (c) three unlike sets with two like objects in each set; (d) three unlike sets with one or two like objects in each set. (e) The sequence is continued until the student demonstrates that he/she can discriminate unlike sets containing from one to five like members.

Verbal operation: When the teacher presents three sets of objects, points to one set and says, "This is a set of (blocks), what is this set?" the student should label the set.

BEHAVIORAL OBJECTIVE 4

When the teacher places two, two member sets with like members in front of the student (e.g., set 1, blocks; set 2, pennies) and says, "Take the set of (blocks)," the student should take the correct set.

Verbal Operation: The same procedure is followed as in objective 4. After the student takes the correct set, the teacher points and says, "What is this set?" and the student should label the set (e.g., "blocks").

BEHAVIORAL OBJECTIVE 5

When the teacher places two, two member sets with unlike members in front of the student (e.g., set 1, block and cup; set 2, penny and pencil), displays a set identical to one presented to the student (e.g., block and cup) and says, "Take the set of (block and cup)," the student should take the correct set.

Verbal operation: The same procedure is followed as in objective 5. After the student takes the correct set, the teacher says, "This is a set of (block and cup). What is this set?" and the student should label the set.

BEHAVIORAL OBJECTIVE 6

When the teacher places three, two member sets with unlike members in front of the student (e.g., set 1, block and cup; set 2, penny and pencil; set 3, bear and cup) and says, "Take the set of (block and cup)," the student should take the correct set.

Instructional sequence: The student should take sets with unlike members when presented with: (a) two, two member sets with unlike members; (b) three, two member sets with unlike members

Verbal operation: The same procedure is followed as in objective 6: After the student takes the correct set, the teacher says, "What is this set?" and the student should label each member of the set (e.g., "block and cup").

BEHAVIORAL OBJECTIVE 7

Given a group of two to four unlike objects (e.g., block, penny, pencil, cup) and when the teacher models making a two-member set (e.g., block and cup) and says, "This is a set of (block and cup). Make a set of (block and cup)," the student should make the correct set.

Verbal operation: The same procedure is followed as in objective 7. After the student makes the set, the teacher points and says, "This is a set of (block and cup). What is this set?" and the student should label each member of the set (e.g., "block and cup").

BEHAVIORAL OBJECTIVE 8

Given a group of four unlike objects (e.g., block, penny, pencil, cup), and when the teacher says, "Make a set of (block and cup), the student should make the correct set.

Instructional sequence: The student should be able to make a two-member set given: (a) a group of two unlike objects, (b) a group of three unlike objects, (c) a group of four unlike objects.

Verbal operation: The same procedure as in objective 8 is followed. After the student makes the correct set, the teacher points and says, "What is this set?" and the student should label each member of the set.

BEHAVIORAL OBJECTIVE 9

Given a group of objects (three to six) which can be made into three separate sets on the basis of color, size or shape, and when the teacher says, "Sort the objects into sets by (color/size/shape)" the student should sort the objects into sets along the dimension of color, size, or shape.

Instructional sequence: The student should be able to sort objects into sets when: (a) given three objects differing along at least one dimension; (b) given six objects of like shape and size which can be sorted into three equal sets by color (cue—sort by color, make sets of different colors); (c) given six objects of like color and shape which can be sorted into three equal sets by size (cue—sort by size, make sets of different sizes); (d) given six objects of like color and size which can be sorted into three equal sets by shape (cue—sort by shape, make sets of different shapes); (e) given six objects all the same shape which may be sorted into three equal sets by color or size (cue—sort by [color/size], make sets of different [colors/sizes]); (f) given six objects all the same color which may be sorted by [shape/size], make sets of different [shapes/sizes]); (g) given six objects, all approximately the same size, which may be sorted into three equal sets by color or shape (cue—sort by [color/shape], make sets of different [colors/shapes]); (h) given six objects which may be sorted into three equal sets by shape, size or color (cue—sort by [color/shape/size], make sets of different [colors/shapes/sizes]).

Verbal operation: The same procedure as stated in objective 9 is followed. After the student correctly responds, the teacher asks, "How did you sort?" and the student should name the appropriate dimension (i.e., color, size, or shape).

C. One–Many

EXAMPLES OF POTENTIAL TASKS:

Potential functional tasks: Throughout the day, students should be required to perform tasks which involve the concept of one and many (e.g., at snack time students could be offered treats and be asked to choose one or many; students who are verbal could be required to ask for one or many; the teacher could ask the students to give him/her one/many crayons; the teacher could ask the students to take one/many balls out to recess).

Potential games: A one-many component could be added to existing card and board games. That is, the students could be required to match cards to representations on the board on the dimension of one-many to advance to another square on the board (e.g.,

start | · | ··· | 🏠 | 🏠 🏠 🏠 | ··· |). See Section B. Sets—

Examples of Potential Tasks for a more detailed description of the games).

Potential tasks which are applicable to repeated practice:
1. Make object sets of one and many in the instructional setting.
2. Make flannel item sets of one and many in the instructional setting.
3. Touch or label pictures of sets as one or many in the instructional setting.

BEHAVIORAL PREREQUISITES:

Motor Imitation, B. Sets (Objective 2).

BEHAVIORAL OBJECTIVE 1

Presented with a model of the correct response and sets of one and many like objects, the student should take the set of one or the set of many when the teacher points to the correct set and says, "Take one" or "Take many."

Instructional sequence: The student should be able to take the set of 1 or many when given a model and presented sets of: (a) objects grouped in sets of 1 and 4; (b) objects grouped in sets of 1 and 3; (c) two-dimensional representations of one or many objects.

Verbal operation: Presented with a set of one or many like objects, and when the teacher points and says, "This is (one/many). Is this one or many?" the should should say, "One" or "Many."

BEHAVIORAL OBJECTIVE 2

Presented with sets of one and many like or unlike objects, the student should take the set of one or the set of many when given the cue: "Take one" or "Take many."

Instructional sequence: The student should be able to take one or many when presented sets of: (a) objects grouped in sets of 1 and 4; (b) objects grouped in sets of 1 and 3; (c) two-dimensional representations of one or many objects.

Verbal operation: Presented with a set of one or many like or unlike objects and asked, "Is this one or many?" the student should say, "One" or "Many."

BEHAVIORAL OBJECTIVE 3

Given a set of six objects and asked, "Take 1" or "Take many," the student should take one or many objects.

Instructional sequence: The student should be able to take a group of one or many objects when given: (a) a set of six like objects, (b) a set of 6 unlike objects.

Verbal operation: The same procedure described in objective 3 is followed. After the student takes the set with one or many objects and the teacher says, "That set has one or many. What does that set have?" and the student should say, "One" or "Many."

D. One-to-One Correspondence

EXAMPLES OF POTENTIAL TASKS

Potential functional tasks:
1. Throughout the day, the student should be required to perform tasks which involve one-to-one correspondence (e.g., give each student a chair, give each student a cookie, put an ice cube in each glass, give each place setting a fork).
2. Students with the requisite skills should perform the potential functional tasks in the format delineated in I. Story Problem, 1. One-to-One Correspondence.

Potential tasks which are applicable to repeated practice:
1. Aligning sets of objects in arrangements which manifest one-to-one correspondence in the instructional setting.
2. Aligning sets of flannel items in arrangements which manifest one-to-one correspondence in the instructional setting.

BEHAVIORAL PREREQUISITE

B. Sets (Objective 2); See I. Story Problems, 1. One-to-One Correspondence.

Behavioral objective 1: The teacher places a set of objects (e.g., cups) in a vertical array and gives another set of objects (e.g., straws) less than or equal in number to the first set to the student. When the teacher says, "Give each (cup) one/a (straw)," the student should assign objects on a basis of one-to-one correspondence between sets. If there was one (straw) for each (cup), the teacher says, "There are enough straws." If there was not a (straw) for each (cup), the teacher could say, "not enough straws'' and wait for the student to ask or gesture for more (straws). When the student has given each (cup) a (straw), the teacher says, "There are enough." If the sets were unequal, the teacher could also say "too many cups" and have the student take away the appropriate number of cups and then say there are enough.

Introductory Activity—Procedure: Students are seated around a table for "milk and cookie break" and a student is to give one cup or one napkin to each of the other seven and put one in his own place: (a) The teacher hands one cup or one napkin to a student and says, "Give one/a cup to Ed," "Give one/a cup to Mary," etc., or "Give one/a napkin to Laura," etc.; (b) The teacher gives eight cups or eight napkins to a student and says, "Give one/a cup to everyone" or "Give one/a napkin to everyone." (Correction procedure: If the student has "leftovers" or gives "too many" to one student, the teacher says, "Look, does everyone have one/a cup and napkin?" or "Look, Ed does not have one/a cup or napkin," etc.); (c) The teacher gives a student more than eight cups and eight napkins and says, "Give one/a cup to everyone," or "Give one/a napkin to everyone."

Instructional Sequence: The student should be able to establish one-to-one correspondence between sets of items which vary in material, relationship of materials, array, and equivalence between sets. The following columns represent these parameters and a potential sequence within each parameter. Then a sequence which integrates the parameters is suggested. There are many steps in the instructional sequence, and teachers should teach each array and set equivalence. However, they may opt not to teach each array across all combinations of materials and materials relationships, as delineated in the suggested sequence.

Materials	*Relationship of Materials*	*Arrays*	*Set Equivalence*
1. Objects	1. Functionally related Items (e.g., cups and saucers, straws and glasses)	1. Vertical (e.g., ⦂)	1. Equivalent sets and the student indicates that there are enough.
2. Flannel items	2. Like Items (e.g., cups and cups	2. Horizontal (e.g., ⦂⦂)	2. Unequal sets and the student indicates that 1 set does not have enough and needs more.

Materials	Relationship of Materials	Arrays	Set Equivalence
3. Pictures	3. Unrelated items (e.g., blocks and bears)	3. Varied arrays and students can align the sets in one-to-one correspondence (e.g., ∴ ∴)	3. Unequal sets and the student indicates that 1 set has too many and items should be taken away.
4. Worksheets		4. Domino configuration e.g., ∷ ∷	4. Unequal sets and the student indicates that 1 set does not have enough, or that the other has too many and solves the problem by adding more or taking away.
		5. Linear arrays (e.g., ⋯ | ⋯ This array is essential to addition.	
		6. Varied arrays and the student is not allowed to move members of the sets (e.g., ∴ .∙∙)	

a. Sets of objects which have a functional relationship (e.g., cups and straws) when the sets are equal in number (enough)
  1. Vertical arrays
  2. Horizontal arrays
  3. Varied arrays and the students align the sets in one-to-one correspondence
  4. Domino configurations

    5. Linear arrays
    6. Varied arrays and the students cannot move the items in the sets
  b. Sets of objects which have a functional relationship when the student's set does not have enough objects
    1. Vertical arrays
    2. Horizontal arrays
    3. Varied arrays and the students align the sets in one-to-one correspondence
    4. Domino configurations
    5. Linear arrays
    6. Varied arrays and the students cannot move the items in the sets
  c. Sets of objects which have a functional relationship when the student set has too many objects.
    1. Vertical arrays
    2. Horizontal arrays
    3. Varied arrays and the students align the sets in one-to-one correspondence
    4. Domino configurations
    5. Linear arrays
    6. Varied arrays and the students cannot move the items in the sets

Throughout the remaining steps, the arrays should be varied between the ones taught above and the student's set should have enough, not enough or too many.

  d. Sets of objects which have a functional relationship
  e. Sets of flannel items or pictures which have a functional relationship (e.g., shirts and pants)
  f. Like sets of objects (e.g., blocks and blocks)
  g. Unlike sets of objects which have no functional relationship (e.g., blocks and bears)
  h. Like sets of flannel items, or pictures (e.g., squares and squares)
  i. Unlike sets of pictures or flannel items which have no functional relationship (e.g., shirts and chairs)

Verbal operation: The teacher presents a set of objects, pictures or flannel items (e.g., cups) in a vertical array and presents another set of objects (e.g., straws) less than or equal to the first set to the student. When the teacher says, "Give each (cup) one/a (straw)," the student should assign objects (straws) on a basis of one-to-one correspondence between sets. Then when the teacher asks, "What can you do?" the student should say, "All done/enough/same" if the sets were equal or

"Add/more" if the sets were not equal. If the student appropriately asks for "more," the teacher should give the student more (straws). When the student has given each (cup) a (straw), the student should then say, "enough/done/same." If the sets were unequal, the student could say "take away" and eliminate the appropriate number of items in response to the "What can you do?" question.

E. Equivalence

EXAMPLES OF POTENTIAL TASKS

Potential functional tasks: Utilize the same tasks that were used for one-to-one correspondence.

Potential games: An equivalence component should be added to existing card and board games. That is, students could be required to match cards on the basis of equivalence. See B. Sets—Examples of Potential Tasks, for a description of the games. Games, such as dominos, which require matching on the basis of numbers should be introduced.

Potential tasks which are applicable to repeated practice:
1. Make equivalent sets of objects in the instructional setting.
2. Make equivalent sets of flannel items in the instructional setting.

BEHAVIORAL PREREQUISITES
C. One-Many; D. One-to-One Correspondence (Objective 1).

BEHAVIORAL OBJECTIVE 1
When the teacher places a selected number of items (from 1 to 10) in his/her set and says, "Make your set equal to my set," the student should use the operation of one-to-one correspondence to make his/her set equal, and then place an equals sign between the two sets, (i.e., the student should match members of his/her set with the teacher's until there are no unmatched members).

Teacher	Student	Teacher	Student

Instructional sequence: The student should be able to make his/her set equal and place an equals sign when the items are arranged in: (a) vertical arrays—: = :; (b) horizontal arrays—‖; (c) varied arrays— : ., .: → :: ; (d) linear arrays—· · · = · · ·

Verbal Operation: Students with verbal skills should be taught rational counting and should be required to solve equivalence problems by counting the number of objects in the teacher's set, then counting out and placing the same number of objects in their set. When the teacher asks, "Are there enough?" or "Are the sets equal?", the students should check their answer by using the operation of one-to-one correspondence to insure that each member of the teacher's set is matched to a member of their set, and then say "enough" or "equal." Verbal students without rational counting skills would not be required to count, but only to say "equal" or "enough" after matching the members of the sets in one-to-one correspondence.

BEHAVIORAL OBJECTIVE 2

Given two pair of equal sets in a selected array and the cue, "Find the sets which are equal," the student should find equal sets by using the operation of one-to-one correspondence (See objective 2) and then put an equals sign between them.

Subobjectives: The student should be able to find equal sets by using the operation of one-to-one correspondence when set members are arranged in vertical, horizontal, or linear arrays.

Verbal Operation: Students with verbal skills should be taught rational counting, and should be required to solve equivalence problems by counting the number of objects in the sets and matching sets with equal numbers. When the teacher asks, "How can you tell the sets are equal?" the students should check their answers by using the operation of one-to-one correspondence to insure that a member of each set is matched to a member of its paired set and then say - "equal." It is not necessary that verbal students be required to count.

F. More and Less

EXAMPLES OF POTENTIAL TASKS

Potential functional tasks: Students should be required to perform tasks which involve the concepts of more and less throughout the day (e.g., at snack time, students could be offered sets of many and few treats and asked to take either the set with more or the set with less; students who are verbal should be required to ask for the set with more or the set with less; the teacher could ask the students if they want more or less treats than another student).

Potential games: Games such as checkers, dominos, and races[6] in which the students align their pieces (e.g., dominos, checkers, or tallies) in a configuration which manifests one-to-one correspondence at the end of the game to ascertain who has more and less to determine the winner.

Potential tasks which are applicable to repeated practice:
1. The students could denote sets of objects as more and less in the instructional setting.
2. The students could denote sets of flannel items as more and less in the instructional setting.
3. The students could denote pictures of object sets as more and less in the instructional setting.

MORE

BEHAVIORAL PREREQUISITES
C. One-Many (Objective 1); B. Sets (Objective 2); D. One-to-One Correspondence (Objective 1); G. Counting (1. Rational, Objective 3); and Equivalence (E. Equivalence, Objective 2).

BEHAVIORAL OBJECTIVE 1
Given two sets unequal in quantity and the cue, "Take/touch more," the student should use the operation of one-to-one correspondence to choose the set with more (i.e., the student should match the objects in the sets in one-to-one correspondence and take/touch the set with at least one object left unmatched).

---

[6]For example, numeral recognition races where teams or individuals compete to call out the numeral name first and a tally is scored for each win, $\frac{\text{Team 1} \mid \quad //// }{\text{Team 2} \mid \quad ///// }$. (See G. Counting—Examples of Potential Tasks, for a more complete description of a numeral recognition game).

Instructional sequence: The student should touch "more:" (a) given sets of 2 and 10 objects in a vertical array aligned in one-to-one correspondence; (b) given sets of 3 and 10 objects in a vertical array aligned in one-to-one correspondence; (c) given sets of 2 and 7 objects in a vertical array aligned in one-to-one correspondence; (d) given sets of 3 and 5 objects in a vertical array aligned in one-to-one correspondence; (e) given sets of 2 and 3 objects in a vertical array aligned in one-to-one correspondence; (f) given sets of 5 and 6 objects in a vertical array aligned in one-to-one correspondence; (g) follow a–f again and the student has to align the sets in one-to-one correspondence; (h) given sets of objects in horizontal, domino, linear, and varied arrays; (i) given sets of 3 and 10 2-D representations; (j) given sets of 3 and 5 2-D representations; (k) given sets of 5 and 6 2-D representations.

Verbal operation: Students with verbal skills should be taught rational counting and be required to solve the "more" problems by counting the objects in each set and saying the number in it. When the teacher points to each set and says, "Which is more, (number) or (number)?" the student should say, "(number) is more." Then, when the teacher says, "How can you tell?" the student should say "match" and match the objects in the sets in one-to-one correspondence, point to the set with at least one object left unmatched and say, "more." Students who are verbal but do not rationally count should follow the procedure articulated in objective 1, then point to the set with more and say, "More."

2. LESS
BEHAVIORAL PREREQUISITE:

F. More and Less (1. More).

BEHAVIORAL OBJECTIVE 1

Given two sets unequal in quantity and the cue, "Take/touch *not* more," the student should use the operation of one-to-one correspondence (as described in "more") and take/touch the set with "*not* more."

$$\vdots \;\; \rightarrow \;\; \vdots \quad\quad \textit{not} \text{ more}$$

Subobjective: The student should be able to take/touch the set with "not more" when presented sets: (a) varying in number from 1 to 10; (b) varying in spacial dimension (See the instructional sequence for "more").

Verbal operation: Same as for "more," except the student must take the set with not more and say, "Not more."

BEHAVIORAL OBJECTIVE 2

Given two sets unequal in quantity and the cue, "Take/touch less," the student should use the operation of one-to-one correspondence (as described in "more") to choose the set with "less."

Subobjective: The student should be able to take/touch the set with less when presented sets: (a) varying in number from 1 to 10; (b) varying in spacial dimension (See the instructional sequence for the "more").

Verbal Operation: Same as for "more," except the student must choose the set with less and say, "less."

3. MORE/LESS
BEHAVIORAL PREREQUISITES

F. More and Less (1. More); F. More and Less (2. Less).

Behavioral objective 1: Given two sets of varying quantities and the cue, "Take/touch (more/less)," the student should use the operation of one-to-one correspondence (as described in "more") to choose the set with more or less.

Instructional sequence: The student should take/touch the set with more or less when presented with sets: (a) varying in number from 1 to 10; (b) varying in spacial dimension (See the instructional sequence for the "more").

Verbal operation: Same as "more,' except the student must choose the set with more or less and say, "more" or "less."

4. CONSERVATION OF NUMBER
BEHAVIORAL PREREQUISITES

F. More and Less (3. More/Less)

Behavioral objective 1: Presented two equivalent sets or two nonequivalent sets from three to nine items aligned in an arrangement which manifests one-to-one correspondence and asked if the sets are equal, the student should use the operation of one-to-one correspondence to determine if they are equal and indicate that they are equal or not equal. When the teacher either spreads all the members of both sets further apart or moves them closer together such that the sets are still arranged in a configuration which manifests one-to-one correspondence and asks if the sets are equal, the student should indicate that the sets are still equal or not equal.

Correction Procedure: If a student errs, the teacher should rearrange the members of the sets in their original configurations, and through the one-to-one correspondence operation demonstrate that the sets are equal or not equal. Then the teacher should help the student change the spatial arrangement of the members of the sets and demonstrate that the sets are still equal or not equal through the one-to-one correspondence operation. Note: Make this task into a fun game.

Instructional sequence: (a) Sets containing three functionally related objects in a vertical array (e.g., ∷→∶ ∶) when the teacher spreads the objects apart. (b) Sets of five functionally related objects in vertical array when the teacher spreads the objects apart. (c) Sets of seven functionally related objects in a vertical array when the teacher spreads the objects apart. (d) Sets of nine functionally related objects in a vertical array when the teacher spreads the objects apart. (e) Sets of three, five, seven, and nine functionally related objects in horizontal (e.g., ∷∷→∶ ∶ ∶) and linear (e.g., · · ·/· · ·→· · ·/· · ·) arrays when the teacher spreads the objects apart. From here on, vary using vertical, horizontal, and linear arrays. (f) Follow steps a–e when the teacher moves the objects closer together. From here on, vary, spreading the objects apart and moving them closer together. (g) Sets of three, five, seven, and nine like objects. (h) Sets of three, five, seven, and nine unlike unrelated objects.

BEHAVIORAL OBJECTIVE 2

Presented two equivalent sets or two nonequivalent sets of from three to nine items aligned in an arrangement which manifests one-to-one correspondence and when the teacher asks if the sets are equal, the student should use the operation of one-to-one correspondence and then indicate that they are equal or not equal. When the teacher either spreads the members of one set apart or moves them closer together, so that the two sets are no longer aligned in a configuration which manifests one-to-one correspondence and asks if the sets are equal, the student should indicate that the sets are still equal or not equal.

Correction Procedure: If a student errs, the teacher should arrange the members of the sets in their original configurations, and through the one-to-one correspondence operation demonstrate that the sets are either equal or not equal. Then the teacher should help the student change the spatial arrangement of the members of one set and demonstrate that the sets are still equal or not equal through the one-to-one correspondence operation. Note: make this task into a fun game.

Instructional sequence: Follow the sequence a–f of objective 1 then: (g) Subgroup the members of one set (e.g., :::::→:ˑ..ˑ.ˑ:.) instead of merely moving the members closer together or spreading them apart. (h) Vary the arrangement of the members of one set (e.g., ::::: → .ˑ:..) instead of merely moving the members closer together or spreading them apart. (i) Sets of three, five, seven, and nine like objects. (j) Sets of three, five, seven, and nine unlike unrelated objects.

BEHAVIORAL OBJECTIVE 3

Presented two equivalent sets or two nonequivalent sets of three to nine items aligned in an arrangement which does not manifest one-to-one correspondence (use arrangements from objectives 2 and 3), and when the teacher asks if the sets are equal, the student should use the operation of one-to-one correspondence to determine if they are equal, and then indicate that the sets are equal or not equal. Then, when the teacher adds one member to each set and asks if the sets are equal, the student should indicate that the sets are still equal or not equal.

Correction procedure: If a student errs, the teacher should take away the additional members and through the one-to-one correspondence operation demonstrate that the sets are equal or not equal. Then the teacher should help the student add one member to each set and demonstrate that the sets are still equal or not equal through the one-to-one correspondence operation.

Instructional sequence: Follow the sequence delineated in objective 1, a–f then: (a) add two members to both sets; (b) add three members to both sets.

BEHAVIORAL OBJECTIVE 4

Presented two equivalent sets or nonequivalent sets of three to nine items aligned in an arrangement which does not manifest one-to-one correspondence (use arrangements from objectives 2 and 3, and asked if the sets are equal, the student should use the operation of one-to-one correspondence to determine if they are equal and then indicate that the sets are equal or not equal. When the teacher adds one member to only 1 set and asks if the sets are equal, the student should use the operation of one-to-one correspondence to determine if the sets are still equal or not equal, and indicate that the sets are either equal or not equal.

Correction procedure: If a student errs, the teacher should take away the addition member, and through the one-to-one correspondence operation, demonstrate that the sets are equal or not equal. Then the teacher should help the student add a member to one set and demonstrate that the sets are equal or not equal through the one-to-one correspondence operation.

Instructional Sequence: Follow the same sequence delineated in objective 1, a–f then: (a) add two members to one set; (b) add three members to one set.

BEHAVIORAL OBJECTIVE 5

Presented two equivalent sets or nonequivalent sets of three to nine items aligned in an arrangement which does not manifest one-to-one correspondence (use arrangements from objective 2 and 3), and the teacher asked if the sets are equal, the student should use the operation of one-to-one correspondence to determine whether they are equal and then indicate that the sets are equal or not equal. When the teacher takes one member away from each set and asks if the sets are equal, the student should indicate that the sets are still equal or not equal.

Correction Procedure: If a student errs, the teacher should add one member to each set, and through the one-to-one correspondence operation demonstrate that the sets are equivalent or nonequivalent. Then the teacher should help the student add one member to each set and demonstrate that the sets are still equal or not equal through the one-to-one correspondence operation.

Instructional Sequence: Follow the sequence delineated in objective 1, a–f then: (g) Take away two members from each set. (h) Take away three members from each set.

BEHAVIORAL OBJECTIVE 6

Presented two equivalent sets or nonequivalent sets of three to nine items aligned in an arrangement which does not manifest one-to-one correspondence (use arrangements from objectives 2 and 3) and asked if the sets are equal, the student should use the operation of one-to-one correspondence to determine whether they are equal, and then indicate that the sets are equal or not equal. When the teacher takes away one member from only one set and asks if the sets are equal, the student should use the operation of one-to-one correspondence and indicate that the sets are either equal or not equal.

Correction procedure: If a student errs, the teacher should add a member to the set subtracted from and through the one-to-one correspondence operation demonstrate that the sets are equal or not equal. Then the teacher should help the student take a member away from one set and demonstrate that the sets are equal or not equal through the one-to-one correspondence operation.

Instructional sequence: Follow the same sequence delineated in objective 1, a–f then: (g) Take away two members from one set. (h) Take away three members from one set.

G. Counting Forward

Counting requires the students to make a verbal approximation of each number. Nonverbal students may be taught to make a gesture or sign to represent each number or to point to representations of each number on a number line, and when appropriate, the object being counted while counting.

EXAMPLES OF POTENTIAL TASKS
Potential Functional Tasks:

1. Throughout the day, the students should be required to use counting operations (e.g., bring me three crayons, get two milks for snack).
2. Students who are learning to order numerals should be required to use the skill throughout the day (e.g., when lining up to go outside the teacher may say, "Tom, you be number one/first, Mary, you be number three/third. Terry, you be number two/ second; when preparing to play a game, the teacher may assign turns by saying, "Mary you be number one/first, etc."; when assigning seats the teacher may say, "Terry, you sit in the first seat, etc.")

Potential Games:

1. Rational counting components should be added to the existing

board games (e.g., the students could shake dice, spin a spinner, or turn over a card with a numeral on it, move their marker
the appropriate number of squares, and then perform the skill
represented on the square to remain in the square, such as label
a numeral | start | 3 | 6 | 8 |).

2. Counting songs which incorporate rational counting, rote counting, and/or numeral recognition should be devised.

3. Numeral recognition races should be employed. These races
could be between individual students or teams. The teacher
could hold up a numeral and the first individual or team to call

out the numeral name would receive a tally $\dfrac{\text{Team 1} \mid ////}{\text{Team 2} \mid //////}$; the

team or individual with the most tallies would win. (See F.
More—Examples of Potential Tasks for a description of how to
use the concept of "more" to determine the winner). The
teacher may design the game so that the same individuals or
team do not consistently win or lose. Students often enjoy rac-
ing and to beat the teacher, or their own best performance.

*Potential tasks which are applicable to
repeated practice:*

Perform counting, numeral recognition, numeral ordering, etc.
using objects, numerals, etc., in the instructional setting.

1. RATIONAL

BEHAVIORAL PREREQUISITE

Verbal Imitation; B. Sets (Objective 2); C. One-Many (Objective 2).

BEHAVIORAL OBJECTIVE 1

Presented a set of one to five objects arranged in horizontal or
vertical arrays and asked, "How many (objects)?" the student should
count the objects assigning a number (at least make a sound) to each
object as he/she touches or moves it.

Instructional sequence: The student should count the objects
when presented: (a) a set of one to three objects in a horizontal array;
(b) a set of three to five objects in a horizontal array; (c) a set of one
to five objects in a horizontal array; (d) a set of one to five objects in a
vertical array.

BEHAVIORAL OBJECTIVE 2

Presented a set of one to five objects in a varied array and asked to
count out a number less than the number in the array, the student

should count out the correct number. (If this is too difficult for the student, he/she should be taught to arrange the objects in a horizontal or vertical array before or while counting.)

Instructional sequence: The student should be able to count out the correct number of objects when: (a) asked to count out a number of objects equal to that presented; (b) asked to count out a number of objects less than that presented.

Note: Throughout this objective, the students should be permitted to put the objects out in a vertical or horizontal array. In the objectives that follow, the teacher may choose to place the objects only in the array the student used in this objective. (See I. Story Problems, 1. One-to-One Correspondence).

BEHAVIORAL OBJECTIVE 3

Presented with one to five objects, six to ten objects, or 11–15 objects in one, two, or three horizontal or vertical arrays and asked, "How many" or "Count the (objects)," the student should count the objects.

Instructional sequence: The student should count the objects when presented: (a) a set of 6–8 objects in two horizontal arrays; (b) a set of 8–10 objects in two horizontal arrays; (c) a set of 6–10 objects in two horizontal arrays; (d) a set of 6–10 objects in two vertical arrays; (e) a set of one–10 objects in one or two horizontal or vertical arrays; (f) a set of 11–15 objects in three horizontal arrays; (g) a set of 11–15 objects in three vertical arrays; (h) a set of 11–15 objects in one, two, three horizontal or vertical arrays; (i) a set of 1–10 in one horizontal or vertical array; (j) a set of 10–20 in two horizontal or vertical arrays; (k) a set of 20–30 in two horizontal or vertical arrays; (l) a set of 1–30 in one, two, or three horizontal or vertical arrays.

BEHAVIORAL OBJECTIVE 4

Presented a varied array of 1–20 objects and asked to count out a number less than the array presented, the student should count out the appropriate number of objects. (If this is too difficult for the student, he/she should be taught to arrange the objects in horizontal or vertical arrays before or while counting.)

BEHAVIORAL OBJECTIVE 5

Presented with objects in crooked horizontal arrays and asked, "How many" or "Count the (objects)," the student should count the objects.

Instructional sequence: Same as in objective 3, except no vertical rows are presented and all rows are crooked.

BEHAVIORAL OBJECTIVE 6

Presented objects which appear and then disappear, such as cars going down the street, the student should tally each object's appearance and then count his/her tallies when asked to, "Count the (objects)."

BEHAVIORAL OBJECTIVE 7

Presented a varied array of 2–30 the student should count the objects without touching or displacing the objects.

Instructional sequence: The student should be able to count varied arrays of objects when presented: (a) 2 to 5 objects when he/she marks each object as it is counted; (b) 2 to 5 objects without marking each object as it is counted; (c) 5 to 10 objects when he/she marks each object as it is counted; (d) 5 to 10 objects without marking each object as it is counted; (e) continue sequence.

2. ROTE
BEHAVIORAL PREREQUISITE

G. Counting (1. Rational, Objective 3).

BEHAVIORAL OBJECTIVE 1

When the teacher says, "Count to (number)," (from one to five), the student should count to the number.

Instructional sequence: The student should count to a number when asked to count to: (a) 2, (b) 3, (c) 4, (d) 5.

BEHAVIORAL OBJECTIVE 2

When the teacher says, "Count from one to a (number)," and then asks, "What are you going to count from?" and "What are you going to count to?" the student should correctly answer the questions and then count.

Instructional sequence: The student should count from one to a number when directed to count to: (a) 3, (b) 4, (c) 5, (d) 6, (e)7, (f) 8, (g) 9, (h) 10.
Vary the number counted to from 1 to 10.

BEHAVIORAL OBJECTIVE 3

When the teacher says, "Count from (number) to (number)," and asks, "What are you going to count from?" and "What are you going to count to?" the student should correctly answer the questions and then count.

Instructional sequence: The student should count from a number to a number when directed to count: (a) from 2 to 5, (b) from 3 to 6, (c) from 1 to 8, (d) from 4 to 9.

Vary the combinations from 1 to 10.

Extended sequence:
a. count to (a number) 1–20
b. from 1 to (any number) 1–20
c. from (any number) to (any number) to 20
d. count to (a number) 1–30
e. from 1 to (any number) 1–30
f. from (any number) to (any number) to 30
g. count to (a number) 1–40
h. from 1 to (any number) 1–40
i. from (any number) to (any number) to 40
j. count to (a number) 1–50
k. from 1 to (any number) 1–50
l. from (any number) to (any number) to 50
m. count to (a number) 1–60
n. from 1 to (any number) 1–60
o. from (any number) to (any number) to 60
p. count to (a number) 1–70
q. from 1 to (any number) 1–70
r. from (any number) to (any number) to 70
s. count to (a number) 1–80
t. count to (any number) 1–80
u. from (any number) to (any number) to 80
v. count to (a number) 1–90
w. from 1 to (any number) 1–90
x. from (any number) to (any number) to 90
y. count to (a number) 1–100
z. from 1 to (any number) 1–100
aa. from (any number) to (any number) to 100

3. NUMERAL RECOGNITION
BEHAVIORAL PREREQUISITE

G. Counting (1. Rational, Objective 3).

BEHAVIORAL OBJECTIVE 1

Given a cue to take/touch a numeral from 1 to 10 when the

numerals are presented in varied arrays the student should take/touch the correct numeral.

Instructional Sequence: The student should be able to take/ touch the correct numeral or math symbol when asked to take/touch numerals (math symbols) from:
   a. 1 to 3 presented on a number line
   b. 1 to 6 presented on a number line
   c. 1 to 10 presented on a number line
   d. "+" or "="[7]
   e. 1 to 3 presented in a varied arrays
   f. 4 to 6 presented in a varied arrays
   g. 7 to 10 presented in a varied arrays
   h. 1 to 10 presented in a varied arrays

Verbal Operation: Presented with a numeral from 1 to 10 and the cue, "What (numeral) is this," the student should be able to label numerals and math symbols when asked to label numerals from:
   a. 1 to 3 presented on a number line
   b. 1 to 6 presented on a number line
   c. 1 to 10 presented on a number line
   d. "+" and "="
   e. 1 to 3 presented in a varied array
   f. 1 to 6 presented in a varied array
   g. 7 to 10 presented in a varied array
   h. 1 to 10 presented in a varied array

Extended Sequence:
   a. 11 to 20 on a number line
   b. 11 to 20 in a varied array
   c. 20 to 30 on a number line
   d. 20 to 30 in a varied array
   e. 1 to 50 on a number line
   f. 30 to 40 in a varied array
   g. 40 to 50 in a varied array
   h. 11–50 in a varied array
   i. 1–70 on a number line
   j. 70
   k. 50–60 in a varied array
   l. 11–60 in a varied array
   m. 60–70 in a varied array
   n. 11–70 in a varied array

---

[7]The students should be taught to discriminate and label "+" as "plus" and "and"; and "−" as "equal" and "is."

  o. 70–100 on a number line
  p. 70–80 in a varied array
  q. 11–80 in a varied array
  r. 80–90 in a varied array
  s. 11–90 in a varied array
  t. 90–100 in a varied array
  u. 11–100 in a varied array

Writing numerals: Students who are learning to write should be taught to write numbers in mixed order when presented the cue "What is this number? Print this number." when a visual cue (model is provided, and when presented the cue "Print _____" when no visual cue is provided. For each step a–z, the students should write numbers in order and after mastering writing numbers in order write them in mixed orders. For example, steps a–b would be as follows: a_1, visual cue 11–20 in order; a_2, visual cue 11–20 in mixed order; b_1, no visual cue 11–20 in order; b_2, no visual cue 11–20 in mixed order.)

  a. visual cue 11–20
  b. no visual cue 11–20
  c. visual cue 20–30
  d. no visual cue 20–30
  e. no visual cue 11–30
  f. visual cue 30–40
  g. no visual cue 30–40
  h. no visual cue 11–40
  i. visual cue 40–50
  j. no visual cue 40–50
  k. no visual cue 11–50
  l. visual cue 50–60
  m. no visual cue 50–60
  n. no visual cue 11–60
  o. visual cue 60–70
  p. no visual cue 60–70
  q. no visual cue 11–70
  r. visual cue 70–80
  s. no visual cue 70–80
  t. no visual cue 11–80
  u. visual cue 80–90
  v. no visual cue 80–90
  w. no visual cue 11–90
  x. visual cue 90–100
  y. no visual cue 90–100
  z. no visual cue 11–100
  aa. no visual cue 1–100

4. MATCHING NUMERALS TO QUANTITIES
BEHAVIORAL PREREQUISITES

G. Counting (1. Rational, Objective 3); G. Counting (3. Numeral Recognition, Objective 1, Instructional Sequence Step 'h').

BEHAVIORAL OBJECTIVE 1

Presented with a numeral from 1 to 10, a set of objects and the cue, "Count out this many," the student should count out the appropriate number of objects.

Instructional sequence: The student should be able to count out the correct quantity given:
a. one numeral from 1 to 3
b. one numeral from 4 to 6
c. one numeral from 7 to 10
d. one numeral from 1 to 10

Subobjectives: The student should be able to match numerals to quantities in a worksheet format and match numerals to lines and figures.

Instructional sequence:
a. match numerals to quantities in worksheet format

b. match numerals to lines

c. match numerals to fingers (this is a prerequisite to addition with fingers)

5. MATCHING QUANTITIES TO NUMERALS

BEHAVIORAL PREREQUISITES

G. Counting (1. Rational, Objective 3); G. Counting (3. Numeral Recognition, Objective 1, Instructional Sequence Step 'h').

BEHAVIORAL OBJECTIVE 1

Given a set of objects from 1 to 10, a number line and the response cue, "Find the numeral which shows this many," the student should count the objects and then choose the appropriate numeral on the number line.

Instructional sequence: The student should be able to match a quantity to a numeral given:
a. one quantity from 1 to 3
b. one quantity from 4 to 6
c. one quantity from 7 to 10
d. one quantity from 1 to 10

Subobjective: The student should be able to match quantities to numerals in a worksheet format and match lines and fingers to numerals.

Instructional sequence:
a. match a quantity to a numeral in a worksheet format

$$2\!\!\nearrow^{\boxed{\cdots}}\ 1$$

b.
match a quantity of lines to a numeral   1 $\searrow^{\boxed{///}}$ 2
c. match a quantity to an equal quantity of fingers (this is a prerequisite to addition with fingers)

6. ORDERING NUMERALS

BEHAVIORAL PREREQUISITES
G. Counting (1. Rational, Objective 3); G. Counting (2. Rote, Objective 2); G. Counting (3. Numeral Recognition, Objective 1).

BEHAVIORAL OBJECTIVE 1
When the teacher places a number card (e.g., $\boxed{1\,|\,2\,|\,3\,|\,4\,|\,5}$) on the table, puts numerals from one to five in front of the student in a varied array and says "Count to five," the student should count to five as the teacher points to the numerals on the number card. Then when the teacher says, "Match the numbers in order from one to five," the student should order his/her numerals by matching them to the numerals on the number card.

BEHAVIORAL OBJECTIVE 2
When the teacher places numerals from one to five in front of the student in a varied array and says, "Put the numerals in order one, two, three, four, five," the student should order the numerals from least to most.

BEHAVIORAL OBJECTIVE 3
When the teacher places numerals from one to five in front of the

student in a varied array and says, "Put the numerals in order, start with one," the student should order the numerals from least to most.

Instructional sequence: (a) same as objective 1 with numerals 1 through 7; (b) same as objective 2 with numerals 1 through 7; (c) same as objective 3 with numerals 1 through 7; (d) same as objective 1 with numerals 1 through 10; (e) same as objective 2 with numerals 1 through 10; (f) same as objective 3 with numerals 1 through 10.

BEHAVIORAL OBJECTIVE 4

When presented with a number line (e.g., 1–5, 1–7, 1–10) with one, two, or three numbers missing, and the teacher says "Look. Count to (5/7/10). What number(s) is/are missing?" the student should tell the teacher which number(s) is/are missing.

Instructional sequence:
a. Set 1:   1 __ 3 4 5
                1 2 __ 4 5
                1 2 3 __ 5
                1 2 3 4__

b. Set 2:   1 __ 3 __ 5
                __ 2 __ 4 5
                __ __ 3 4 5
                1 2 __ __ 5
                1 2 3 __ __

c. Set 3:   1 __ __ __ 5
                __ __ __ 4 5
                __ __ 3 __ __
                __ 2 __ __ 5
                1 __ __ 4 5

BEHAVIORAL OBJECTIVE 5

When presented with a number line with one, two, or three numbers missing and the teacher says, "What number(s) is/are missing?," the student should say which number(s) is/are missing.

Instructional sequence: Same as in objective 4.

BEHAVIORAL OBJECTIVE 6

This objective is appropriate for students who can write numbers in sequence (i.e., 1–3, 1–7, 1–10) dot to dot (e.g., 1 __ __ __ __ __ 7).

When presented with a number line (e.g., 1 _ _ _ _ _ 7) with one, two, or three numbers missing and the teacher says, "Count what number(s) is/are missing. Print the missing number(s)," the student should print in the missing numbers.

Instructional sequence: Same as objective 4.

BEHAVIORAL OBJECTIVE 7

When presented with a number line (e.g., 1–5, 1–7, or 1–10) and the teacher says, "Touch the number that comes after ( ), what number comes after ( )?" the student will touch and label a number which comes after a given number.

BEHAVIORAL OBJECTIVE 8

When presented with a number line one (e.g., 1–5, 1–7, or 1–10) and asked, "What number comes after ( )?" the student will label and number which comes after the given number.

BEHAVIORAL OBJECTIVE 9

When the teacher asks, "What number comes after ( )?" the student should label the number that comes after the given number.

Instructional sequence for before, more, and less:
a. Same as objective 7 except the teacher says, "Touch the number(s) which come(s) before ( ). What number(s) come(s) before ( )?"
b. Same as objective 8 except the teacher asks, "What number(s) come(s) before ( )?"
c. Same as objective 9 except the teacher asks, "What number(s) come(s) before ( )?"
d. Same as objective 7 except the teacher says, "Touch the number(s) which is/are more than ( ). Tell me some/a number(s) which is/are more than ( )?"
   Note: Number lines of the following form should facilitate the instruction of the concepts of "More" and "Less."

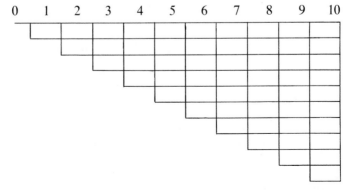

e. Same as objective 8 except the teacher asks, "Tell me some/a number(s) which is/are more than ( )?"

f. Same as objective 9 except the teacher asks, "Tell me some/a number(s) which is/are more than ( )?"

g. Same as objective 7 except the teacher says, "Touch the number(s) which is/are less than ( ). Tell me some number(s) which is/are less than ( )?"

h. Same as objective 8 except the teacher asks, "Tell me some/a number(s) which is/are less than ( )?"

i. Same as objective 9 except the teacher asks, "Tell me some/a number(s) which is/are less than ( )?"

7. ORDERING QUANTITIES

BEHAVIORAL PREREQUISITES

F. More and Less; G. Counting, 6. Ordering Numerals.

BEHAVIORAL OBJECTIVE 1

Presented with from one to five sets of unequal quantities (varying from one to five), and asked to, "Order the sets of (objects) or (2-D representations)," the student should count the number of objects in each set and place the set with more objects (the number which comes after in counting) to the right of the set with less (the number which comes before in counting). The student should then check this ranking by matching the objects in the sets using the one-to-one correspondence operation to insure that a set with at least one left over was placed to the right of the matched set.

Instructional sequence: The student should be able to order sets when given: (a) two sets varying in quantity from 1 to 2; (b) three sets varying in quantity from 1 to 3; (c) four sets varying in quantity from 1 to 4; (d) five sets varying in quantity from 1 to 5.

H. Addition

The addition objectives articulated here require the students to use the operation of rational counting in solving the problems. As described in the rational counting objectives, this operation requires the students to make a verbal approximation of each number as they touch the objects being counted. Nonverbal students could be taught to solve addition problems by making gestures to represent each number or number statement or by pointing to representations of each number or number statement.

EXAMPLES OF POTENTIAL TASKS

Potential Functional Tasks: 1. Students who have the requisite skills should be required to use addition in the format delineated in I. Story Problems, 2. X + Y = __ and/or 3. X + __ = Y.

Potential Games: 1. An addition component should be added to the existing board and card games (e.g.,

| start | 1 + 1 = __ | 2 + 3 = __ | 5 + 1 = __ |).

That is, when students land on a square they should be required to solve an addition problem in order to remain on the square.

2. Students who are learning math facts should participate in math fact races.

Potential Tasks Which are Applicable to Repeated Practice: Performing addition problems with objects, flannel items, lines, numerals, and fingers in the instructional setting.

COGNITIVE TASKS

Mastery of these tasks is not a prerequisite to a student's being taught addition. In fact, it is not expected that students will have met the prerequisites for these tasks before they are taught addition. After students have mastered the prerequisites for these tasks, they should be taught them across many materials with various numbers of objects in the sets. Do not skip these tasks. They are essential to a student's mastery of the underlying conceptual base of addition. That is, the concept that the sum of two sets is greater/more than either component set.

BEHAVIORAL PREREQUISITES

F. More/Less (4. Conservation of Number, Objective 6); G. Counting (1. Rational, Objective 3); G. Counting (3. Numeral Recognition); G. Counting (4. Matching Numerals to Quantities); G. Counting (5. Matching Quantities to Numerals); G. Counting (6. Ordering Numerals, Objective 9).

BEHAVIORAL OBJECTIVE 1

When the teacher places a number line with removeable numerals, a set of (2) (cups) and a set of (3) (saucers) in front of the student and asks:

a. "How many (cups) are there?" the student should count the (cups), state the number and place the correct numeral from the number line next to a picture of a (cup).

    b. "How many (saucers) are there?" the student should count the (saucers), state the number and place the correct numeral from the number line next to a picture of a (saucer).

    c. "Join/give each (cup) a (saucer)," the student should join the sets, count the total number of objects, and place the correct numeral from the number line next to a picture of (cups and saucers).

    d. "Are there more (cups/saucers) or more (cups and saucers)?" (Note: Frequently reverse the order of the question such that the correct response is not always the second portion of the question, e.g., "Are there more (cups and saucers) or more (cups/saucers)?") The student should say, "There are more (cups and saucers)." Then when the teacher asks, "How can you tell?" the student should say "(5) (cups and saucers) is more than (number) (cups/saucers)."

BEHAVIORAL OBJECTIVE 2

    When the teacher places a set of (2) (cups) and a set of (3) (saucers) in front of the student and asks, "Are there more (cups/saucers) or more (cups and saucers)?" (Note: Again, frequently reverse the order of the question). The student should say, "There are more (cups and saucers)." Then when the teacher asks, "How can you tell?" the student should say "(5) (cups and saucers) is more then (number) (cups/saucers)."

1. ADDITION WITH OBJECTS

BEHAVIORAL PREREQUISITES

    B. Sets (Objective 8); E. Equivalence (Objective 2); and G. Counting (1. Rational, Objective 3).

BEHAVIORAL OBJECTIVE 1

    Given two sets of objects (e.g., cups, cups) and when the teacher points and says, "This is a set of (cups) and this is a set of (cups), (plus/join) the sets," the student should join the sets. Then when the teacher says, "Now you have one set of (cups). Point to the set of (cups)," the student should point to the set of (cups).

    Instructional sequence: The student should join sets of: (a) boys, girls, (b) objects, (c) flannel items.

Verbal operation: Same as described in objective 1. After the student joins the sets the teacher says, "Now you have a set of (cups)," "What is this set?" and the student should say, "A set of (cups)."

BEHAVIORAL OBJECTIVE 2

Given two sets of objects (e.g., blocks, blocks) and when the teacher points to one set and says:

a. "How many (blocks) are there?" (the teacher points to the first set) the student should count the (blocks) and state the number.

b. "How many (blocks) are there?" (the teacher points to the second set), the student should count the (blocks) and state the number.

c. "Plus/join the sets of (blocks) and (blocks) the student should joint the sets.

d. "How many (blocks) are there?" the student should count the (blocks) and state the number.

2. NUMERALS AND OBJECT

BEHAVIORAL PREREQUISITES

G. Counting (3. Numeral Recognition, Objective 1); G. Counting (4. Matching Numerals to Quantity, Objective 1); G. Counting (Matching Quantities to Numerals, Objective 1); G. Counting (1. Rational, Objective 3); H. Addition (1. Addition With Objects, Objective 2).

BEHAVIORAL OBJECTIVE 1

Presented with two factor boxes containing a selected number of like objects (1–10) (e.g., balls, balls), a number line from 1–10 with removable numerals, and the cue, "Find the numeral that shows how many," the student should:

$$\boxed{\,\cdot\cdot\,} + \boxed{\,\cdot\cdot\,} =$$

a. Count the number of objects in each factor box and place the correct numeral under it.

$$\underset{2}{\boxed{\,\cdot\cdot\,}} + \underset{2}{\boxed{\,\cdot\cdot\,}} =$$

b. Move the objects from the factor boxes to the sums box.

$$\boxed{\cdot\cdot} + \boxed{\cdot\cdot} = \boxed{\cdot\cdot\cdot}$$
$$\quad 2 \qquad 2$$

c. Count the objects in the sum's box and place the correct numeral under it.

$$\square + \square = \boxed{\cdot\cdot\cdot}$$
$$2 \qquad 2 \qquad 4$$

d. Point to each numeral and math symbol and say: "(2) (balls) (and/plus) (2) (balls) (is/equals) (4) (balls)." or "(2) (and/plus) (2) (is/equals) (4)."

e. When the teacher asks, "Does (number) and (number) equal (number)" the student should label the numeral under each factor box, count out that number of objects and place them in each factor's box, and then align the items in the factors' boxes and the items in the sums box in one-to-one correspondence and say, "(number) plus (number) equals (number)."

$$\boxed{\cdot\cdot} + \boxed{\cdot\cdot} = \boxed{\cdot\cdot\cdot}$$
$$2 \qquad 2 \qquad 4$$

Instructional sequence: The student should perform steps a–d when: (a) the teacher cues or prompts each step; (b) without teacher cues or prompts.

3. NUMERALS AND LINES

Note: Teachers sometimes opt to skip addition with lines and go directly to "5. Fingers" because addition with fingers is a more functional skill across environmental configurations.

BEHAVIORAL PREREQUISITES

H. Addition: (2. Numerals and Objects, Objective 1), motor ability to draw lines.

BEHAVIORAL OBJECTIVE 1

Presented with two factor boxes containing a selected number of lines (1–10), a number line from 1 to 10 with removable numerals and the response cue, "Find the number that shows how many," the student should: (a) count the number of lines in each factor box and put the correct numeral under it; (b) count the number of lines in both factor boxes and draw the number of lines counted to in the sum's box; (c) place the correct numeral under the sum's box; (d) point to each numeral and symbol and say, "(2) and/plus (2) is/equals (4)."

$$[// + // = \underline{\quad}] \quad [// + // = \underline{\quad}] \quad [// + // = ////]$$
$$ 2 \quad\quad 2 \quad\quad\quad 2 \quad\quad 2 \quad\quad 4$$

Self-Correction Procedure: At this point, the student should be taught a procedure for checking his/her answer. After the student has completed objective 1, the teacher points to each side of the equal sign and asks, "Are the sides equal?" And when the student responds, "Yes/No," the teacher asks, "How can you tell?" and the student should count the lines on each side of the equal sign and say, "(4) equals (4)." (The student could also match the objects or lines on each side of the equals sign in one-to-one correspondence to show that the sides are equal.)

Instructional Sequence: The student should perform steps a–d when: (a) the teacher cues or prompts each step, (b) without teacher cues or prompts.

4. NUMERALS

BEHAVIORAL PREREQUISITES
    H. Addition (3. Numerals and Lines).

BEHAVIORAL OBJECTIVE 1
    Given an equation of the form 2 + 2 = __, a number line with removeable numerals and the cue, "Find the number which shows how many," the student should: (a) draw the appropriate number of lines under each of the factor boxes; (b) count all the lines and state the number; (c) draw the nuumber of lines stated under the sum's box; (d) place the appropriate numeral (from the number line) in the sum's box; (e) point to each numeral and math symbol and say "(2) plus (2) equals (4)."

$$[2 + 2 = \underline{\quad}] \to [2 + 2 = \underline{\quad}] \to [2 + 2 = \underline{\quad}] \to [2 + 2 = 4].$$
$$ // \quad // \quad // \quad // \quad //// \quad // \quad // \quad ////$$

Self Correction Procedure: Same as described in Addition With Numerals and Lines.

Instructional Sequence: The student should perform steps a–c when: (a) the teacher cues or prompts each step; (b) without cues or prompts.

See I. Story Problems, 2. X + Y = ____

5. FINGERS

BEHAVIORAL PREREQUISITES

H. Counting (2. Rote, Objective 3).

BEHAVIORAL OBJECTIVE 1

Given an equation of the form 2 + 3 = ___ when the teacher asks the student:

a. "Which side do you start counting on?" the student should touch the side without the empty box (i.e., the side to the right of equals sign).

b. "What do you count to?" the student should count on his finger(s) to the number in the second factor box (e.g., 3), and then while holding up those finger(s) (3) and starting with the number in the first factor box (e.g., 2), the student should count the fingers held up (e.g., 3—4—5), say the number counted to (5), and place it in the sums box;

c. "What does (two) plus (three) equal (___)?" the student should say, "(two) plus (three) equals (five)."

[2 + 3 = __]   [2 + 3 = 5]

Self-Correction Procedure: After the student completes Objective 1 and when the teacher asks, "How can you tell," the student should draw lines under each numeral and use the correction procedure described in "Addition With Numerals and Lines."

BEHAVIORAL OBJECTIVE 2

The student should be able to perform the behaviors listed in objective 1 (a–c) without teacher cues.
See I. Story Problems, 2. X + Y = ____.

BEHAVIORAL OBJECTIVE 3

Given an equation of the form ___ + 2 = 5 or 2 + ___ = 5, and when the teacher asks the student the following:

a. "Which side do you start counting on?" the student should touch the side without any empty box.

b. "What do you count *to*?" the student should point to the numeral on the side of the equation without an empty box and label it (e.g., 5).

c. "What number do you start counting from?" the student

should point to the numeral on the side of the equals sign with an empty box and label it (e.g., 2).

d. "(2) plus how many equals (5)?" the student should start counting with the numeral on the side of the equals sign with an empty box (e.g., 2) and count up to the numeral on the side of the equals without an empty box (e.g., 5), holding up a finger (or drawing a line) for each number he/she counts (e.g., 3, 4, 5). Then the student should count the fingers he/she is holding up, say the number counted to (e.g., 5) and place this numeral in the sum's box.

e. (2) plus how many equals (5)?" the student should say "(2) plus (3) equals (5)."

Instructional sequence: The student should add with his/her fingers given problems of the form: (a) 2 + __ = 5; (b) __ + 3 = 5.

Self-Correction: After the student completes objective 3, and when the teacher asks, "How can you tell?" the student should draw lines under each numeral and use the correction procedure described in "Addition With Numerals and Lines."

BEHAVIORAL OBJECTIVE 4

Given an equation of the form __ + 2 = 5 or 2 + __ = 5, the student should be able to perform the behaviors listed in Steps a through e (behavioral objective 3) correctly and in sequence without any teacher cues. See I. Story Problems, 3. X + __ = Y.

6. FACTS[8]

BEHAVIORAL PREREQUISITES

G. Counting (2. Rote, Objective 3); H. Addition (4. Numerals, Objective 1), and/or H. Addition (5. Fingers, Objective 2).

BEHAVIORAL OBJECTIVE 1

When orally presented problems of the form zero plus one, one plus one, two plus one . . . up to nine plus one, the student should state the answer for each problem.

Instructional sequence: The student should be able to state the answer when given the problems: (a) in sequence (i.e., one plus one,

---

[8]These objectives should be taught through group and individual drills. There should be an emphasis on rapid rates of responding. Races which emphasize rate should be utilized to teach math facts. Races are fun and because they require rapid and accurate responding; they should facilitate rote memorization of facts.

two plus one, etc.) presented visually; (b) in sequence presented orally; (c) in random order.

BEHAVIORAL OBJECTIVE 2

When presented orally in sequence with problems of the form: $5 + 0 = 5, 5 + 1 = 6, 5 + 2 = \_\_, 5 + 3 = \_\_$, etc., the student should be able to state the answer for each problem.

> *Instructional sequence:*
> a. Problems presented visually (e.g., on the blackboard) and orally $5 + 0 = 5; 5 + 1 = 6; 5 + 2 = \_\_; 5 + 3 = \_\_$.
> b. Problems presented orally.

BEHAVIORAL OBJECTIVE 3

When orally presented with a problem where the first factor is more than the second factor (e.g., $5 + 2 = \_\_$), the student should derive the answer by performing a series of problems starting with $X + 0 = X$. (e.g., $5 + 0 = 5, 5 + 1 = 6, 5 + 2 = 7$).

> *Instructional sequence:*
> a. Problems presented visually (e.g., on the blackboard) and orally

$$5 + 0 = 5$$
$$5 + 2 = \_\_ \rightarrow 5 + 1 = 6$$
$$5 + 2 = 7$$

> b. Problems presented orally.

BEHAVIORAL OBJECTIVE 4

When orally presented with number pair problems such as one plus one, two plus two . . . up to 10 plus 10, the student should state the answer.

BEHAVIORAL OBJECTIVE 5

When orally presented with a problem where the first factor is less than the second factor (e.g., $4 + 5 = \_\_$) the student should derive the answer by using an addition sequence starting with the number pair of the first factor

$$4 + 4 = 8$$
$$4 + 6 = \_\_ \rightarrow 4 + 5 = 9$$
$$4 + 6 = 10$$

Instructional sequence:

a. Problems presented visually (e.g., on the blackboard) and orally of the form:

1. 0
   1
   2
   3
   4
   5
   4 + 6 =

2. and the teacher points and says, "What does four plus six equal?" "What number should we start counting with?" the student should find the number pair of the first factor and say 4 + 4 and go through the sequence from 4 + 4 = 8 to 4 + 6 = 10 as the teacher writes it out.

3. 0
   1
   2
   3
   4 + 4 = 8
   4 + 5 = 9
   4 + 6 = 10

b. Problems presented visually (e.g., on the blackboard) and orally of the form:

1. 4 + 6 =

2. and the teacher asks, "What does four plus six equal?" the student should go through the sequence, starting with the number pair of the first factor as the teacher writes the sequence on the board.

3. 4 + 4 = 8
   4 + 5 = 9
   4 + 6 = 10

c. Problems presented orally.

Behavioral objective 6:   When orally presented addition problems with sums up to 10, the student should state the answer.

I. Story Problems

EXAMPLES OF POTENTIAL TASKS:

POTENTIAL FUNCTIONAL TASKS:

Students should be required to solve problems in the story problem formats delineated below throughout the day (e.g., when students are passing out pencils to four students and they only have two pencils, they must figure out how many more pencils they need, $2 + \_\_ = 4$; when an item costs ten cents and students only have eight cents, they should figure out how many more cents they need, $8 + \_\_ = 10$; students who have six cents and are given five cents should figure out how many cents, they have altogether $6 + 5 = \_\_$; students who have won five checkers and then win two more should figure out how many checkers they won altogether, $5 + 2 = \_\_$).

1. ONE-TO-ONE CORRESPONDENCE

BEHAVIORAL PREREQUISITES

Motor Imitation; B. Sets (Objective 2); G. Counting (1. Rational, Objective 2).

BEHAVIORAL OBJECTIVE 1

When the teacher presents a set (e.g., students) and presents a student with a set of objects (e.g., cookies) less than, equal to, or more than the first set and says, "Give each (student) one/a (cookie)," the student should assign objects (cookies) in an arrangement which manifests one-to-one correspondence between sets. When the teacher asks, "Were there enough (cookies) or not enough (cookies)?" the student should say "enough," "not enough," or "too many." If there were "not enough," then the teacher asks, "What can you do?" the student should say "Add"/"More" or "Add (number)/(number) more." If there were "too many," the student should say "Take away" or count and say "Take away (number)."

Instructional sequence: The student should be able to establish one-to-one correspondence between sets of items which vary in material, relationship of materials, array and equivalence between sets. The following columns represent these parameters and a potential sequence within each parameter. Then a sequence which integrates the parameters is suggested. There are many steps in this instructional sequence, and teachers should teach each array and set equivalence. However, they may opt not to teach each array across all combinations of materials and material relationships, as delineated in the suggested sequence.

Materials	Relationship of Materials	Arrays	Set Equivalence
1. Objects	1. Functionally Related Items (e.g., cups and saucers, straws and glasses)	1. Vertical (e.g., ∷)	1. Equivalent sets and the student indicates that there are enough.
2. Flannel Items	2. Like items (e.g., cups and cups)	2. Horizontal (e.g., ∷∷)	2. Unequal sets and the student indicates that one set does not have enough, and needs (number) more or add (number).
3. Pictures	3. Unrelated items (e.g., blocks and bears)	3. Varied arrays and students can align the sets in one-to-one correspondence (e.g., ∴ ∴)	3. Unequal sets and the student indicates that one set has too many and (number) items should be taken away.
4. Worksheets		4. Domino configuration (e.g., ∷ ∷)	4. Unequal sets and the student indicates that one set does not have enough or that the other has too many and solves the problem by adding more or taking away.
		5. Linear arrays (e.g.,··· | ···) This array is essential to addition.	
		6. Varied arrays and the student is not allowed to move members of the sets (e.g., ∴ ∵)	

a. Sets of objects which have a functional relationship (e.g., cups and straws) when the sets are equal in number (enough).
   1. Vertical arrays
   2. Horizontal arrays
   3. Varied arrays and the students align the sets in one-to-one correspondence
   4. Domino configurations
   5. Linear arrays
   6. Varied arrays and the students cannot move the items in the sets
b. Sets of objects which have a functional relationship when the student's set does not have enough objects. Throughout the remaining objectives, the student having enough or not enough objects should be randomly varied.
   1. Vertical arrays
   2. Horizontal arrays
   3. Varied arrays and the students align the sets in one-to-one correspondence
   4. Domino configurations
   5. Linear arrays
   6. Varied arrays and the students cannot move the items in the sets
c. Sets of objects which have a functional relationship when the student's set has too many objects.
   1. Vertical arrays
   2. Horizontal arrays
   3. Varied arrays and the students align the sets in one-to-one correspondence
   4. Domino configurations
   5. Linear arrays
   6. Varied arrays and the students cannot move the items in the sets
   Throughout the remaining steps, the arrays should be varied between those taught above and the student's set should have enough, not enough, or too many items.
d. Sets of objects which have a functional relationship.
e. Sets of flannel items or pictures which have a functional relationship (e.g., shirts and pants).
f. Like sets of objects (e.g., blocks and blocks).
g. Unlike sets of objects which have no functional relationship (e.g., blocks and bears).
h. Like sets of flannel items, or pictures (e.g., squares and squares).

i. Unlike sets of pictures or flannel items which have no functional relationship (e.g., shirts and chairs).

2. X + Y = __

BEHAVIORAL PREREQUISITES

H. Addition (4. Numerals, Objective 1 and/or 5. Fingers, Objective 2—If the student meets the fingers prerequisite, have him/her solve all problems using fingers.)

BEHAVIORAL OBJECTIVE 1

When the teacher presents a story problem of the form 2 + 2 = __ and says we can make stories into math problems, watch:
   a. Using a student or him/herself as a model, the teacher says, "Tom has two records" and points to the records. "What can we write down" and the student should say "two." Then the teacher writes the numeral two and says, "Write two."
2

   b. The teacher gives Tom two more records and says "I give Tom two records. If I give what do you do?" and the student should say "Plus/add." Then the teacher writes a plus and says, "Write a plus."
2 +

   c. The teacher says, "How many records did I give Tom?" and the students should say "Two." The teacher says, "What should we write?" and the students should say "Two." Then the teacher writes two and says, "Write two."
2 + 2

   d. The teacher says, "Do you know how many records? No. What do you write?" and the students should say "Equals." The teacher then writes an equals and says, "Write equals."
2 + 2 =

   e. The teacher says, "We can find out how many records Tom has by counting or by solving the problem 2 + 2 = __. "Solve the problem." and the students should draw two lines under the second numeral 2 + 2 = __. Start counting from the first numeral (2) and count up on the line (3, 4) and say "Four" and write "Four" in the blank.
2 + 2 = 4
//

   f. The teacher says, "How many records does Tom have?" and the students should say, "Four." Then the teacher says, "Let's check," counts the records, says "Four" and then says, "Right, Tom has four records and our problem says Tom has four records."

BEHAVIORAL OBJECTIVE 2

The students should solve the problems when the teacher does not write them or state answers prior to the students' solving the entire problem.

BEHAVIORAL OBJECTIVE 3

The students should solve the problem using fingers instead of lines (See H. Addition, 5. Fingers, Objective 2).

BEHAVIORAL OBJECTIVE 4

The students should solve the problems when the teacher orally presents the problems (no object prompts) such as, "Tom has two balls and I gave him two balls. How many balls does he have? Solve the problem."

BEHAVIORAL OBJECTIVE 5

Students who can read should be taught to solve story problems that are presented in printed form.

3. $X + \underline{\quad} = Y$

BEHAVIORAL PREREQUISITES

H. Addition (5. Fingers, Objective 4).

BEHAVIORAL OBJECTIVE 1

When the teacher presents a story problem of the form $2 + \underline{\quad} = 4$ and says, "We can make stories into math problems, watch:"
   a. "Using a student or him/herself as a model, the teacher says, "Tom has two spoons" and points to the spoons. "What can we write down?" and the students should say "Two." Then the teacher writes the numeral two and says, "Write two."
$$2$$
   b. The teacher holds up four spoons and says, "Tom needs four spoons. Do you know how many spoons Tom needs? Yes. What do you write?" and the students should say, "Equals four." The teacher then writes equals four and says, "Write equals four."
$$2 \quad = 4$$
   c. The teacher says, "What should we do?" and the students should say, "Count from two to four." Next, the teacher

says, "When we count from two to four, what do we write?" and the students should say, "Add/plus/count up." Then the teacher should write a plus and say, "Write plus."

$$2 + \quad = 4$$

d. The teacher says, "Solve the problem" and the student should start counting from two, hold up a finger for each number he/she counts (e.g., 3, 4), stop at (four), count his/her fingers and say, "(Two)" and place that numeral in the empty slot to the left of the equals.

$$2 + 2 = 4$$

e. The teacher says, "(Two) count up how many equals (four)?" and the student should say, "(Two) count up (two) equals (four)."

f. The teacher says, "How many spoons does Tom need?" and the student should say "(Two)."

BEHAVIORAL OBJECTIVE 2

The students should solve the problems when the teacher does not write or state the answer prior to the students' solving the entire problem.

BEHAVIORAL OBJECTIVE 3

The students should solve the problems when the teacher orally presents the problems (no object prompts) such as, "Tom has two spoons and needs four. How many more spoons does Tom need? Solve the problem."

BEHAVIORAL OBJECTIVE 4

Students should be able to solve functional problems, such as when setting the table and they need four spoons but only have two, they get two more spoons.

BEHAVIORAL OBJECTIVE 5

Students who can read should be taught to solve story problems that are presented in printed form.

REFERENCES

Becker WC, Engelmann S, Thomas DR: Teaching: A Course in Applied Psychology. Chicago, Science Research Associates, 1971

Brunner J: Organization of early skilled action. Child Develop, 44:1–11, 1973

Resnick LB, Wang, MC, Kaplan J: Task analysis in curriculum design: A hierarchically sequenced introductory mathematics curriculum. J Appl Behav Anal, 6:679–701, 1974

Nick Certo,
Richard Schwartz, and
Lou Brown[2]

C

Community Transportation: Teaching Severely Handicapped Students to Ride a Public Bus System[1]

This program was designed to teach severely handicapped students to ride a public bus system independently. Bus riding was taught as a functional skill which might provide a means to obtain such vital commodities as food, clothing, recreation, and medical and dental assistance. The students who participated ranged in age from 14 through 18 years, and were enrolled in Badger School, a self-contained public school for severely handicapped students in Madison, Wisconsin.

This program can be viewed as comprising two skill levels. Within the first level (Phases I, II, and III), students were taught to ride city buses to specific destinations supplied by the classroom teacher. The second level (Phase IV) entails more complex skills, in that it was essentially a problem-solving component designed to accommodate to individual transportation needs both current and future. Stated another way, Phase IV was an attempt to control for the possibility of a student becoming dependent upon the particular instructional materials and teacher assistance used in Phases I, II and III. This assistance, of course, would not be present in, or may not be relevant to, future transportation settings.

[1]The development and dissemination of this paper was supported in part by Madison Public Schools, Federal Contract No. OEC-0-74-7993, and in part by Grant No. OEG-0-73-6137 to the University of Wisconsin-Madison from the Department of HEW, Bureau of Education for the Handicapped, Division of Training Programs, Washington, D.C.

[2]The authors wish to thank Alan Ginsberg for his help in organizing and implementing the video tape components of this program.

Obviously, functional bus riding skills are only one of many very complex skill clusters that severely handicapped individuals must acquire in order to act independently and efficiently in diverse, demanding, complex, changing community environments. Thus, the skills referred to here should be viewed only as components of a more comprehensive and complex independent community functioning curriculum.

However, as part of an independent community functioning curriculum, this program attempted to provide severely handicapped students with the skills necessary to use one mode of transportation (buses) in order to get to grocery stores, doctors' offices, theaters, restaurants, and parks. Other programs, some already operative, have been designed to teach these students to use such facilities once they arrive, to use money to make purchases, to tell time so that they can determine when a movie begins or when to honor a doctor's appointment, etc.

Problems inherent in the complexities created by changing community environments surfaced continually. The Madison Metro bus system, although a good system from the point of view of the number of buses in operation, coverage of the city, and hours per day in service, has many inconsistencies. Many nonhandicapped persons may adapt to these inconsistencies with little, if any, disruption. Most severely handicapped students, however, must be taught how to adapt to them. For example, Madison bus stops generally have a particular sign stationed at a painted curb. At a number of bus stops, though, the format of the signs vary; the curbs are not painted or are painted in a variety of colors; and bus stop signs are not always placed in the same part of a city block.

Attempts were not made to teach students to adapt to all inconsistencies they might possibly encounter. However, attempts were made to provide some experience with potential problems by occasionally placing students in inconsistent situations as they rode buses and allowing them to make errors. It was hoped that with repeated interactions, they would adapt to many real or potential problem situations across a variety of bus riding conditions.

The structure of the bus system was not the only source of problems. Since the most important phases of the program involved the students riding an actual city bus, large blocks of time had to be spent outside the classroom. This, of course, reduced the time available for acquiring other equally important skills. Generally, an afternoon school session (approximately 3 hr) was required to complete one round trip on a city bus and the return to school. In an effort to attenuate this problem, a video tape component was developed in which students were presented with video tapes of bus routes in an attempt to reduce the need for teachers riding with and pointing out various destinations when instruction on a real bus route was in progress.

The extent to which parents would allow their children to use the buses independently once they learned the skills was also an issue of concern. The classroom teacher hoped to circumvent possible difficulties in this area by continually explaining the goals and procedures of the program to the parents. Parents were also informed of their children's progress in related programs that were being implemented which would eventually require a transportation component for their completion. This was done to stress further the functional aspect of bus riding to the students and to demonstrate their safe, efficient, and competent use of this mode of transportation for their parents. For example, parents were kept abreast of their childrens' progress in a program designed to teach the arranging and keeping of extraschool social appointments with classmates. Ultimately, the means by which students would keep these appointments would be the public bus system. In this way, additional independent community functioning skills were taught, extending and emphasizing potential uses of public buses, while hopefully dispelling parental fears.

The school principal, realizing the potential importance of independent transportation skills, was quite cooperative. Money was made available to help implement the program; time away from school was allowed and supported, etc. Thus, many potential administrative concerns which often impede programs such as this were avoided.

Finally, although this program was designed for use within the Madison Metro bus system, hopefully it can be modified and used to teach severely handicapped students to ride bus systems in other cities with minimal difficulty.

METHOD

Students (Ss)

The ten Ss who participated in the program were enrolled in classes for the severely handicapped at Badger School, a public school in Madison, Wis. Chronological ages ranged from 14.4 to 18.8 years ($\overline{X}$ CA = 17.0). Full scale intelligence test scores from either the Weschler Intelligence Scale for Children (WISC) or Stanford Binet (Form L-M) ranged from 47 through 75 ($\overline{X}$ I.Q. = 50.0). Medical and psychological classifications included Down's syndrome, athetoid cerebral palsy, hearing impaired, schizophrenic, brain damaged, and severe seizure involvement.

General Instructional Procedures

TEACHING PROCEDURES

1. The teacher *(T)* presented each cue once. If *S* responded correctly, *T* followed each correct response with praise.
2. If *S* did not respond, *T* repeated the cue. If *S* still did not respond, *T* repeated the cue and modeled the correct response. *T* then presented the cue again. This procedure was repeated until *S* emitted the correct response. A correct response, when using this procedure, was followed by praise.
3. If *T* presented a cue and *S* responded incorrectly, *T* quickly said, "No." *T* then implemented procedure B above.
4. During baseline trials *T* presented a cue and made the phrase "Thank you" contingent upon correct, incorrect or no responses.

Data Collection and Criterion Performance

Whether during baseline or teaching trials, each correct or incorrect response was recorded on a data sheet (See Appendix IV). In addition, if *S* failed to emit a response, an incorrect response was recorded. When *S* responded correctly after a correction procedure was employed, no data was recorded. A criterion of three consecutive correct occurrences of each response or sequence of responses without assistance from *T* was required before *S* was judged to have mastered the skill or skills of a particular phase or step.

At the beginning of each new phase and step, baseline information was secured. Baseline measures consisted of a presentation of all the cues in a particular step for three consecutive trials. If *S* performed at criterion during baseline trials, instruction was not considered necessary. If *S* responded incorrectly, he/she received instruction after the three baseline trials were completed.

During teaching components of a particular phase or step, if *S* responded correctly to all the cues for three consecutive trials, he/she had reached criterion and moved on to the next step.

Materials

buzzer—12 v D.C.
rope
cardboard
paint—white, gray, blue, black, red
red and yellow adhesive tape
3 x 6 index cards without lines

picture of a Madison Metro Bus
Madison Telephone Directory
map with bus routes drawn in of the city of Madison, Wisconsin
wooden poles
combinations of 15 and 25 cents
videotape recorder
videotape camera
batteries (Size D)
continuous contact switches
videotape monitor
various lengths of electrical wire
light bulbs (small 6 V D.C.)

A simulated cardboard Madison Metro bus was constructed for use in the classroom. This bus was large enough to serve as a functional facsimile of a city bus (6 ft x 12 ft x 5½ ft), although it was stationary. The bus was painted white, blue and gray, and seats were placed inside. the interior also contained a black coin box, a driver's seat with a steering wheel and gauges drawn on cardboard placed in front of it, and a buzzer which was connected to a rope running the length of the bus. A bus stop was constructed outside the bus. It consisted of red and yellow tape attached to the floor to simulate the coloring of the curb at some bus stops along with a sign that read, *"No Parking Bus Stop"* in red letters on a white background.

Vocabulary words taught during various steps in the program were printed individually on white index cards. These cards were also used for the printing of individual bus route cards (Appendix I). One bus route card was printed for each bus route. A bus route card consisted of the names of the bus route going to and coming from "Capitol Park."[3] It also listed the names of five places *S* could go to along each route.

Program Design and Task Analysis

PHASES

I. Teaching *S*s to ride a simulated city bus in the classroom.

II. Teaching *S*s selected places in the city of Madison where food, clothing, opportunities for recreation, and other services can be obtained, and to determine what bus to take in order to reach those places from Capitol Park.

---

[3]"Capitol Park" and "Capitol Square" will be used interchangeably throughout the program. These words refer to the circular drive in the center of Madison where the State Capitol building is located, and where all the Madison Metro bus routes originate and end.

III. Teaching *S*s to ride an actual city bus to and from Capitol Park to obtain the food, clothing, recreation opportunities, or other services listed on the bus route cards.

IV. Teaching *S*s to determine what buses to take to places that do not appear on bus route cards.

Phase I: Teaching *S*s to ride a simulated city bus in the classroom.

Step 1—*S* tells *T* the differences between a school bus and a city bus and what is meant by the term destination.

Step 2—*S* labels the various parts of a Madison Metro bus, recognizes a bus stop and demonstrates knowledge of the student fare.

Step 3—*S* emits the following behaviors in sequence after *T*'s cues have been faded using a simulated Madison Metro bus:

a. *S* says where he/she wants to go
b. *S* walks to a bus stop
c. *S* waves bus to a stop
d. *S* reads destination sign on front of bus
e. *S* enters the bus by front door
f. *S* hands the driver the bus route card and says: "Let me off near _____."
g. *S* pays fare
h. *S* sits or stands (varies)
i. *S* rings buzzer and goes to a door on cue from driver
j. *S* gets off.

Phase II: Teaching *S*s selected places in the city of Madison, Wisconsin, where food, clothing, opportunities for recreation, and other services can be obtained and what bus to take to reach the destination from Capitol Park.

Step 1—*S* demonstrates the ability to label eight "sight words" individually presented (These are words which will appear on individual bus route cards. Each bus route card should be considered a set of eight words).

Step 2—*S* points to the eight words appearing on the bus route card learned in step 1 of this phase on cue from *T*.

Step 3—*S* tells *T* the name of the bus route that would appear on the bus' destination sign when traveling between two points listed on the bus route card.

Step 4—*T* asks the *S* to view a videotape of a bus route and names a destination where *S* should get off. *S* responds by throwing a switch which lights a bulb when the appropriate stop flashes on the monitor.

Phase III: Teaching *S*s to ride an actual city bus to and from

Capitol Park to obtain the food, clothing, recreational opportunities, or other services listed on the bus route cards.

Step 1—*S*s choose one of the bus routes they have learned. *T* chooses the last stop on this route as *S*s' destination. Using their bus route cards, *S*s determine the name of the route leaving and returning to Capitol Park from the destination chosen. *S*s verbally rehearse the stops along this route. They find the proper bus stop at Capitol Square.

Step 2—*S*s, starting at Capitol Park, take the appropriate bus to the destination chosen in Step 1 and return. They travel in a small group with *T*.

Step 3—Same as step 2, except *S*s travel without *T* in a small group.

Step 4—Same as step 2, except *S*s travel alone.

Step 5—The *S*s perform the prerequisite skills necessary to transfer buses in the classroom.

Step 6—Using their bus route cards in the classroom, *S*s gain experience at finding the buses they need to take when transferring.

Step 7—*S*s ride a city bus, traveling in a small group with *T*, choosing two destinations and transferring to reach them.

Step 8—Same as step 7, except *S*s travel in a small group without *T*.

Step 9—Same as step 7, except *S*s travel alone.

Step 10—*S*s perform the prerequisite skills for taking a city bus from their house to Capitol Park and returning home in the classroom.

Step 11—*S* chooses a destination, takes a city bus from his/her home traveling with *T* to Capitol Park, transfers to the destination and returns home.

Step 12—Same as step 11, except *S* rides alone.

Phase IV: Teaching *S*s how to determine what bus to take to places that do not appear on bus route cards.

Step 1—Teaching *S*s to label cards with the names of major streets in the city of Madison (This is done to facilitate labeling addresses in later stages of this phase.).

Step 2—*S* looks up one of the streets acquired in step 1 of this phase in the *Street Index* on the back of a map of Madison, Wis. He/She then labels the coordinates listed next to the name of the street located.

Step 3—*S* gains experience at finding streets on a map of Madison, Wis.

Step 4—Teaching *S*s how to use the Madison Telephone Directory to find addresses and phone numbers of places they would like to go to. *S* also writes down the address and phone number that he/she finds.

Step 5—*S* calls Directory Assistance to find out the phone number of a place he/she has been unable to locate in the phone book. *S* then calls the number to find the address.

Step 6—*S* uses an actual phone to call Directory Assistance to find a phone number. *S* calls this number and writes down the address.

Step 7—*S* finds an exact location on a map of Madison, using the numerical component of the address.

Step 8—*S* gains experience at finding exact locations on the map.

Step 9—*S* is taught the names of various bus routes listed on the map.

Step 10—*S* gains experience finding bus routes on the map.

Step 11—*S* learns how to find the closest route to a particular street address he/she has located on the front of the map.

Step 12—*S* gains experience at finding the appropriate bus route for various addresses, using a map of Madison.

Step 13—*S* looks up an address in the phone book, locates the closest bus route, and rides the bus to the destination with *T* and a small group of *S*s.

Step 14—Same as step 13, except *S*s travel in a small group without *T*.

Step 15—Same as step 13, except *S* travels alone.

Instructional Program

Phase I:

Teaching *S*s to ride a simulated city bus in the classroom.

Step 1—S tells *T* the differences between a school bus and a city bus and what is meant by the term destination.

Materials: No material needed.

Data Collection: Whether on baseline or reinforcement, responses 9–13 should be recorded on the data sheet. *S*'s name should appear in the column at the left and the responses for 9–13 should be written in at the top. Criterion, then, for the teaching trials would be the five correct responses in a row for three consecutive trials. Baseline would consist of the presentation of the cues for these five responses for three consecutive trials.

Sequence of Cues and Responses:

Teacher's Cues	*Student's Responses*
1. What do you call the bus that takes you to school?''	1. School bus
2. "Who has ridden on a city bus?"	2. Various

3. "What's different about a city bus and a school bus?"

3. Color; pay for city bus; city bus doesn't stop at house

4. "Who rides the city bus with your parents and/ or friends?"

4. Various

5. "Who rides a city bus by themselves?"

5. Various

6. "Where do you go when you ride a city bus?" (of those who ride the city bus)

6. Various

7. "How often do you ride a city bus?"

7. Various

8. "We are going to learn to take a city bus when we want to go somewhere. A place you want to go is called a destination."

8. No response (R)

9. "When you get on a bus, the place you want to go is called a (_____)."

9. Destination

10. "If you were home and you wanted to take a bus to the Capitol Park, the Capitol Park would be your (_____)."

10. Destination

11. "What would be your destination?"

11. Capitol Park

12. "We are going to learn to take a city bus to a (_____)."

12. Destination

13. "What is a destination?"

13. Where you want to go

14. "When we finish, we'll choose a destination, take a city bus there and buy something. But first, we'll have to learn

14. No R.

what a city bus looks
like, where you pay
your money, where
you sit, and when to
get off.''

Step 2—*S* labels the various parts of a Madison Metro bus, recognizes a bus stop, and demonstrates knowledge of the student fare.
Materials: picture of Madison Metro bus
              simulated bus and bus stop
              bus route card
              money for fare
Data Collection: Whether on baseline or teaching the following
responses should be recorded: 1, 3, 4, 6, 8, 10, 17, 19, 21, 25, 27,
28, 36, 38, 42, 44, 45, 46, 49, 55, 56, 57. The *S*'s name should appear
in the column at the left and the responses should be written in at
the top. Baseline would consist of the presentation of the cues for
these 21 responses for three consecutive trials. Criterion, then, for
the teaching trials would be the 21 correct responses in a row for
three consecutive trials.

Sequence of Cues and Responses:

Teacher's Cues	*Student's Responses*
1. Point to the front of the bus in the picture and say: "This is the (_____) of the bus."	1. Front
2. Point to the destination sign on the front of the bus and say: "This is a destination sign; it tells you where a bus is going."	2. No R.
3. Point to the destination sign and say: "What is this sign called?"	3. Destination sign
4. "What does this sign tell you?"	4. Where the bus is going
5. "A city bus does not stop at your house. When you want to ride a city bus, you have to walk to a bus stop."	5. No R.

6. "Where do you walk to
   if you want to ride a
   city bus?"

6. Bus stop

7. Point to bus stop sign
   in bus mock-up and
   say: "A bus stop has
   a sign that looks like
   this."

7. No R.

8. "What does this sign
   say?"

8. *No Parking Bus Stop*

9. "At some bus stops they
   not only have a sign
   that says, (_____),
   but they also paint the
   curbs."

9. *No Parking Bus Stop*

10. Point to the simulated
    curb and say: "They
    paint the curbs
    (_____)."

10. Red and yellow

11. "When you get to a bus
    stop, you wait right
    by the bus stop sign
    until the bus comes.
    Sometimes a bus will
    come right away, but
    sometimes you may
    have to wait for as
    long as 20 minutes."

11. No R.

12. "When you take a city
    bus, where do you
    walk to?"

12. Bus stop

13. "How do you know when
    you are at a bus stop?"

13. Sign—*No Parking Bus
    Stop* and red and
    yellow curb

14. "Where do you wait for
    the bus?"

14. At bus stop—next to
    sign

15. Displaying the picture
    of the bus say: "Point
    to the front door."

15. *S* points to front door
    in picture.

16. "Point to the back
    door."

16. *S* points to back door
    in picture.

17. "Do you use the front
    door or back door to
    go in the bus?"

17. Front door

18. Point to the back door   18. Back
    and say: "Which door
    is this?"

19. Point to the back door   19. No
    and say: "Can you use
    this door to go in the
    bus?"

20. "Which door can you use   20. Front
    to go in the bus?"

21. "Which doors do you   21. Front or back
    use to get off the
    bus?"

22. "Are bus rides free?"   22. No

23. "It costs 25¢ for   23. No R.
    adults and 15¢ for
    students to ride the
    bus."

24. "Are you an adult or   24. Student
    a student?"

25. "How much do you pay   25. 15¢
    to ride the bus?"

26. "The money you pay   26. No R.
    to ride the bus is
    your fare."

27. "What is the money you   27. Fare
    pay to ride the bus
    called?"

28. Hand student a combi-   28. Student takes 15¢ in
    nation of dimes,   any combination.
    nickels, quarters
    and pennies and say:
    "Take your fare."

29. Model other combina-   29. No R.
    tions of 15¢, e.g., three
    nickels, one dime,
    and five pennies, etc.,
    and say: "You could
    also use one dime and
    five pennies, etc., to
    equal your 15¢ fare."

30. "When you ride the   30. No R.
    bus, you have to
    have exactly 15¢. If

you have more than
15¢ you can't ride
the bus, and if you
have less than 15¢
you can't ride the
bus.''

31. "When you leave   31. No R.
Badger School next
year or 2 years or
3 years from now,
you won't be a
student. You'll be
an adult.''

32. "How much do adults   32. 25¢
pay to ride the city
buses?''

33. "How much will you   33. 25¢
have to pay when you
leave Badger School?''

34. "But as long as you're   34. 15¢
at Badger School, your
fare is (_____).''

35. "As soon as you get on   35. No R.
the bus, you tell the
driver where you want
to get off; then you
pay your fare.''

36. "When do you pay your   36. After tell driver where
fare?''   want to get off.

37. Pointing to the coin   37. No R.
box in the bus mock-up
say: "This is a fare
box; this is where
you pay your fare.''

38. "What is this called?''   38. Fare box

39. "Where do you pay your   39. Fare box
fare?''

40. "When do you pay your   40. After tell driver where
fare?''   want to get off.

41. Holding up a bus route   41. No R.
card say: "Whenever
you want to take a
bus, you must look up

your destination on
the bus route card."

42. "What is this card   42. Bus route card
    called?"

43. "If you want to go to   43. No R.
    McDonald's, you hand
    the bus driver the bus
    route card, point to
    the name McDonald's
    and say: "Let me off
    near McDonald's,
    please."

44. "What do you say to   44. "Let me off near
    the driver when you   McDonald's, please."
    show him your bus
    route card?"

45. "When do you show the   45. As soon as you get on
    driver the bus route   the bus
    card?"

46. "When you ride the bus,   46. Sit down
    you tell the driver
    where you want to
    get off, pay your
    fare and then
    (_____)."

47. "You should always try   47. No R.
    to sit close to the
    driver so he can tell
    you when to get off."

48. "When you ride a city   48. Sit next to the driver
    bus, you should
    (_____)."

49. "If there are a lot of   49. Stand up
    people sitting in the
    bus and there is no
    seat left for you to
    sit in, you will have
    to (_____)."

50. "When will you have to   50. When there are no seats
    stand up?"   left

51. "If you have to stand   51. No R.
    up, you should hold on
    to a seat so that you
    don't fall down."

52. "If you have to stand up, you should (_____) so you won't fall down."	52. Hold on to a seat
53. "When the bus driver tells you that the next stop is your destination, it's time to get off the bus."	53. No R.
54. "When it's time to get off the bus, you should get up and walk to either the front or back door."	54. No R.
55. "When the driver says that the next stop is your destination, you should (_____)."	55. Walk to front or back door
56. "When will the driver open the door?"	56. When bus stops
57. "When the bus driver opens the door, you (_____)."	57. Get off

Step 3—*S* emits the following behaviors in sequence after *T*'s cues have been faded, using a simulated Madison Metro bus:

   a. *S* says where he/she wants to go.
   b. *S* walks to bus stop.
   c. *S* waves the bus to a stop.
   d. *S* reads the destination sign on the front of the bus.
   e. *S* enters the bus by the front door.
   f. *S* hands the driver the bus route card, points to his/her destination, and says: "Let me off near _____."
   g. *S* pays fare.
   h. *S* sits or stands (varies with condition, three trials of each).
   i. *S* rings buzzer and goes to a door on cue from the bus driver.
   j. *S* gets off the bus.

Materials: bus and bus stop mock-up
                    bus route card

Data Collection: Data should be collected for responses 1, 2, 7, 10, 12, 13, 14, 16, 18, 19, 20. Baseline should consist of three trials when there is a seat available on the bus, and three trials when no seats are available and the *S* must stand. After these trials are completed, the teaching trials begin. Criterion is three trials of 11 correct responses in a row for standing and three for sitting. Each response should be written across the top of the data sheet, with the *S*'s name appearing in the left column.

Sequence of Cues and Responses:

Teacher's Cues	*Student's Responses*
1. Ask *S*, "Where do you want to go?"	1. McDonald's[4]
2. *T* is standing at the simulated bus stop and asks the student to: "Come over and ride the bus."	2. *S* walks to the bus stop
3. "Where are you?"[5]	3. At a bus stop
4. "How do you know you're at a bus stop?"	4. Sign—*No Parking Bus Stop* and red and yellow curb
5. "If you are at a bus stop and your bus is coming and you want it to stop so you can get on, you must wave your arm (model) to make sure the driver stops."	5. No R.
6. "What do you do to make sure the bus will stop."	6. ". . wave your arm. ." (verbal R)
7. "Do it."	7. Waves arm
8. Point to the destination sign on the front of the bus and say: "This is the (_____)."	8. Destination sign
9. "It tells you (_____)."	9. Where the bus is going
10. "Where is this bus going?"	10. Capitol Park

---

[4]This answer will vary with *S*, but McDonald's will serve as an example in this step.
[5]Cues 3–18 should be faded.

11. "What door do you use to go in the bus?"

11. Front

12. "Go in."

12. Walks in front door

13. "Show the driver your bus route card and point to your destination (the destination is McDonald's)."

13. Shows driver card and points to McDonald's

14. "When you show the driver your card you say: "(_____).""

14. "Let me off near McDonald's, please."

15. "After you ask the driver to let you off at your destination, you (_____)."

15. ". . pay your fare"

16. "Pay your fare."

16. Deposits 15¢ in fare box

17. "What do you do now?"

17. "Sit down" or "Stand up" (varies with trial)

18. "Do it."

18. Stands or sits close to driver (varies with trial)

19. Driver says: "Next stop, McDonald's (this cue will not be faded)."

19. Rings buzzer, gets up and walks to either front or back door.

20. Open front or back door, where student is waiting.

20. Walks out

Phase II: Teaching *S*s selected places in the city of Madison, Wisconsin, where food, clothing, opportunities for recreation, and other services could be obtained and what bus to take to reach the destination from the Capitol Park.

Step 1—S demonstrates the ability to label eight "sight words," individually presented (Sight words by category are listed in Appendix I and II. These are words which will appear on individual bus route cards. Each card should be considered a set of eight words.[6]).

---

[6]The words that appear in Appendix I and II correspond to destinations along bus routes in Madison, Wisconsin. *T*s interested in implementing this step of the program would, of course, need to make up lists of destinations which correspond to places along bus routes in his or her town.

Materials: Each of the eight words that appear on a bus route card are printed individually on an index card.

Data Collection: Record *S*'s response to cue 2 for each "sight word" presented. Each response should be written across the top of the data sheet with *S*'s name at the left. Baseline would consist of three presentations of all eight cards. Criterion for the teaching trials would be eight correct responses in a row for three trials.

Sequence of Cues and Responses:

Teacher's Cues	Student's Responses
1. "On each of these cards is printed the name of a place you can go to or the name of a bus that will take you to places in Madison. We're going to learn the names of each of these places."	1. No R.
2. *T* holds up card with word printed on it (e.g., McDonald's) and says: "Read the card."	2. Labels word
3. Repeat cue 2 for each card to be taught.	3. Labels words
4. After *S* reaches criterion on the set of eight cards, explain to *S* what each place is, what can be purchased there, etc.	4. No R.

Step 2—S points to the eight words appearing on the bus route card learned in Step 1 on cue from *T*.

Materials: Bus route card

Data Collection: Print the eight words across the top of the data sheet and record *S*'s responses to cue 6. Three trials, asking *S* to point to and label the eight words to only cue 6, would comprise the baseline phase. Criterion for teaching would be 100% correct responses for three consecutive trials.

Sequence of Cues and Responses:

Teacher's Cues	*Student's Responses*
1. Give each S a printed bus route card (see list at end) and say: "This card is called a bus route card."	1. No R.
2. "What is this card called?"	2. Bus route card
3. "This is the bus route card for the (add route name, e.g., Johnson St./Nakoma Rd.) bus route."	3. No R.
4. "Which bus route is this?"	4. e.g., Johnson St./ Nakoma Rd.
5. "There are six places you can go to on the bus written on the card. There are also the two names for the bus route. Depending upon which way you are going, the destination sign on the bus will read (e.g., Johnson St.) or (e.g., Nakoma Rd.)."	5. No R.
6. Randomly ask S to point to one of the six places to go to, or one of the two bus route names until S has responded to all eight items on the card.	6. Points to appropriate word on cue from T.

Step 3—S tells *T* the name of the bus route that would appear on the bus destination sign when travelling between two points listed on the bus route cards.

Materials: Bus route cards

Data Collection: The ten combinations of destinations with the appropriate bus route name should be written at the top of the data sheet. *S*'s responses to cue 11 should be recorded under these headings. Baseline would consist of three presentations of these ten combinations to cue 11 alone.

If *S* gets all ten correct for three consecutive presentations, he/she has reached criterion for the teaching trials. Data should be taken whether or not cues 7–10 have been faded. If the objective is to teach *S* to use these cards independently of *T*, fading these cues must be an added contingency for the criterion during the teaching trials.

Sequence of Cues and Responses:

Teacher's Cues	*Student's Responses*
1. Give *S* a bus route card, and say in reference to the name of the bus route written at the top: "What color is the name (e.g., Johnson St.)?"	1. Green (Note—the route at the top of the card will always be green.)
2. "Does the green arrow (See route cards at end) point up or down?"	2. Down (Note—the green arrow will point down on all the bus route cards.)
3. "What color is the name (e.g., Nakoma Rd.)?"	3. Red (Note—the bottom route will always be red.)
4. "Does the red arrow (See route card at end) point up or down?"	4. Up (Note—red arrow will always point up.)
5. "Let's say that you're at (e.g., Capitol Park, any place listed on bus route card); point to it."	5. *S* points as cued.
6. ". . . and you want to go to (e.g., East Towne Mall, any place other than that in No. 5); move that same	6. *S* moves finger as cued.

finger until you
come to (e.g., East
Towne Mall)."

7. "Are you reading up
or down?"[7]

7. Down or up, depends
upon places chosen;
the response would be
down in the example.

8. "Which colored arrow
points (either up or
down, depending upon
choices in No. 5 and 6)?"

8. Red or green, depends
upon places chosen.

9. "Put your finger on the
(e.g., green, depends
on places chosen) arrow."

9. S puts finger on the
tip of appropriate arrow.

10. "Now follow that arrow
back until you come to
the (e.g., green) bus
route name."

10. S moves finger back as
cued.

11. "What would be the
name of the destina-
tion sign on the
bus?"

11. e.g., Johnson St.;
depends upon places
chosen.

12. Repeat the above cues
5–11 until S has
responded to ten
combinations of places
to go for each of the
two bus route names.

12. Various

Note: After teaching S a particular bus route with Steps 1–3,
start back at Step 1 with another bus route until all
eight bus routes have been taught.

Step 4—This step involves the use of videotapes to present a simulated bus ride. Each tape was made while riding in a car, traveling the
exact route a bus would take. During the course of the taping the
camera would focus in on the bus' destination sign and the five destinations that appeared on the bus route card. Since traveling a bus
route one way involves a 15–30 min ride, the tapes were edited to
increase their usefulness in the classroom. The essential setting surrounding each destination was kept intact, along with some of the
rides between stops. It was felt that the final tapes presented the

---

[7]Cues 7–10 should be faded.

salient cues of the routes, while successfully eliminating some of the boredom that might have resulted from presenting an exact mirror image of the route to S.

In the teaching sessions, T told S where, during the taped ride, he/she should get off the bus. S responded by throwing a switch which turned on a light. A correct response entailed turning on the light as the destination cued by T flashed across the monitor.

Materials: videotapes of the bus routes
videotape recorder with monitor
desk with portable switch and
light bulb placed on top
appropriate bus route cards

Data Collection: The names of the five destinations which appear on S's bus route card for the route being viewed should be written across the top of the data sheet in random order. S's responses to cue 10 should be recorded under the appropriate destinations. Baseline would consist of three presentations of a tape for each of the five destinations. If S gets all five correct for three consecutive presentations, he/she has reached criterion for the teaching trials. Cues 1–8 should be faded.

Sequence of Cues and Responses:

Teacher's Cues	*Student's Responses*
1. "We are going to look at a movie of the Johnson St./Nakoma Rd.[8] bus route on T.V."	1. No R.
2. "What bus route are we going to see on T.V.?"	2. Johnson St./Nakoma Rd.
3. "Let's look at the movie (T shows videotape)."	3. S views T.V.
4. T hands S the appropriate bus route card and says, "What bus route card is this?"	4. Johnson St./Nakoma Rd.
5. "What bus route are we going to see in the movie?"	5. Johnson St./Nakoma Rd.

---

[8]The Johnson St./Nakoma Rd. bus route will be used as an example throughout the teaching steps.

6. "From now on, when I			6. No R.
show you the movie,
I'm going to ask you
to get off the bus at
one of the destinations
printed on the Johnson
St./Nakoma Rd. bus
route card."

7. "When you see the desti-		7. No R.
nation in the movie,
it will be time to get
off the bus. You can
show me when you should
get off the bus by
flipping this switch
(*T* demonstrates)."

8. "Flip the switch to see		8. *S* flips switch.
how it works."

9. "You're at Capitol Park,		9. Johnson St.
and you want to get
off at Tenney Park.
What would be the des-
tination sign on the
bus?"

10. "Watch the movie and		10. *S* flips switch and
get off at Tenney			lights bulb when *Tenney*
Park. When you see			*Park* appears on the
Tenney Park, flip the		monitor.
switch to show me
where you want to
get off."

Note: Repeat this sequence showing both directions of each
bus route to be taught.

Phase III: Teaching *S*s to ride an actual city bus to and from
Capitol Park to obtain the food, clothing, recreational opportunities,
or other services listed on the bus route cards.

*Step 1—S*s choose one of the bus routes they have learned. *T*
chooses the last stop on this bus route card as *S*s' destination.
Using their bus route cards, *S*s determine the name of the route
leaving Capitol Park and going to their destination. They also determine the route coming back to Capitol Park. *S*s verbally re-

hearse the stops along the route they have chosen. This section also functions as a review of the procedure for riding a bus with the inclusion of additional information needed to find the proper bus stop at Capitol Square.

Materials: Bus route cards

Data Collection: This step is used to foreshadow the bus ride on the following day. Because of this, all *S*s' responses required in this step will have been acquired in previous phases. There is only one new response to be learned; the response to cue 13. Data need only be taken for this response in this step. Baseline would be three presentations of this question as it occurs in sequence with the rest of the cues in this step. The teaching criterion would be simply three correct responses in a row to cue 13.

Sequence of Cues and Responses:

Teacher's Cues	*Student's Responses*
1. "We're going to go out and ride a real city bus tomorrow. I would like you to choose a bus route to go on."	1. No R.
2. "What bus route would you like to ride?"	2. *S*s name route—choose route that most want to go on.
3. "We are going to start out at the Capitol Park and go to East Towne Mall. When we're at East Towne Mall, we can buy a record to use at school. Each of you will ride the bus with one teacher and two other students."[9]	3. No R.
4. Give *S* a Johnson St./ Nakoma Rd. bus route card.[10]	4. No R.
5. "What is the name of the bus route at the top of the card?"	5. Johnson St.

---

[9]The Johnson St./Nakoma Rd. bus route will be used as an example.
[10]Cues 4–13 are a modified version of Step 3 of Phase II.

6. "What is the name of the bus route at the bottom of the card?'

6. Nakoma Rd.

7. "(S's name), you will be at the Capitol Park and you will want to go to East Towne Mall. What will be the destination sign on the bus?"

7. Johnson St.

8. "(S's name), when you get to East Towne Mall, we'll get off the bus and buy a record. then we will have to come back to the Capitol Park."

8. No R.

9. "(S's name), you will be at East Towne Mall, and you will want to go to the Capitol Park. What will be the destination sign on the bus?"

9. Nakoma Rd.

10. "Now when we're at the Capitol Park, what's the first thing we will have to do in order to ride the bus?"

10. Walk to a bus stop.

11. "How do you know when you're at a bus stop?"

11. Sign—*No Parking Bus Stop* and red and yellow curb

12. "At the Capitol Park, the bus stops not only have red and yellow curbs and a sign that says *No Parking Bus Stop,* but they also have another sign that will have the names of the buses that stop there."

12. No R.

13. "So if you are at the
Capitol Park and you
want to take the
Johnson St. bus, you
would have to walk
to a bus stop with
a red and yellow
curb, a sign that
says, *No Parking
Bus Stop* and a sign
under that that
says (_____)."

13. Johnson St.

14. "Tell me what you do
when you get on the
bus."[11]

14.
  a. Wave bus to stop.
  b. Go in front door.
  c. Show driver route
     card
  d. "Let me off at
     East Towne Mall,
     etc."
  e. Pay fare—15¢
  f. Sit down
  g. Rings buzzer and
     goes to door when
     driver says, "Next
     stop, East Towne
     Mall, etc."
  h. Get off

15. "Look at your bus
route cards. If
you are on the
Johnson St. bus
traveling to East
Towne Mall, what
will be the first
place you will see
after you leave the
Capitol Park?"

15. Tenney Park

16. "What will be next?"
17. ". . . next?"
18. ". . . next?"
19. ". . . next?"

16. East High School
17. McDonald's
18. Shakey's Pizza
19. East Towne Mall

---

[11]Prompt responses *S*s fail to make.

20. "When you are travel-   20. Shakey's Pizza
    ing back to the
    Capitol Park from
    East Towne Mall,
    what will be the
    first stop you will
    see?"
21. ". . . next?"   21. McDonald's
22. ". . . next?"   22. East High School
23. ". . . next?"   23. Tenney Park
24. ". . . next?"   24. Capitol Park

*Step 2—S*s, starting out at Capitol Park, take the appropriate bus to the destination chosen in Step 1 of this phase. They travel in a small group with *T*. *T* insures that each *S* recognizes each of the five stops listed on their bus route card as they pass them. While at their destination, *S*s perform the behaviors required by the place they have traveled to (e.g., if they go to East Towne Mall, they could make a small purchase). *S*s then take the appropriate bus back to Capitol Park. *T* again makes sure that *S*s recognize the five stops along the way.

Materials: Appropriate bus route card

Data Collection: Since the final goal is to teach *S*s to independently ride the bus and due to the difficulties in collecting data in this situation, data will only be collected in Step 4 when *S* rides the bus alone.

Sequence of Cues and Responses:

Teacher's Cues	*Student's Responses*
1. After *S*s arrive at the Capitol Park with the Johnson St./Nakoma Rd. bus route card, *T* says: "We're at the Capitol Park and we want to go to East Towne Mall. What will be the destination sign on the bus?"[12]	1. Johnson St.

---

[12]The Johnson St./Nakoma Rd. card will again serve as an example in this section.

2. "In order to catch the Johnson St. bus, first we have to walk to a (_____)."

2. Bus stop

3. "How do we know when we're at the right bus stop?"

3. Sign—*No Parking Bus Stop;* Sign—Johnson St. and red and yellow curb.

4. "Find a bus stop where you can catch the Johnson St. bus."

4. *S*s find Johnson St. bus stop.

5. "We'll wait here until the bus comes with Johnson St. as the destination sign; then we'll get on."

5. *S*s wait

6. Johnson St. bus arrives (no cue from *T*).

6. *S*s get on front door.

7. Sight of driver (no cue from *T*).

7. *S* hands bus driver route card, points to East Towne Mall and says: "Let me off near East Towne Mall."

8. Sight of fare box (no cue from *T*).

8. *S* pays 15¢ fare in fare box.

9. Sight of seats (no cue from *T*).

9. *S* sits down.

10. "Look at your bus route cards. What's the first place we will pass?"

10. Tenney Park.

11. "Watch for Tenney Park."

1. *S* watches.

12. If *S*s do not recognize Tenney Park as the bus approaches, say: "What's that place to your left?"

12. Tenney Park

13. Repeat cues 11 and 12, substituting the names of the remaining four stops (East High School, McDonald's, Shakey's Pizza, East

13. Various places listed on route cards.

Towne Mall), if
necessary.

14. On the cue from the driver: "Next stop East Towne Mall. . ." (*T* supplies cue if driver fails to.)	14. *S* rings buzzer and walks to either front or back door.
15. Door opens (no cue from *T*).	15. *S* gets off.
16. *T* shows *S*s East Towne Mall and lets *S*s purchase a record.	16. Various
17. "Take out your bus route cards."	17. *S* takes out card.
18. "We're at East Towne Mall and we want to go back to the Capitol Park. What will be the destination sign on the bus?"	18. Nakoma Rd.
19. "If we want to take the Nakoma Rd. bus back to the Capitol Park, first we have to walk to a (_____)."	19. Bus stop
20. "Find the nearest bus stop."	20. *S*s find the bus stop.
21. "We have to wait for the bus whose destination sign reads, (_____)."	21. Nakoma Rd.
22. Bus arrives (no cue from *T*).	22. *S*s get on via front door.
23. Sight of driver (no cue from *T*).	23. *S* hands bus driver route card, points to Capitol Park and says: "Let me off near the Capitol Park."
24. Sight of fare box (no cue from *T*).	24. *S* pays 15¢ fare in fare box.
25. Sight of seats (no cue from *T*).	25. *S* sits down.

26. "Look at your bus
    route cards. What's
    the first place we
    will pass?"

26. Shakey's Pizza

27. "Watch for Shakey's
    Pizza."

27. S watches.

28. If S does not recognize
    Shakey's Pizza as the
    bus approaches, say:
    "What's that place to
    your left?"

28. Shakey's Pizza

29. Repeat cues 27 and 28
    substituting the names
    of the remaining four
    stops (McDonalds,
    East High School,
    Tenney Park, Capitol
    Park).

29. Various places listed
    on route cards.

30. On the cue from the
    bus driver, "Next
    stop, Capitol Park. . ."
    (T supplies cue if
    driver fails to).

30. S rings buzzer and
    walks to either
    front or back door and
    gets off when bus stops.

Step 3—*S*s, starting out at Capitol Park, take the appropriate bus to
the destination chosen in step 1 of this phase. They travel in a small
group without a teacher. While at their destination, *S*s perform the
behaviors required by the place they have traveled to (e.g., if they go
to East Towne Mall, they could make a small purchase). *S*s then take
the appropriate bus back to the Capitol Park.

Materials: Appropriate bus route card
Data Collection: No data collected during this step.

Sequence of Cues and Responses:

Teacher's Cues	*Student's Responses*
1. After *S*s arrive at the Capitol Park with the Johnson St./Nakoma Rd. bus route card, *T* says: "We're at the Capitol Park and we want to go to East Towne Mall.	1. Johnson St.

What will be the des-
tination sign on the
bus?''[13]

2. "In order to catch the
Johnson St. bus, first
we have to walk to a
(_____).''

2. Bus stop

3. "How do we know when
we're at the
right bus stop?''

3. Sign—*No Parking Bus
Stop;* Sign—Johnson St.
and red and yellow curb

4. "Find a bus stop where
you can catch the
Johnson St. bus. When
the Johnson St. bus
comes, take it to
East Towne Mall. After
you get off at East
Towne Mall, look for
(T's name). T's name
will take you to buy
a record. (*T* then
leaves *S*s and
observes from a
distance).''

4. *S* finds Johnson St. bus
stop and gets on the
first Johnson St. bus.

5. Sight of Johnson St.
bus (no cue from *T*).

5. *S* gets on front door,
shows route card, pays
fare, sits down.

6. Sight of bus stop at
East Towne Mall; *T*
stays hidden so that
S does not respond to
T's presence as cue
to get off.

6. *S* gets off.

7. *T* takes *S*s to make a
purchase.

7. Various

8. "Take out your bus
route cards.''

8. *S* takes out card.

9. "You're at East Towne
Mall, and you want to
go to the Capitol

9. Nakoma Rd.

---

[13]The Johnson St./Nakoma Rd. card will serve as an example in this section.

Park, What will be
the destination sign
on the bus?"

10. "If you want to take · the Nakoma Rd. bus back to the Capitol Park, first we have to walk to a (_____)."	10. Bus stop
11. "Find a bus stop. When the Nakoma Rd. bus comes, take it to the Capitol Park. Get off at the first bus stop at the Capitol Park."	11. *S* goes to bus stop.
12. Sight of Nakoma Rd. bus (no cue from *T*).	12. *S* gets on front door, shows route card, pays fare, sits down.
13. Sight of first stop at Capitol Park; *T* stays hidden.	13. *S* gets off.

Step 4—S, starting out at Capitol Park, takes the appropriate bus to the destination chosen in step 1 of this phase. *S* travels alone. While at his/her destination, *S* performs the behaviors required by the place he/she has traveled to (e.g., if *S* goes to East Towne Mall, he/she could make a purchase). *S* then takes the appropriate bus to the Capitol Park.

Materials: Appropriate bus route card

Data Collection: The responses to cues 4–6 and 11–13 should be written at the top of the data sheet with *S*'s name at the left side. Data should be collected for these responses. Since *S* will gain practice at riding all eight bus routes alone, the criterion for each route will be only one perfect trial. Because of the two previous steps and the difficulty in separating the generalization effects from those situations, baseline information will not be taken.

Procedure: The occurrence of behaviors 1–6 and 8–13 should be recorded. Each correct response should be followed by praise, except when *S* enters the bus. In these cases, *T* should praise when *S* gets off at the appropriate stop.

Sequence of Cues and Responses:

Teacher's Cues	*Student's Responses*

Cues 1–13 in Step 3 of this phase should be used. Repeat Steps 1–4 until each bus route has been taught. After each route is learned, then move on to Step 5.

Step 5—During this step *S*s learn how to transfer buses. They choose two of the bus routes they have learned. *T* chooses one place on each card as destinations. Using their bus route cards, *S*s determine the name of the route leaving Capitol Park and going to each of the two destinations. They also determine the routes coming back to Capitol Park. This section functions as a review of the procedure for riding a bus, with the inclusion of additional information needed to transfer from one route to another.

Materials: Appropriate bus route cards

Data Collection: Data should be collected for the following responses: 5, 9, 10, 11, 12, 13, 15, 17, 19, 20, 23, 24, 26. Each response should be listed across the top of the data sheet with *S*'s name at the left. Baseline will consist of three presentations of the 13 cues appropriate to the responses listed above. Criterion for teaching would be three trials of the 13 correct responses in a row.

Sequence of Cues and Responses:

Teacher's Cues	*Student's Responses*
1. We're going to go out and ride a city bus tomorrow, and we're going to learn how to transfer buses. I'd like you to choose two bus routes to go on."	1. No R.
2. "What bus routes would you like to ride?"[14]	2. *S* names two routes, e.g., Johnson St./ Nakoma Rd., and Highland Park/Sherman Ave.

---

[14]The Johnson St./Nakoma Rd. and Highland Park/Sherman Ave. bus routes will serve as examples in this step.

3. "We are going to start   3. No R.
   out at the Capitol
   Park and go to
   McDonald's for lunch.
   Then we are going to
   go back to the
   Capitol Park and
   transfer to the bus
   that takes us to
   PDQ Grocery Store.
   We'll buy some Coke
   at PDQ to bring
   back to class and
   then take the bus
   back to the Capitol
   Park."

4. Give Ss both bus route   4. S takes cards.
   cards.

5. "(S's name), you will   5. Johnson St.
   be at the Capitol
   Park, and you will
   want to go to
   McDonald's for lunch.
   What will be the
   destination sign on
   the bus?"

6. "When you get to   6. No R.
   McDonald's, you'll
   have your lunch; then
   you will want to go
   to PGQ Grocery Store
   to buy some Coke to
   bring to class."

7. "In order to get to   7. No R.
   PDQ Grocery Store, you
   will have to take one
   bus to the Capitol
   Park and then transfer
   to the bus that goes
   to PDQ."

8. "To transfer means to   8. No R.
   change buses to get to
   your destination."

9. "What does transfer mean?"

9. To change buses to get to your destination.

10. "Now you will be at McDonald's, and you want to go to PDQ Grocery Store to buy some Coke. First you will have to take a bus to the (_____).''

10. Capitol Park

11. "Then you have to (_____) buses."

11. Transfer

12. "You will be at the Capitol Park, and you want to go to PDQ Grocery Store to buy some Coke. What will be the destination sign on the bus you transfer to?"

12. Highland Park

13. "After you buy the Coke at PDQ, you will want to go back to the Capitol Park. What will be the destination sign on the bus?"

13. Sherman Ave.

14. "Whenever you get on a city bus and you need to transfer to another bus, you should ask the bus driver for a transfer right after you pay your fare."

14. No R.

15. "When should you ask the bus driver for a transfer?"

15. Right after pay fare, when need to change to a second bus.

16. "A transfer is a small piece of paper with printing on it that looks like this (demonstrate)."

16. No R.

17. Hold up transfer and
    say: "What is this?"

17. Transfer

18. "When you transfer from
    one bus to another bus,
    all you have to do is
    give the bus driver
    this (show transfer),
    a transfer. You
    won't have to pay
    the 15¢ fare to ride
    the second bus if
    you have a transfer."

18. No R.

19. "Do you have to pay
    the 15¢ fare to ride
    the second bus if you
    have a transfer?"

19. No

20. "What do you do instead
    of paying the fare
    when you ride the
    second bus?"

20. Give bus driver the
    transfer.

21. "Tomorrow when you're
    at Capitol Park and
    you want to go to
    McDonald's, will you
    have to ask the bus
    driver for a transfer?"

21. No

22. "Right, because you
    will only be taking
    one bus to get to
    McDonald's."

22. No R.

23. "But when you finish
    eating at McDonald's
    and you want to go to
    PDQ Grocery Store to
    buy some Coke, will
    you have to ask the
    bus driver for a
    transfer?"

23. Yes

24. "You will have to ask
    the driver for a trans-
    fer because you need
    to take (_____)
    buses to get to PDQ."

24. Two

| 25. "Will you have to pay the 15¢ fare to ride the second bus to PDQ Grocery Store?" | 25. No |
| 26. "You will have to give the bus driver a (_____) to ride the bus to PDQ Grocery Store." | 26. Transfer |

Step 6—Using their bus route cards, *S*s gain experience in the classroom at finding the buses they need to take when *transferring*.

Materials: Appropriate bus route cards

Data Collection: Responses 2–5 should be written across the top of the data sheet. Baseline consists of three trials, where the cues for these responses are presented. Criterion for the teaching trials would be *S* emitting the four correct responses for three consecutive trials.

Sequence of Cues and Responses:

Teacher's Cues	Student's Responses
1. *T* hands out two different bus route cards and says: "What bus routes are these?"[15]	1. Johnson St. Highland Park
2. "You're at East Towne Mall and you want to go to PDQ Grocery Store. First you have to go to the (_____)."	2. Capitol Park
3. "What would be the destination sign on the first bus?"	3. Nakoma Rd.
4. "Now you're at the Capitol Park and you have to transfer buses to go to PDQ Grocery Store. What would be the destination sign on the second bus?"	4. Highland Park

[15]Johnson St. and Highland Park will serve as examples.

5. "You're at PDQ Grocery Store and you want to go back to the Capitol Park. What would be the destination sign on the bus?"	5. Sherman Ave.

Repeat cues 1–5 until *S* has reached criterion for ten random combinations of destinations on the two bus route cards. Then move on to two different bus route cards. Repeat this procedure until *S*s have had trials with destinations from all the bus route cards.

*Step 7—S*s, starting out at Capitol Park, take the appropriate bus to the first destination chosen in step 5 of this phase. They travel in a small group with *T*. While at their destination, *S*s perform the behaviors required by the place they have traveled to (e.g., if they go to McDonald's, they eat). *S*s then take the appropriate bus back to Capitol Park, where they transfer to the bus they need to take to the second destination chosen in step 5. *S*s perform the behaviors required by the second place they have traveled to (e.g., if they go to PDQ Grocery Store, they buy something). After are finished, they travel back to Capitol Park.
   Materials: Appropriate bus route cards
   Data Collection: No data collected during this step.

Sequence of Cues and Responses:

Teacher's Cues	*Student's Responses*
1. After *S*s arrive at Capitol Park with the two bus route cards *T* says: "You're at the Capitol Park and you want to go to McDonald's for lunch. What would be the destination sign on the bus?"[16]	1. Johnson St.
2. "When we want to take a bus, first we have to find the right bus stop."	2. No R.

---

[16]The Johnson St./Nakoma Rd. and Highland Park/Sherman Ave. bus routes will be used as examples in this step.

3. "Go find the Johnson St. bus stop and wait for the Johnson St. bus."

3. *S* finds bus stop and waits.

4. Sight of bus (no cue from *T*).

4. *S* enters front door; shows driver route card and says: "Let me off near McDonald's."; pays fare; sits down.

5. Sight of McDonald's; driver: "Next stop, McDonald's."

5. *S* rings buzzer and goes to back door.

6. Door opens (no cue from *T*).

6. *S* gets off.

7. "Let's have lunch (i.e., whatever is required by destination)."

7. *S* eats lunch, etc.

8. After lunch *T* says: "You're at McDonald's and you want to go to PDQ Grocery Store to buy some Coke to bring back to class."

8. No R.

9. "In order to get to PDQ you will have to (_____) Buses."

9. Transfer

10. "So you're at McDonald's and you want to go to PDQ Grocery Store to buy some Coke. First you will have to go to the (_____)."

10. Capitol Park

11. "You're at McDonald's. To go to the Capitol Park, you have to take the (_____) bus."

11. Nakoma Rd.

12. "You will be at the Capitol Park and you want to go to PDQ Grocery Store to buy some Coke. What will be the destination sign on the bus you transfer to?"

12. Highland Park

13. "In order to catch the Highland Park bus at the Capitol Square, you will have to walk to a (_____) . . ."

13. Bus stop

14. ". . . with two signs that say (_____) and (_____)."

14. *No Parking Bus Stop Highland Park*

15. "Since you have to transfer buses at the Capitol Park, when you get on the Nakoma Rd. bus you must ask the driver for a (_____)."

15. Transfer

16. "When you get on the Highland Park bus at the Capitol Square, do you have to pay the 15¢ fare?"

16. No

17. "You give the bus driver a (_____)."

17. Transfer

18. "You're at McDonald's and you want to go to PDQ Grocery Store."

18. No R.

19. "First you walk to a (_____)."

19. Bus stop

20. "You wait for the (_____) bus."

20. Nakoma Rd.

21. "When you get on the Nakoma Rd. bus, after you pay your fare, you ask for a '(_____)."

21. Transfer

22. "When you come to the Capitol Park you (_____)."

22. Get off bus

23. "Then you have to transfer to the (_____) bus."

23. Highland Park

24. "To catch the Highland Park bus, you have to walk to a (_____)

24. Bus stop; *No Parking Bus Stop; Highland Park*

with two signs that
say: (_____) and
(_____)."

25. "When you get on the Highland Park bus, you don't have to pay the fare. You hand the driver the (_____)."	25. Transfer
26. "Find a bus stop, take the Nakoma Rd. bus to the Capitol Park; find the Highland Park bus stop and transfer to go to PDQ."	26. S responds as directed.

Step 8—Ss, starting out at Capitol Park, take the appropriate bus to the first destination chosen in step 5 of this phase. They travel in a small group without T. While at their destination, Ss perform the behaviors required by the place traveled to. Ss then take the appropriate bus back to Capitol Park, where they transfer to the bus they need to take to the second destination chosen in step 5. Ss perform the behaviors required by the place they have traveled to. After they are finished, they travel back to Capitol Park.
Materials: Appropriate bus route cards
Data Collection: No data collected during this step.

Sequence of Cues and Responses:

Teacher's Cues	*Student's Responses*

Repeat cues 1–26 that appear in step 7 of this phase. T should stay hidden as Ss get on or off a bus and should come out to greet them after they get off.
Step 9—S, starting out at Capitol Park, takes the appropriate bus to the first destination chosen in step 5 of this phase. S travels alone. While at his/her destination, S performs the behaviors required by the place traveled to. S then takes the appropriate bus back to Capitol Park, where he/she transfers to the bus needed to reach the second destination. S performs the behaviors required by the place traveled to and returns to Capitol Park.
Materials: Appropriate bus route cards
Data Collection: Record only S's responses to cue 26 appearing

in step 7. No baseline data will be taken, and criterion for the teaching trials will be one perfect trial.

Sequence of Cues and Responses:

    Teacher's Cues   *Student's Responses*

Repeat cues 1–26 that appear in step 7 of this phase. After *S* has reached criterion in this step, repeat steps 7–9 until *S* has transferred, using each bus route.

Step 10—Since all city buses originate at Capitol Park, *S* learns how to take a city bus from the vicinity of his/her house to Capitol Park and return home.

  Materials: *S*'s own "home-bus-route card" (See Appendix II, e for example).

  Data Collection: The responses for cues 29–34 should be written across the top of the data sheet with *S*'s name in the left column. Baseline would consist of three presentations of cues 29–34 in sequence as they occur in this step. Criterion for the teaching trials would be six correct responses to these cues in a row for three consecutive trials.

Sequence of Cues and Responses:

Teacher's Cues	*Student's Responses*
1. "Whenever you are home and you want to take a city bus to go some place, for example, McDonald's, you will first have to take a bus from your house to Capitol Park. Sometimes when you arrive at the Capitol Park, you will have to transfer to another bus to go to your destination. And sometimes the place you want to go to will be on the same bus route you would take	1. No R.

to go to the Capitol
Park."

2. "When you are home   2. Capitol Park
   and you want to take
   a city bus to go some
   place, you have to
   first take a bus to
   (_____)."

3. "When you arrive at the   3. Transfer
   Capitol Park, sometimes
   you will have to
   (_____) buses."

4. "And sometimes the   4. Same
   place you want to go
   to will be on the
   (_____) bus you
   take to the Capitol
   Park."

5. "(S's name), where   5. S's address
   do you live?"

6. "The first thing you   6. Bus stop
   do when you want to
   take a city bus is
   walk to a (_____)."

7. "How do you know when   7. Sign—*No Parking Bus
   you're at a bus stop?"   Stop;* red and yellow
                                     curb

8. "*S's name,* when you want   8. No R.
   to go to the Capitol
   Park to catch a bus you
   should walk to the bus
   stop at the corner (if
   corner applies) of
   (_____) (St./Ave.)
   and (_____)
   (St./Ave.)."

9. "When you want to go to   9. _____(St./Ave.) and
   the Capitol Park, your   _____(St./Ave.)
   bus stop is at the
   corner of (_____)
   (St./Ave.) and
   (_____) (St./Ave.)."

10. "The destination sign   10. No R.

on the bus that you
take is (route that
applies).''

11. "When you want to go   11. _____(St./Ave.) and
to the Capitol Park,   _____(St./Ave.)
you walk to the bus
stop at the corner of
(_____) (St./Ave.)
and (_____)
(St./Ave.).''

12. "And you wait for the   12. Bus route name
(_____) bus.''

13. "When you get home   13. No R.
tonight, ask your
parents to walk with
you to the bus stop
at the corner of
(_____) (St./Ave.)
and (_____)
(St./Ave.).''

14. "When you arrive at the   14. Transfer
Capitol Park, you may
have to transfer to get
to your destination.
If you do, when you
get on the bus at your
house to come to the
Capitol Park, you
should ask the driver
for a (_____).''

15. "When you get to the   15. No R.
Capitol Park, get off
the bus and transfer
to the next bus going
to your destination.
If you don't have to
transfer, stay on the
bus until you reach
your destination.''

16. "When you want to go   16. No R.
back home, you will
have to take a bus to
the Capitol Park and

transfer to the bus
that goes to your
house. But some-
times the bus you
take back from your
destination will be
the same one that
goes to your house.''

17. "*S's name*, the route
that you take to go
home is (route that
applies).''

17. No R.

18. "What route do you
take home from the
Capitol Park?''

18. Route name that
applies

19. "When you are at the
Capitol Park and you
have to transfer to
the (route name) bus,
you will have to walk
to a (_____).''

19. Bus stop

20. "How do you know that
you're at the right
bus stop?''

20. Sign—*No Parking Bus
Stop;* Sign—Bus route
name

21. "*S's name,* the bus
stop where you get
off to walk to your
house is at the
corner of (_____)
(St./Ave.) and
(_____) (St./Ave.)''

21. No R.

22. "When you want to go
home from the Capitol
Park, you take the
(bus route name) bus,
and you get off at the
corner of (_____)
(St./Ave.) and
(_____) (St./Ave.).''

22. *Bus route name*
_____(St./Ave.)
_____(St./Ave.)

23. Ask your parents
tonight to show you
the bus stop at the
corner of (_____)

23. No R.

(St./Ave.) and
(_____) (St./Ave.),
the place where
you get off the bus
when you're coming
  home from the Capitol
Park.

24. *T* hands *S* new bus   24. No R.
route card to be used
for trips from the
Capitol Park to *S*'s
house and says: "This
bus route card tells
you the destination
sign on the bus when
you are going from
your house to the
Capitol Park and back to
your house.

25. "What is the name of   25. _____(St./Ave.)
the bus route at the
top of the card?"

26. "What is the name of   26. _____(St./Ave.)
the bus route at the
bottom?"

27. "This card also tells   27. No R.
you the corner where
the bus stop is when
you are going to the
Capitol Park."

28. *T* points to the name   28. _____(St./Ave.)
at the top of the   _____(St./Ave.)
card and says: "When
you are going to the
Capitol Park, you
catch the bus at the
corner of (_____)
(St./Ave.) and
(_____) (St./
Ave.)."

29. *T* points to the   29. _____(St./Ave.)
name of the bus stop   _____(St./Ave.)
at the bottom of the

card and says: "When
you are coming home
from the Capitol
Park, you get off
at the corner of
(_____) (St./
Ave.) and (_____)
(St./Ave.)."

39. "You're at S's address
and you want to go to
the Capitol Park.
What would be the
destination sign on
the bus?"

30. *bus route at top of card*
(St./Ave.)

31. "Where would the bus
stop be where you catch
the *bus route at top*
(St./Ave.) bus?"

31. _____(St./Ave.)
_____(St./Ave.)

32. "You're at the Capitol
Park and you want to
go to your home, S's
address. What would be
the destination sign
on the bus?"

32. *bus route at bottom on card*
(St./Ave.)

33. "What would be the bus
stop where you get off
the bus route at bottom
(St./Ave.) bus?"

33. _____(St./Ave.)
_____(St./Ave.)

Step 11—S chooses a destination, starts out from his/her house with
T, transfers at the Capitol Park and arrives at the destination. *S*
performs the behaviors required by the place he/she has traveled to.
S then returns home, transferring at the Capitol Park.

Materials: S's "home-bus-route-card"
Route card appropriate to the destination

Data Collection: No data collected.

Sequence of Cues and Responses:

Teacher's Cues	Student's Responses
1. *T* arrives at *S*'s house and says: "I have two tickets to the football game at Camp Randall	1. Yes (hopefully)

Stadium. Would you
like to go? (This is
an example).''

2. "Take out all your bus
   route cards."

   2. *S* complies.

3. "Find the bus route
   that stops at Camp
   Randall Stadium."

   3. *S* locates Nakoma Rd./
   Johnson St. route card.

4. "In order to go to
   Camp Randall Stadium,
   you will have to take
   a bus from your house
   to (_____) and
   (_____) buses."

   4. Capitol Park
   transfer

5. "Take out the bus route
   card that tells you
   what bus to take to
   the Capitol Park from
   your house."

   5. *S* complies.

6. "You're at home, *S*'s
   address, and you want
   to go to the Capitol
   Park. What will be
   the destination sign
   on the bus?"

   6. *S* labels St./Ave. listed
   on "home—bus—route
   card."

7. "What corner will you
   catch the bus at?"

   7. _____(St./Ave.)
   _____(St./Ave.)

8. After you get on the
   bus and pay the fare
   you ask for
   (_____)."

   8. Transfer

9. "Once you get to the
   Capitol Park, you will
   want to transfer to the
   bus that takes you to
   Camp Randall Stadium."

   9. No R.

10. "You'll be at the
    Capitol Park and you
    want to go to Camp
    Randall Stadium.
    What will be the
    destination sign on
    the bus?"

    10. Nakoma Rd.

11. "In order to catch the Nakoma Rd. bus to go to Camp Randall Stadium, first you have to walk to the right (_____).''

11. Bus stop

12. "How will you know when you're at the right bus stop?''

12. Sign—*No Parking Bus Stop;* Sign—Nakoma Rd.

13. "Will you have to pay 15¢ to ride the Nakoma Rd. bus?''

13. No

14. "You pay with a (_____).''

14. Transfer

15. "What is the name of the corner where the bus stop is to catch bus route at top of card (St./Ave.) bus?''

15. _____(St./Ave.) _____(St./Ave.)

16. "Go find the bus stop and wait for the bus route at top of card (St./Ave.) bus.''

16. *S* finds bus stop.

17. Sight of bus (no cue from *T*)

17. *S* gets on front door.

18. Sight of driver (no cue from *T*)

18. *S* shows driver route card and says: "Let me off near the Capitol Park.''

19. Sight of fare box (no cue from *T*)

19. Pays 15¢ fare.

20. Sight of transfers (no cue from *T*)

20. Asks driver for a transfer.

21. Sight of seats (no cue from *T*)

21. Sits down

22. Sight of Capitol Park; driver says: "Next stop, Capitol Park.''

22. *S* rings buzzer and goes to either door.

23. Door opens (no cue from *T*)

23. *S* gets off.

24. "Now you're at the Capitol Park and you want to go to Camp

24. Nakoma Rd.

Randall Stadium.
What will be the des-
tination sign on the
bus?''

25. "Find a bus stop where   25. *S* complies.
the Nakoma Rd. bus
comes and wait for
the bus."

26. Sight of Nakoma Rd.   26. *S* boards bus through
bus (no cue from *T*)   front door, asks:
                                        "Let me off at Camp
                                        Randall Stadium"; pays
                                        fare and sits down.

27. Sight of Camp Randall   27. *S* rings buzzer and
Stadium; driver: "Next   goes to door.
stop, Camp Randall
Stadium."

28. Door opens (no cue   28. *S* gets off.
from *T*)

29. *T* takes *S* to the   29. Various
football game.

30. "You're at Camp Randall   30. Johnson St.
Stadium and you want to
go to the Capitol Park
to transfer buses to go
home. What will be the
destination sign on the
bus?''

31. "If you want to go to   31. Bus stop
the Capitol Park,
first you have to
walk to (_____)."

32. "Find a bus stop and   32. *S* complies.
wait for the Johnson St.bus."

33. Sight of Johnson St.   33. *S* goes in front door;
bus.   shows route card and
                                        says: "Let me off
                                        near the Capitol Park";
                                        pays fare; asks for
                                        transfer; sits down.

34. Sight of Capitol Park;   34. *S* rings buzzer and
driver says: "Next   walks to a door.
stop, Capitol Park."

35. Door opens.	35. *S* gets off.
36. "Now you're at the Capitol Park and you have to transfer buses to go home, *S's address*. What will be the destination sign on the bus?"	36. Route name at top of card (St./Ave.)
37. "If you want to catch the *route name at top of card* bus, first you walk to the right (_____)."	37. Bus stop
38. "How will you know if you're at the right bus stop?"	38. Sign—*No Parking Bus Stop;* Sign—*Bus route name*
39. "Find the bus stop and wait for the (_____) (St./Ave.) bus."	39. *S* complies.
40. Sight of (_____) (St./Ave.) bus (no cue from *T*)	40. *S* gets on front door; shows route card and says: "Let me off near *S's address*"; hands driver transfer; sits down.
41. Sight of bus stop near *S's* house; driver: "We're at *S's address*."	41. *S* rings buzzer and goes to a door.
42. Door opens.	42. *S* gets off.

Step 12—*S* chooses a destination, starts out from his/her house alone, transfers at Capitol Park and arrives at the destination. *S* performs the behaviors required by the place he/she has traveled to. *S* then returns home, transferring at Capitol Park.

    Materials: *S's* "home-bus-route-card"
                  Route card appropriate to the destination

    Data Collection: The following responses should be listed across the top of the data sheet: 16, 17, 23, 25, 26, 28, 32, 33, 35, 39, 40, 42. Baseline data will not be taken. Criterion for the teaching trials would be three completely correct trials when transferring and three correct trials when the *S* does not need to transfer.

Sequence of Cues and Responses:

Teacher's Cues   *Student's Responses*

Repeat cues 1–33 in step 10 of this phase. *T* should monitor *S*'s behavior to insure that the *S* gets on and off the right buses. *T* should remain concealed while monitoring and should come out to greet *S* only after he/she has emitted the required behaviors. This step should be repeated, choosing two more destinations for which *S* needs to transfer, and three for which he/she does not.

Phase IV: Teaching *S*s how to determine what bus to take to places that do not appear on bus route cards.
  Step 1—Teaching *S*s to label cards with the names of major streets in the city of Madison (This is done to facilitate labeling addresses in later stages of this phase.).
  Materials: The names of various streets in the city of Madison, grouped in sets of ten, printed on white index cards (See Appendix III for list of streets).
  Data Collection: The name of each street that forms the set should be written across the top of the data sheet. Baseline would consist of three presentations of these cards. Criterion for the teaching trials would be 100% correct responses for three consecutive trials.

Sequence of Cues and Responses:
            Teacher's Cues   *Student's Responses*
  1. Show *S* card and say: 1. *S* reads card.
     "Read the card."

          Continue this procedure until *S* learns to label all the streets in the sets.
  Step 2—*S* looks up one of the streets acquired in Step 1 of this phase in the *Street Index* on the back of a map of Madison, Wisconsin. He/She then labels the coordinates listed next to the name of the street located.
  Materials: Index cards
              Map of Madison, Wisconsin
  Data Collection: The name for each street that forms the set should be written across the top of the data sheet. Data should be recorded for responses 8, 15, 16, and 17. Baseline would consist of three presentations of the cues for each street in the set. Criterion for teaching trials would be the correct performance of responses 8, 15, 16, and 17 on three consecutive occasions for each street in the set.

Sequence of Cues and Responses:

Teacher's Cues	*Student's Responses*
1. Hold up map of Madison and say: "This is a map of Madison."	1. No R.
2. "What is this?"	2. Map of Madison
3. Show side with streets and landmarks drawn in and say: "This is the front of the map."	3. No R.
4. "Which side of the map is this?"	4. Front
5. Turn map over to side with Street Index and say: "This is the (_____) of the map."	5. Back
6. "The back of the map has all the streets in the city written down."	6. No R.
7. Point to words Street Index and say: "All the streets are written in the Street Index. Read this."	7. Street Index
8. Hold up a card with the name of the street learned in step 1 of this phase (e.g., Atwood Ave.) and say: "Read this card and find it in the Street Index."	8. Atwood Ave.; *S* locates cued word.[17]
9. "What letter does the word Atwood start with?"	9. A.
10. "Point to the letter A in the Street Index and leave your finger there."	10. *S* points to A.
11. "Whenever you want to look up a street, first	11. No R.

---

[17]If *S* fails to find the street in the Street Index, use cues 9–14 to teach the skill. Cues 9–14 should eventually be faded.

you look at the first
letter in the word.
Then you find the
column in the Street
Index that starts
with the letter."

12. "Once you find the   12. No R.
    column that starts
    with the same letter
    as the name of the
    street, you move your
    finger down that
    column until you come
    to the second letter."

13. "What is the second   13. T.
    letter in Atwood?"

14. "Move your finger until   14. S moves finger until
    you come to the first   first AT word.
    word that starts with
    AT and stop."

Note: Continue this procedure until S has located the word writ-
       ten on the card.

15. When S finally locates   15. Atwood Ave.
    the word written on the
    card, say: "Read the
    word."

16. "Now move your finger   16. S moves finger.
    to the right along the
    dotted line until you
    come to a letter and
    a number."

17. "Read them."   17. E–9

18. "The letter and number   18. No R.
    are called coordinates."

19. "What are the letter   19. Coordinates
    and number called?"

20. "You can use the coor-   20. No R.
    dinates to find a street
    on the front of a map."

Note: Continue this procedure until S can locate all the
       streets listed in the three sets in Appendix III and label
       their coordinates.

Step 3—S gains experience at finding streets on a map of Madison, Wisconsin.

Materials: Index cards
                 Map of Madison, Wisconsin

Data Collection: Responses to cue 2 should be written across the top of the data sheet. Baseline would consist of three presentations of cue 2. Criterion for the teaching trials would be 100% correct responses to cue 2 for three consecutive trials. Baseline and teaching procedures should be repeated for each of the five streets in the three sets listed in Appendix III.

Sequence of Cues and Responses:

Teacher's Cues	*Student's Responses*
1. Give each student a map; hold up an index card with the name of a Madison street written on it and say: "What street is this?"	1. *S* names street.
2. "Look up *name of street* in the Street Index; find the coordinates and then find the street on the front of the map."	2. *S* performs the following:[18] a. looks up st. in St. Index b. finds coordinates c. turns map over d. puts right finger on letter e. puts left finger on number f. moves fingers until they meet g. finds st. at junction and notifies *T*
3. "Turn to the front of the map."	3. *S* turns to front.
4. "A coordinate is made up of a letter and a number. The letter part of a coordinate is located at the sides of the map."	4. No R.

[18]If *S* responds incorrectly to cue 2, cues 3–20 should be implemented. Cues 3–20 should eventually be faded so that *S* eventually performs the chain of responses in response 2 without *T*'s assistance.

5. "Point to the letters at the sides of the map."	5. *S* points to letters.
6. "Read the letters."	6. *S* reads letters.
7. "The number part of the coordinate is located at the top and bottom of the map."	7. No R.
8. "Point to the numbers."	8. *S* points to numbers.
9. "Read the numbers."	9. Reads the numbers.
10. "Whenever you want to find a street on the front of the map, first you look up the name of the street in the Street Index."	10. No R.
11. "Look up Atwood Ave. in the Street Index."	11. *S* finds Atwood Ave.
12. "The next thing you do is find the coordinates for the street."	12. No R.
13. "What are the coordinates for Atwood Ave.?"	13. E–9
14. "Then you turn your map to the front."	14. *S* turns to front.
15. "What is the letter part of the coordinates for Atwood Ave.?"	15. E.
16. "Put one of the fingers of your right hand on the letter E at the right side of the map."	16. *S* puts finger on E as directed.
17. "What is the number part of the coordinates for Atwood Ave.?"	17. 9
18. "Put one of the fingers of your left hand on the number 9 at the top of the map."	18. *S* puts finger on 9 as directed.

19. "Now move the finger
on the letter E to the
left, and the finger
on 9 down until your
fingers meet, then
stop."

19. *S* moves fingers until
they meet, then stops.

20. "Find the street that
says Atwood Ave. (show
card)."

20. *S* finds Atwood Ave.

Step 4—Teaching *S*s how to use the Madison Telephone Directory to
find the address and phone number of a place they would like to go to.
S also writes down the address and phone number that he/she finds.

Materials: Pencil
                Paper
                Madison Telephone Directory

Data Collection: List the responses across the top of the data
sheet for the following: 10–23. Baseline would consist of finding
three words all starting with the same letter. Criterion for teaching
trials would be the correct performance of responses 10–23 for
three consecutive trials.

Sequence of Cues and Responses:

Teacher's Cues	*Student's Responses*
1. "Sometimes you will want to take a city bus to a place that is not on your bus route cards. When this happens, you will have to know the address of the place you want to go to. We are going to learn to use the Madison phone book to find these addresses."	1. No R.
2. *T* holds up Madison phone book and says: "What is this?"	2. Madison phone book
3. "Whenever you want to find the address of a	3. No R.

place you want to go
to, you will first have
to print the name on
a piece of paper.''

4. ''What's the first   4. Print name on paper
   thing you do?''

5. ''If you don't know how   5. No R.
   to print the name of
   the place you want to
   go to, then you will
   have to ask someone to
   print it for you.''

6. ''You could ask your   6. No R.
   mother, father, friend,
   of, if you are out,
   you could ask someone
   walking down the
   street.''

7. ''Hand a person some   7. No R.
   paper and a pencil
   and just say: ''Would
   you please print
   (name of place you
   want to look up) for
   me?''

8. ''If you needed a   8. Hand person pencil
   name printed, what   and paper and say,
   would you do?''   ''Would you please
                                  print (name of place)
                                  for me?''

9. ''Once you have the   9. No R.
   name printed on
   paper, open the phone
   book and find the page
   that starts with the
   first letter of the
   word you want to
   look up.''

10. *T* writes down Arby's   10. Arby's Roast Beef
    Roast Beef on a piece
    of paper and says:
    ''Read the card.''

11. ''If you wanted to look   11. A.
    up Arby's Roast Beef,

you would have to find
the page that started
with an (_____).''

12. ''Turn to the page that   12. *S* complies.
     starts with an A.''

13. ''What's the next letter   13. R.
     in Arby's Roast Beef?''

14. ''Put your finger on the   14. *S* complies.
     first word after all
     the abbreviations
     under the letter A.''

15. ''Now move your finger   15. *S* complies.
     until you come to the
     first word that starts
     with AR and then stop.''

16. ''What's the next letter   16. B.
     after AR in Arby's?''

17. ''Move your finger   17. *S* complies.
     until you come to the
     first word that starts
     with ARB and stop.''

     Note: Continue with this procedure until *S* locates the word
            that *T* has written down.

18. ''When *S* finally locates   18. Arby's Roast Beef
     the word that was
     written down say:
     ''Read the word.''

19. ''Move your finger   19. *S* complies.
     to the right until
     you come to the
     address that is
     printed next to the
     name Arby's Roast
     Beef.''

20. ''Read the address.''   20. 1609 S. Park

21. ''Leave your finger   21. *S* prints 1609 S. Park
     on the address and
     use your other hand
     to print the address
     on the piece of
     paper under the name
     Arby's Roast Beef.''

22. "Now move your finger   22. *S* moves finger to
    to the right again   phone number.
    until you come to the
    phone number."
23. "Leave your finger on   23. *S* prints 257-9934 under
    the phone number and   the address for Arby's.
    use your hand to print
    the phone number on
    the piece of paper
    under the address for
    Arby's Roast Beef."

Note: Continue until *S* has found three addresses for every
        letter in the alphabet.

Step 5—S acquires the skills necessary to call Directory Assistance
to find the phone number of a place he/she has been unable to locate
in the telephone book. Next, *S* acquires the skills necessary to call
the place to find out its address.
Materials: None
Data Collection: Data should be collected for the following responses: 2, 4, 6, 8, 10, 11, 13, 16, 18, 19, 21, 23. These responses
should be listed at the top of the data sheet with *S*s' names in the
column on the left side. Baseline would consist of the presentation
of cues 2, 4, 6, 8, 10, 11, 13, 16, 18, 19, 21, and 23 for three
consecutive trials. Criterion for teaching trials would be the correct
performance of the responses listed for these cues for three trials in
a row.

Sequence of Cues and Responses:

            Teacher's Cues   *Student's Responses*
1. "Sometimes you won't   1. No R.
   be able to find the
   place you are looking
   for in the phone book.
   Some places aren't
   printed in the phone
   book. And sometimes
   you might just make
   a mistake. So if you
   can't find a place
   in the phone book,
   you should call
   Directory Assistance."

2. "Who do you call when you can't find a place in the phone book?"

2. Directory Assistance

3. "Whenever you can't find a place listed in the phone book and you have to call Directory Assistance, first you should print the name of the place where you want to go."

3. No R.

4. "What's the first thing to do when you want to call Directory Assistance?"

4. Print name of place where want to go.

5. "If you don't know how to print it ask your parents, brothers or sisters, friends, or even someone you don't know to spell the name for you. Then you should print the name as they spell the letters."

5. No R.

6. "If you can't print the name of the place where you want to go, who could you ask to spell it?"

6. Parents, brothers, sisters, friends or strangers.

7. "Once you print the name, you have to call Directory Assistance. The phone number is 411."

7. No R.

8. "What is the phone number for Directory Assistance?"

8. 411

9. "Let's say that you couldn't find Rendahl's Super Market in the phone book."

9. No R.

10. "The first thing you do is (_____)."

10. Print Rendahl's Super Market on paper.

11. "Next you dial
    (_____)."

11. 411

12. "When the person
    answers they will
    say: 'Directory
    Assistance, for
    what city?' "

12. No R.

13. "When they asked . . .
    'for what city?', you
    should say (_____)."

13. Madison

14. "After you say
    'Madison,' you have to
    ask for the phone num-
    ber of the place you
    want to go."

14. No R.

15. "If you want the number
    for Rendahl's Super
    Market, you should
    say: 'May I have the
    phone number for
    Rendahl's Super
    Market?' "

15. No R.

16. "How would you ask
    for the phone number
    for Rendahl's Super
    Market?"

16. "May I have the phone
    number for Rendahl's
    Super Market."

17. "When the person tells
    you the phone number,
    you should print it
    on the same piece of
    paper that your des-
    tination is written
    on."

17. No R.

18. "Now that you have the
    phone number of the
    place you want to go
    to, how do you find
    the address?"

18. Call the place and ask.

19. "What would you say
    when someone answers
    your phone call?"

19. "What is your address,
    please?"

20. "When they tell you
    the address, write it

20. No R.

down on the piece of
paper that has the
phone number and the
name of the place
where you want to go."

Teacher's Cues	Student's Responses
21. "There are two parts to an address. One is the (_____), and the other is (_____)."	21. Number, name of street
22. "When the person tells you the address, write down the number part, and if you can't spell the name of the street ask them: 'Please spell *Park St.* for me.'"	22. No R.
23. "If you can't spell the street, what do you say?"	23. "Please spell *Park St.* for me."
24. "Then as the person spells it, you print it next to the number part of the address."	24. No R.

Step 6—S places a call to Directory Assistance and asks for the phone number of a place he/she could not find in the phone book. *S* writes this number down, then calls the place and asks for their address. *S* writes this address down.

Materials: Pencil
Paper
Actual working telephone

Data Collection: The responses listed after cue 1 should be written across the top of the data sheet. Baseline would consist of three presentations of cue 1. The criterion for the teaching trials would be three correct trials in a row in response to cue 1. Baseline and teaching should be repeated for each of ten places chosen.

Sequence of Cues and Responses:

Teacher's Cues	Student's Responses
1. "Find the phone	1. The *S* does as follows:

number and address
for: *Rendahl's Super
Market."*

a. asks *T* to spell the
   name
b. writes Rendahl's as
   T spells
c. calls Directory
   Assistance
d. responds with
   Madison to question
   "for what city?"
   from operator
e. "May I have the
   phone number for
   *Rendahl's Super
   Market."*
f. writes down number
g. hangs up
h. *S* calls Rendahl's
i. *S* says: "What is
   your address, please?"
j. *S* prints number
   component
k. *S* asks: Please
   spell *Park St."*
l. *S* writes Park St.
   as it is spelled.

Note: Continue this procedure until *S* reaches criterion for ten
different places.

Step 7—The *S* learns how to find an exact location on a map of
Madison, using the numerical component of the address.
Materials: Index cards
               Map of Madison, Wisconsin, with street numbers
Data Collection: Responses 1, 2, 6–14 should be written at the
top of the data sheet with *S*s' names in the left hand column.
Baseline would consist of three presentations of cues 1, 2, 6–14.
Criterion for teaching trials would be the correct performance of
the responses listed for these cues on three consecutive occasions.

Sequence of Cues and Responses:

Teacher's Cues	*Student's Responses*
1. Hold up an index card with 3452 Atwood Ave.	1. 3452 Atwood Ave.

written on it and say:
"Read the address."

2. "Look up Atwood Ave.
in the Street Index.
Find the coordinates
and then find the
street on the map."

2. *S* performs the following:
   a. looks up street in
      Street Index
   b. finds coordinates
   c. turns map over
   d. puts right finger on
      letter
   e. puts left finger on
      number
   f. moves fingers
      until they meet
   g. finds St. at junction
      and notifies *T*

3. "Do you see the small
numbers written on
Atwood Ave.?"

3. Yes

4. Those numbers are
like the number part
of an address."

4. No R.

5. "Read some of the
numbers."

5. 2100, 2200, etc.

6. Hold up the card,
3452 Atwood Ave. and
say: "What are the
first two numbers in
3452?"

6. 34

7. "How many numbers are
in 3452?"

7. 4

8. "Add zeroes after 34
until you have four
numbers."

8. *S* writes 3400 on
a card.

9. "If you add two zeroes
after 34 it becomes
(_____)."

9. 3400

10. "What comes after 34?"

10. 35

11. "How many numbers in
3452?"

11. 4

12. "Add zeroes after 35
until you have four
numbers."

12. *S* writes 3500 on
a card.

13. "If you add two zeroes

13. 3500

after 35 it becomes
(_____).''

14. Hold up card and say: "This address falls between 3400 and 3500. Move your finger along Atwood Ave. until it is between 3400 and 3500."	14. *S* complies.
15. "This is where 3452 is."	15. No R.

Step 8—S gains experience at finding exact locations on a map of Madison, Wis.

    Materials: Index cards

                Map of Madison, Wisconsin, with street numbers

Data Collection: Write five addresses across the top of the data sheet. Baseline would consist of presenting three trials of the five addresses. Criterion for the teaching trials would be finding all five addresses for three consecutive trials.

Sequence of Cues and Responses:

Teacher's Cues	*Student's Responses*
1. Hold up index card with address (number and st.) written on it and say: "Read the address."	1. *S* reads address.
2. "Find the street in the Street Index; look up the coordinates and locate the street on the front. Then move your finger along the street until you come to the number part of the address. Stop there."	2. *S* looks up st., locates st. on front, moves finger along street address.

    Note: Continue this until *S* has found five different addresses for three consecutive trials.

Step 9—S is taught the names of the various bus routes listed on the front of the map.

Materials: Map of Madison, Wis., with street addresses.
Data Collection: Responses 2, 4, 6, and 7 should be written across the top of the data sheet with *S*s' names in the left hand column. Baseline would consist of three presentations of cues 2, 4, 6, and 7. Criterion for teaching trials would be the correct performance of the responses listed for these cues on three consecutive occasions.

Sequence of Cues and Responses:

Teacher's Cues	Student's Responses
1. "All the streets that the buses travel on are written in red on the map. These red streets also have a letter in a red circle printed on them."	1. No R.
2. "What are the red lines?"	2. Streets the buses travel on.
3. "The letter in the circle tells you what bus route travels down the street in red."	3. No R.
4. "What does the letter tell you?"	4. Bus route
5. "In order to find out which bus route the letter stands for, you have to look up the letter in the box at the top right hand side of the map."	5. No R.
6. "Read all the letters and the bus routes they stand for in the box."	6. *S* reads routes: A G B E C H R X U
7. "Find a street in red and tell me the name of the bus route."	7. *S* complies.

Step 10—S gains more experience finding bus routes on the map of Madison.

Materials: Map of Madison, Wis.

Data Collection: List all the names of the bus routes across the top of the data sheet. Baseline would consist of three trials of finding each route in response to cue 1. The criterion for the teaching trials would be finding each route for three consecutive trials.

Sequence of Cues and Responses:

Teacher's Cues	*Student's Responses*
1. "Find a street in red and tell me the name of the bus route."	1. *S* complies.

Note: Continue this until *S* has found all the city bus routes for three consecutive trials.

Step 11—S learns how to find the closest bus route to a particular street address *S* has located on the front of the map.

Materials: Map of the city of Madison with numbers

Data Collection: Data should be collected for responses 1, 2, 3, 4, and 6 for both baseline and teaching trials. Baseline would consist of three presentations of cues 1, 2, 3, 4, and 6. Criterion for teaching trials would be the correct performance of the responses for these cues on three consecutive occasions.

Sequence of Cues and Responses:

Teacher's Cues	*Student's Responses*
1. Hold up a card with an address on it (e.g., 2100 W. Washington Ave.), and say: "Read the address."	1. *S* labels 2100 W. Washington Ave.
2. "Find the exact place where 2100 W. Washington Ave. is on the map."	2. *S* complies.
3. "Now if you want to find out what bus you could take from the Capitol Square to the place written on the card, just look at the	3. *S* finds line.

closest red line to
the address you have
found on the map."

4. "What letter is printed   4. G.
   on the line?"

5. "When the place you   5. No R.
   have found is to the
   left of the Capitol
   Park, you read the
   second bus route name.
   When it is to the
   right, you read the
   top bus route name."

6. "What would be the   6. Highland Park
   closest bus route to
   take from the Capitol
   Square to 2100 W.
   Washington Ave.?"

Step 12—S gains experience at finding the appropriate bus route for
various addresses, using a map of Madison, Wisconsin.
   Materials: Index cards
                  Map of Madison with numbers
   Data Collection: List the five addresses with bus routes at the
top of the data sheet. Baseline information would consist of presenting the five addresses three times to *S*. Criterion for the teaching trials would be finding the five addresses and bus routes for
three consecutive trials.

Sequence of Cues and Responses:

Teacher's Cues	*Student's Responses*
1. Holding up a card with an address, *T* says: "Read the card."	1. *S* labels card.
2. "Find *address* on the map and tell me what is the closest bus to take to get there from the Capitol Park."	2. *S* locates address and finds closest bus route.

   Note: Continue this until *S* has found five new addresses
           with bus routes for three consecutive trials.

Step 13—*S* looks up an address in the phone book, locates the closest bus route, rides the bus to the destination with *T* and a small group of *S*s.

Materials: Phone book
                    Map of Madison

Data Collection: Data for both baseline and teaching trials should be collected on responses 1, 2, and 3.

Sequence of Cues and Responses:

Teacher's Cues	Student's Responses
1. "Look up Arby's Roast Beef in the phone book and find the bus route you would take to get there on the map."	1. *S* complies.
2. (At Capitol Park) "Wait for the _____ bus and take it to Arby's."	2. *S* complies.
3. While on bus *T* says: "Look at the addresses. When you see the addresses are getting close to Arby's address, ring the buzzer and get off."	3. *S* complies.

Step 14—Same as step 13, except *S*s travel in a small group without *T*.

Materials: Phone book
                    Map of Madison

Data Collection: Data for both baseline and teaching trials should be collected on responses 1–3.

Sequence of Cues and Responses:

Teacher's Cues	Student's Responses
Repeat cues 1 and 2 from Step 13.	

Step 14—Same as Step 13, except *S* travels alone.

Materials: Phone book
                    Map of Madison

Data Collection: List responses 2 and 3 from step 13 across the top of the data sheet. No baseline necessary. Criterion for the teaching trials would be three correct trials in a row.

Sequence of Cues and Responses:

| *Teacher's Cues* | *Student's Responses* |

Repeat cues 1 and 2 from Step 13.

RESULTS

A summary of the criterion performance of each S in Phases I–III is presented in Table 1. It should be noted that attempts to teach steps 10–12 of Phase III were not made because of the impending end of the school year. These steps involved taking a bus from an individual S's home and transferring to another bus in order to reach a destination. These tasks required that considerable time be spent in one-to-one teaching situations outside of school. Unfortunately, such time and staff could not be allocated at the end of the school year. Thus, it was concluded that it would be more useful to attempt to teach steps that could be completed under the time restrictions than to begin steps which could not. In addition, steps 4–15 of Phase IV were not attempted because the school term ended. The deleted and untaught steps in Phases III and IV will be implemented during the subsequent school year.

As can be determined from Table 1, Ss 1–4 reached criterion on all steps of Phases I and II, but only on steps 1–3 of Phase III. Thus, Phase IV for Ss 1–4 was not initiated. Although in Phase III, step 4, Ss 1–4 were not able to ride the actual buses alone, they did reach criterion when bus riding was performed in conjunction with T (step 2) or with a small group of Ss (step 3).

Like Ss 1–4, Ss 5 and 6 did not acquire the skills necessary to ride buses alone (Phase III, steps 4 and 9), but did reach criterion on all other steps, including steps 1–3 of Phase IV.

Ss 7–10 performed at criterion on all steps of Phases I and II; on Steps 1–9 of Phase III; and on steps 1–3 of Phase IV.

Figures 1–3 provide information regarding the savings in the number of teaching trials needed to attain criterion performance across related tasks within steps. Figure 1 depicts the performance of S_6 on the sitting and standing tasks of step 3, Phase I. Although S_6 required six teaching trials to reach criterion on the sitting task of Step 3, teaching the standing task was unnecessary, since S_6 performed without error during baseline trials.

Figure 2 represents the performance of S_7 during two sight word reading tasks of step 1, Phase II, and the two complimentary tasks of labeling these same sets of sight words as they occurred vertically on bus route cards in step 2, Phase II. S_7 required six teaching trials to attain

Table 1.

Each "X" indicates that S reached criterion for a particular step in the program. Shaded areas represent parts of the program that were not taught.

Students	Phase I Step 1	Phase I Step 2	Phase I Step 3	Phase II Step 1	Phase II Step 2	Phase II Step 3	Phase II Step 4	Phase III Step 1	Phase III Step 2	Phase III Step 3	Phase III Step 4	Phase III Step 5	Phase III Step 6	Phase III Step 7	Phase III Step 8	Phase III Step 9	Phase III Step 10	Phase III Step 11	Phase III Step 12	Phase IV Step 1	Phase IV Step 2	Phase IV Step 3	Phase IV Step 4	Phase IV Step 5	Phase IV Step 6	Phase IV Step 7	Phase IV Step 8	Phase IV Step 9	Phase IV Step 10	Phase IV Step 11	Phase IV Step 12	Phase IV Step 13	Phase IV Step 14
1	X	X	X	X	X	X	X	X	X	X																							
2	X	X	X	X	X	X	X	X	X	X																							
3	X	X	X	X	X	X	X	X	X	X										X	X	X											
4	X	X	X	X	X	X	X	X	X	X										X	X	X											
5	X	X	X	X	X	X	X	X	X	X	X	X	X	X	X					X	X	X											
6	X	X	X	X	X	X	X	X	X	X	X	X	X	X	X					X	X	X											
7	X	X	X	X	X	X	X	X	X	X	X	X	X	X	X	X				X	X	X											
8	X	X	X	X	X	X	X	X	X	X	X	X	X	X	X	X				X	X	X											
9	X	X	X	X	X	X	X	X	X	X	X	X	X	X	X	X				X	X	X											
10	X	X	X	X	X	X	X	X	X	X	X	X	X	X	X	X				X	X	X											

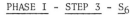

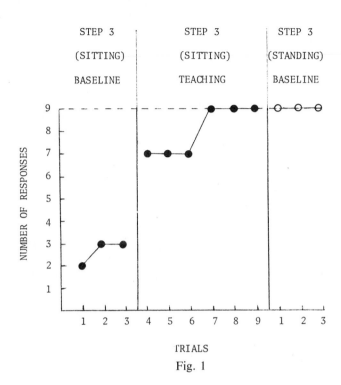

Fig. 1

criterion on the first sight word task of step 1 (Johnson St.), and nine teaching trials on the second sight word task of step 1 (Highland Park). Once criterion was reached on the two tasks of step 1, S_7 was immediately given the opportunity to perform the two tasks of step 2 and performed without error during baseline trials.

Similar results are depicted in Fig. 3 for S_{10}. Figure 3 represents the performance of S_{10} on two tasks in Phase IV, steps 2 and 3: locating two sets of streets in the street index of a map of Madison, and finding these same two sets of streets on the front of the map. S_{10} required six teaching trials to reach criterion on the first set of streets for step 2, but required only three teaching trials to achieve criterion on the second set. In step 3, S_{10} reached criterion after ten teaching trials on the first set of streets while needing three teaching trials for the second set. In contrast to the data depicted in Figs. 1 and 2, S_{10} did not perform without error during the baseline trials on either of the second tasks. S_{10} emitted four errors during the three baseline trials on the second task of step 2 and one error for the three baseline trials on the second task of step 3.

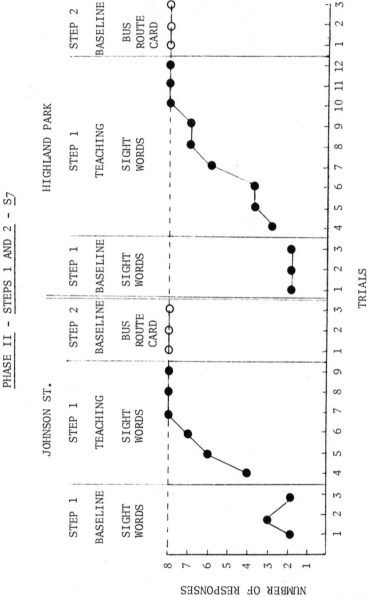

PHASE II – STEPS 1 AND 2 – S7

Fig. 2

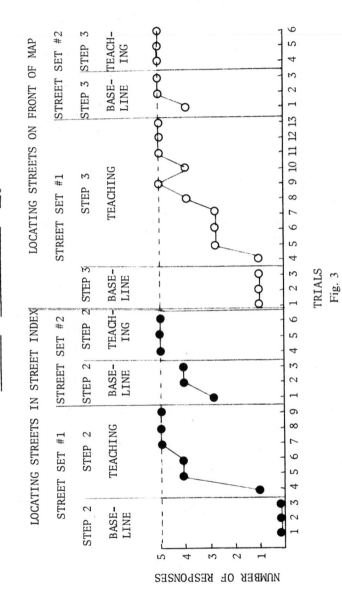

PHASE IV - STEPS 2 AND 3 - S_{10}

Fig. 3

The inclusion of these figures is by no means exhaustive of all data collected. The information was chosen selectively as representative of perhaps the two most salient performance characteristics: (a) that the students progressed differentially through the task analysis, and (b) that many students manifested transfer of training in the form of savings in teaching trials to criterion across similar tasks and unexpectedly good performance on selected untaught tasks.

DISCUSSION

Bus riding skills were acquired by all ten students, although the extent to which the skills were acquired varied in degree within and between students. The program appears to have discriminated two groups of students along at least two dimensions. One dimension seemed to be the degree of independence from adults achieved. Students 1–4 were not, at the end of the school year, able to ride the buses alone, but were able to ride with a small group of their peers to a chosen destination.

Students 5 and 6 did not acquire the skills necessary to ride buses without adult supervision. One student had a severe visual impairment (previously undetected) which made it impossible for her to read the destination signs on the buses as they approached bus stops. This student's vision, though, did not interfere with reading at the close distances used in the classroom phases of the program. The other student exhibited "anxious" behavior whenever required to ride alone. These behaviors were sufficiently disruptive to interfere with taking a bus alone. Attempts made to desensitize the student to riding a bus alone met with little success. However, anecdotal information indicated that when this student rode a bus with a teacher present, she was able to get off at the appropriate stops without a direct cue from the teacher. It is concluded that this student would have been able to ride independently had the "anxious" behavior been eliminated.

In contrast to students 1–6, students 7–10 were able to ride public buses to chosen destinations without assistance from either peers or teachers. In summary, six students (students 1–6) achieved independence from adult supervision, although still remaining dependent upon their peers, and four students (students 7–10) acquired the skills necessary for complete independence. Thus, it can be concluded that the objective of teaching the riding of public buses to chosen destinations, independent from adult supervision, was achieved in part.

Another dimension along which students' performance varied seemed to be related to the degree of task complexity. Students 1–4 were able to acquire the skills necessary to ride one bus to and from one destination. These same students did not acquire the skills necessary to transfer buses and to use maps. In comparison to riding one bus, the added component requiring the utilization of two buses when transferring seemed to represent a substantial increase in task complexity. Students 7–10, who performed successfully on all steps related to the riding of a single bus, also performed successfully when transferring buses was required. Students 5 and 6, with the exception of riding alone, also acquired the rudiments of transferring. In addition, students 5–10 were able to perform the beginning components of the map reading skills. It is apparent that the instructional sequence, as written, was sufficiently detailed to enable some students to acquire the requisite skills, but not others. Whether additional trials or a finer breakdown of the instructional components would have reduced the complexity of the transfer task and enabled students 1–4 to acquire the necessary skills cannot be concluded at this time. Further implementation of this program during the current school year will attempt to examine these and other questions.

In addition to the manner in which the program apparently discriminates within and between students, the data presented in Figs. 1–3 seem to support the conclusions that the program teaches some skills that are generalizable, resulting in a savings in trials to criterion. Figure 1 shows the differences between the number of trials needed to reach criterion during the program when a sequence of ten bus riding responses were being taught using the simulated bus. The only variations between the two sets of trials was the final response in the sequence of either standing or sitting, and the imposed condition that, on standing trials, all the seats were occupied when the student boarded the simulated bus. The sequence of responses is considered to have generalized, since once the student acquired all the skills necessary in the sitting component, the standing skills were executed without direct teaching. The successful transfer from sitting to standing seems to be a function of teaching students a general class of bus riding skills that are adaptable to various riding conditions. The high performance level of the standing trials cannot be attributed to scheduled reinforcement, since they were conducted under baseline conditions. The skills acquired during the sitting trials then seem to have generalized to standing, and were maintained in the absence of direct reinforcement.

Figures 2 and 3 contain data which also support a conclusion regarding the existence of generalization across altered stimulus conditions. The data in Fig. 2 shows that once student 7 had mastered each set of individually presented sight words, he was able to label these same words when they were presented under an entirely different format—the format of the bus route cards. As in the standing trials of Fig. 1, the presentation of the route cards was done under baseline conditions. The labeling responses acquired in the first step appeared to have generalized to the new stimulus situation in the absence of scheduled reinforcement. Likewise, the data presented in Fig. 3 for student 10 suggests that after the components of looking up a street name and finding its coordinates had been performed to criterion for one set of streets, the necessary skills were emitted for the second set of streets with relatively few errors. This pattern also was apparent for the step which utilized these coordinates to find street locations on the front of the maps. The fact that a few errors occurred during the baseline component when each of the second set of streets were presented was probably a function of the difficulty of the map reading phase when compared to the other two phases for which data are presented. Three perfect trials were required before the students were considered to have reached criterion for all the steps in the program. Admittedly, this is not a very stringent criterion. The errors emitted by student 10 indicate the possible need for a more demanding criterion performance when teaching the complex skills of Phase IV.

In addition, the fact that all of the students were very familiar with the mechanics of sight-reading may also have led to this difference in errors emitted. It is significant, though, that there is a greater number of errors in the first baseline (i.e., with the first set of streets) in the map reading data than those found during the baseline for the second set of streets for each skill taught. The data seem to suggest the existence of general classes of skills that are generalizable across varying stimulus conditions. Since students will be expected to respond to varying conditions when they are using public transit, the generalizable skills taught may have crucial practical value. Furthermore, the real success of such a program may lie solely in its ability to teach students skills that are functional under changing conditions.

SUGGESTIONS FOR IMPLEMENTATION

In addition to the points brought up in the introduction, the following suggestions may be useful:

1. In step 5 of Phase IV, a template was used to help some of the students zero in on the quadrant where the street they were required to find was located. The template was a square piece of cardboard which simply formed a border around the area in which the students were looking. The template was faded as quickly as possible so that the students would not become too dependent upon it.

2. The use of videotapes in step 4 of Phase II is not a necessary component of the program. This step may be eliminated without

disrupting the task sequence. It was initiated in order to save some trials when actually riding the buses. After the students had gained some experience riding actual city buses, the use of videotape resulted in the elimination of the first step of riding, the step that sends them with the teacher, and enabled them to begin right away riding in a small group.

3. When presenting the videotape in step 4 of Phase II, the tape was stopped after the destination in question had flashed across the monitor. This not only simulates what would happen during an actual bus ride, but also decreases the time it takes to conduct a trial.

4. Because of the difficulty some students encountered with the transfer phase, it is necessary to make some suggestions about how this problem might be avoided. First of all, transferring buses could be simulated through a role playing situation in the classroom. This might facilitate acquisition. Videotape presentation of two routes where transferring is necessary to reach the cued destination may also be helpful.

5. When the students were out riding a bus, they always went to a destination for a specific purpose. They went to movies, parks, and bought items in stores. This was done to emphasize the functional reason for taking a bus, whether for business or pleasure.

APPENDIX I

Examples of bus route cards:
a. *Johnson St./Nakoma Rd.*[19]

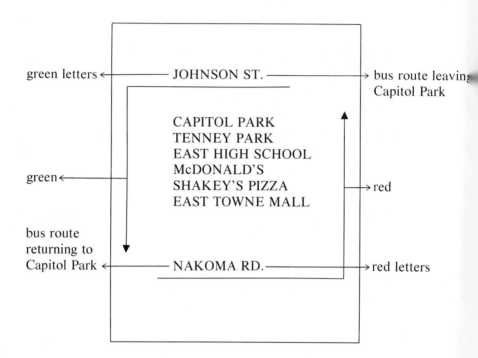

green letters ← JOHNSON ST. → bus route leaving Capitol Park

CAPITOL PARK
TENNEY PARK
EAST HIGH SCHOOL
McDONALD'S
SHAKEY'S PIZZA
EAST TOWNE MALL

green ←

→ red

bus route returning to Capitol Park ← NAKOMA RD. → red letters

3 x 6 index card with destinations written in black

_____

[19]The card above and the ones that follow represent those originally used in the program. The prosthetic cues built into the card were eventually faded, yielding a final set of cards having no arrows or color cues.

b. *Highland Park/Sherman Ave.* (color and layout same as Johnson St./ Nakoma Rd. card)

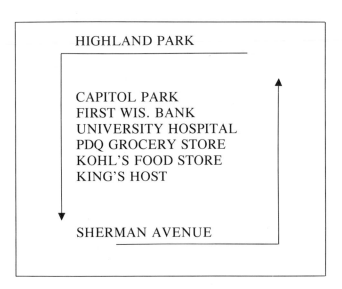

c. *Park St./North St.* (color and layout same as Johnson St./Nakoma Rd. card)

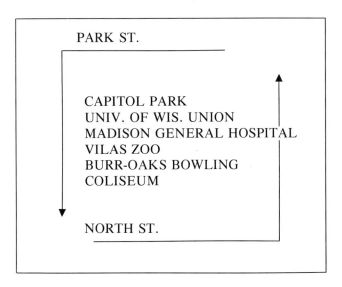

d. Nakoma Rd./Johnson St. (color and layout same as Johnson St./
Nakoma Rd. card)

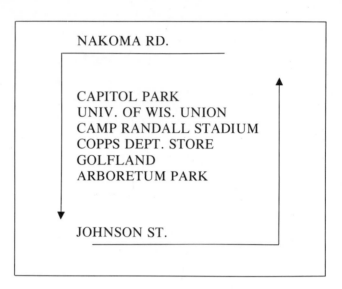

e. Example of a "home-bus-route-card" (color and layout same as
Johnson St./Nakoma Rd. card)

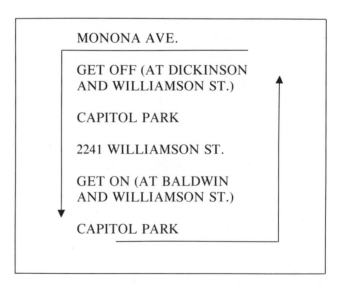

APPENDIX II

Below is a listing of places that the students were taught to take a bus to. Some of those listed were within walking distance of the Capitol Park. This information was shown to the students on individual "bus route cards" which consisted of a white 3× 6 index card with the name of the bus route written at the top and bottom and each place they could go to along that route. In the following listing the names of the appropriate bus routes appear after the destination.

Services

HEALTH

Near Eastside Health Center (Monona Ave./Capitol Park)
Dane County Mental Health Center (Capitol Park)
Dane County Dental Clinic (Capitol Park)
Wisconsin Central Colony (Sherman Ave./Highland Park)

SOCIAL

Dane County Social Services (Sherman Ave./Highland Park)

LEGAL

Legal Services Center (Capitol Park)

REHABILITATION

Madison Opportunity Center (Monona Ave./Capitol Park)

BANKS

First Wisconsin National Bank (Highland Park/Sherman Ave.)
American Exchange Bank (Capitol Park)

MISCELLANEOUS

Madison Area Association for Retarded Citizens (Sherman Ave./ Highland Park)
Post Office (main) (Capitol Park)
Police Station (main) (Capitol Park)
Public Library (main) (Capitol Park)

Food

RETAIL GROCERY

PDQ Grocery Store (Highland Park/Sherman Ave.)
Kohl's Food Store (Highland Park/Sherman Ave.)

PREPARED

McDonald's (Johnson St./Nakoma Rd.)
Shakey's Pizza (Johnson St./Nakoma Rd.)
King's Host (Highland Park/Sherman Ave.)

General Merchandise and Clothing

Copps Department Store (Nakoma Rd./Johnson St.)
East Towne Mall (Johnson St./Nakoma Rd.)
Treasure Island (Ridgewood)
Penney's Department Store (Capitol Park)
Kresge's 5–10¢ (Capitol Park)
Rennebohm's Drug Store (Capitol Park)

Recreation

PARKS

Tenney Park (Johnson St./Nakoma Rd.)
Vilas Zoo (Park St./North St.)
Arboretum Park (Nakoma Rd./Johnson St.)

THEATERS

Capitol Theater (Capitol Park)
Esquire Theater (Capitol Park)
Strand Theater (Capitol Park)
East Towne Cinema I & II (Johnson St./Nakoma Rd.)
University of Wisconsin Union (Park St./North St.)

SPORTS

See parks
Camp Randall Stadium (Nakoma Rd.(Johnson St.)
YMCA (Capitol Park)
East High School (Johnson St./Nakoma Rd.)
Golfland (Nakoma Rd./Johnson St.)
Burr-Oaks Bowling (Park St./North St.)

APPENDIX III

The following is a list of streets in the city of Madison taught to the students.

Set 1	Set 2	Set 3
Johnson St.	Sherman Ave.	Packers Ave.
Nakoma Rd.	Milwaukee St.	Fair Oaks Ave.
Midvale Blvd.	Atwood Ave.	Westmorland Blvd.
Mineral Point Rd.	S. Park St.	Wilson Dr.
University Ave.	E. Washington Ave.	Williamson St.

Fig. 1.   This figure shows the performance of S_6 under the baseline and teaching conditions of Phase I, step 3. The dotted line represents criterion performance for step 3 sitting and step 3 standing tasks.

Fig. 2.   This figure depicts the performance of S_7 during the sight word and bus route card trials of Phase II, steps 1 and 2. The dotted line represents the criterion for these trials. The same criterion applies to both steps.

Fig. 3   This graph shows the performance of S_{10} during the map reading trials of Phase IV, steps 2 and 3. The dotted line represents the criterion for these trials. The same criterion applies to both steps.

APPENDIX IV

Example of a data sheet:

Description of responses goes here.

Name	McDonald's	Tenney P.	Shakey's Pizza								
J.S.	+	+	+								
N.J.	+	−	+								
B.T.	−	−	+								

Sidney M. Levy,
David J. Pomerantz, and
Marc W. Gold

D

Work Skill Development

INTRODUCTION

This chapter is designed to provide a current account of the research on work skill development of the severely handicapped which has been going on at Children's Research Center, University of Illinois at Urbana–Champaign since 1969. Those activities which have been described in other publications or are currently being prepared for publication will not be included. The focus of attention here will be on pilot activities and recent developments which are not likely to find their way into publication in the near future. The three separate areas to be covered include pilot work on skill training with young children; pilot work on the acquisition of the necessary skills to assemble printed circuit boards with many components, and a detailed discussion of the concept of job enlargement from the industrial psychological literature, which provides some insights into worker motivation and productivity which might be of use to our field, and perhaps some information which can provide strategies for the inclusion of the severely handicapped into existing industrial organizations.

Preparation of this paper was supported by NICHHD Program Project Grant No. HD05951 to Children's Research Center, University of Illinois at Urbana-Champaign.

MANUAL SKILL TRAINING OF CHILDREN

Until 1974, research activities in work skill development were carried out with adults only. The rationale for this was that studies of manual skill development would be clearer if a developmental effect was minimized by avoiding the use of younger individuals, where such a factor would have to be accounted for. We felt that the information generating from that research would be applicable to younger children, even though adults were used to obtain the information and to generate the strategies. Anecdotal information from the field has tended to support that position. Many public school personnel are using our procedures and, according to their verbal reports, have found the techniques useful. This past year, we began working with younger children in an attempt to more systematically assess the applicability and limitations of our procedures with school-age children. Part of this decision related to a long range goal of developing a prevocational training program for public school use.

Two general attitudes underlie the work conducted by this program. First, we recognize the primary importance of a technology of training developed from basic and applied research. Data from such research can provide educative agencies with the instructional expertise required to give to the severely handicapped the skills needed to live with dignity within their home communities. The second philosophical foundation of our work is a bit more disturbing. Developing effective ways of teaching the retarded is not in itself an adequate strategy for solving their problems. In fact, many of these problems can be most meaningfully conceptualized as existing outside of the handicapped individual (Gold, 1975). They are reflected by inappropriately low levels of expectation commonly held in society and a general tendency to exclude deviant people from the mainstream rather than to adapt to their special needs. If we are to engineer meaningful change, farsighted social action strategies in addition to pedagogic skill are essential.

One such intervention plan focuses on economic reality. If the severely handicapped can be molded into a labor force able to meet industrial demands, the chances would significantly improve for them to be assimilated into the social structure as productive citizens. In the past, our research has attempted to demonstrate the potential of the retarded for economic viability. The studies have utilized 14- and 24-piece bicycle coaster brakes, as well as electronic circuit board assemblies. These represent considerably more difficult tasks than are usually associated with the severely handicapped, and are therefore useful for demonstrating the large discrepancy between the current level of functioning and unknown potential of retarded persons. The assemblies are also useful as research tools because they have considerable face validity. Watching subjects produce bicycle brakes or circuit boards, one sees a clear example of the retarded engaged in activity that is typically wage-generating.

The subjects who participated in the majority of studies of vocational skill development were sampled from unscreened populations of moderately and severely handicapped adolescents and adults. After an average of less than 2 hr cumulative training time, they were demonstrating a vocational competence, as indicated by high quality performance in production of complex tasks. It is clear that the severely retarded can acquire skills under appropriate training conditions. If their level of functioning can be dramatically elevated after 2 hr of intervention, what are the possible outcomes of well-planned, comprehensive training opportunities provided consistently from an early point in the lifespan? Most severely handicapped persons do receive some form of special educational or professional "helping" services during childhood. If such services were characterized by an orientation toward training and building of skills, application of powerful instructional techniques, and accountability for positive behavior change, clients would display much larger repertoires of competencies by adolescence than they do at present.

It is within this context of unfulfilled potential that the goals and techniques of this program are being extended to younger age ranges within the population of severely handicapped persons. Five through 12-year-olds from trainable classes in the public schools have received training on complex vocational assemblies. These studies represent an effort to assess the modifications in training procedure and strategy that are necessary for intervention with younger children. Also, this expansion of research involvement should provide momentum for the development of prevocational components for public school curriculum planning and programming. Society appears to be accepting its responsibility to provide quality services to the severely handicapped, and much of this responsibility is being delegated to the public schools (Brown and York, 1974). The clearest indications of change are the judicial and legislative actions of several states guaranteeing to all children the right to public education (Gilhool, 1973). If economic viability is to be considered a long range objective of educational services, the schools will have to provide a systematic progression of prevocational experiences over an extended period of time. Researchers will have to begin looking at the many unanswered questions associated with prevocational training. What kinds of experiences will be most facilitative for future vocational training and placement? The rapidly changing nature of the vocational structure in a technologically advanced society, as well as the great degree of variability across work situations make these issues quite complex. Deficiencies in knowledge and experience characterize much of the prevocational area at the present time, and are particularly evident in reference to elementary curricula. Baroff (1974) has proposed a set of basic objectives for elementary prevocational programs. These include (1) developing manual skills, (2) making small objects, (3) developing concern for the quality of tasks performed, (4) creating an awareness of the importance of task completion, and (5) strengthening work-related personality characteristics. Although the training described in this chapter is conceived as a preliminary search 'for information and not a prevocational program, it could be considered an appropriate activity for working toward all of these objectives.

Originally, our plans called for the use of the 14-piece coaster brake in studies with young children. This assembly was considered ideal for pilot research because of our extensive experience with it. A high degree of task familiarity serves to emphasize the particular needs of a subject population. Also, it facilitates flexibility on the part of the trainer, so that the procedures can be readily adapted to meet these needs. The well-developed level of organization of bicycle brake training techniques was indicated in previous extensions of our research involving institutionalized deaf–blind severely retarded, as well as profoundly retarded persons. Although the original training method included 24 steps in the content task analysis, it was readily apparent that further refinement, in the form of other, intermediate steps, had to be added in addition to changes in the kinds of feedback that were given. Experimenters were able to isolate the precise junctures where modifications were needed, and have alternative methods available because they knew the task well. Thus, the pilot studies with trainable children were conceived as a further broadening of the scope of the vocational skill development program in terms of populations involved. An effort was made to hold other parameters of the research environment (e.g., setting, basic format of training, and task) constant. Information regarding generalizability of our methods in reference to the other parameters is equally important, and research concerning these issues has been included in our plans. A careful progression of study should provide a basic understanding of the factors important in effective training of the severely handicapped.

The following anecdotal data are based on a pilot study conducted over a 7-mo period. Twelve school children (mean chronological age = 8.5 years, mean I.Q. = 40) from two trainable classes served as subjects. Within the first 2 days of training, it became evident that there were serious architectural barriers to manual skill training of small children in school. It was difficult to find a table–chair combination that was size-appropriate. Despite numerous attempts to circumvent the problem (including seating subjects on the trainer's lap), it was never adequately resolved. From our perspective, this kind of difficulty is quite important. The training techniques employed in these studies of vocational skill development stress stimulus control, or manipulation of response probability through arrangement of antecedent conditions in the training environment. The physical format of training is a major determinant of efficiency. If such physical limitations of the instructional setting are common in public school classrooms, they could obstruct the development of high quality elementary prevocational training programs.

A large proportion of the procedural modifications attempted were necessitated by the size of the learners' hands. It was most difficult for the children to hold up the brake while performing the fine manipulations involved in its assembly. One remedial strategy relied on the trainer to support the weight of the task, and to gradually reduce his assistance as the learner's proficiency and/or strength increased. Under these conditions, the two choice discriminations involved in the bicycle brake were learned relatively quickly, but manipulative skill never developed to the desired level. It seemed that the children had been taught too well to depend on the trainer, and that this pattern was most difficult to reverse. The withholding of physical assistance led to slower rates of acquisition (i.e., learning the discriminations), but higher quality skills resulted in the final analysis. A promising alternative method is to use simple jigs to support the brake as the child works on its assembly. These kind of data illustrate the importance of flexibility in the task analyses for application to different populations. Even during its original formulation, an instructional plan must consider alternative ways to break down a task.

In terms of the system developed within the research program described in this chapter, training format and feedback procedures are considered in the process task analysis. Format refers to the manner in which instruction is sequenced and to the layout of materials. In the usual brake training procedures, the parts are arranged in a left to right order. Identical pieces are grouped together in a compartment of the assembly tray, and the learner must bring one piece from each compartment to the front of the tray before starting the assembly. Commonly, retarded individuals have learned to perform this aspect of the task very rapidly, after observing one demonstration. Although the tray was uncomfortably large for all of the children involved, format adaptations were needed for only two of them. These particular children tended to grab randomly at parts in the tray, seriously disrupting the continuity of the training process in its early stages. Control over the situation was increased by leaving the parts of only one brake at a time in the tray. Physical prompts toward the correct piece successfullly eliminated the disruptive behavior, so that many more trials per session were possible. After gradual fading of the prompts, the children consistently approached the task in correct sequence.

Much of this research effort has been directed toward determination of the kinds of feedback that will facilitate skill acquisition by trainable children. The instructional techniques which provided encouraging acquisition data with adolescents and adults were relatively nonverbal in nature. Trainers relied mostly on modeling and manipulation of the learners' hands, rather than spoken instructions and reinforcement. One verbal phrase, "try another way," was consistently used to cue the necessity of a correction, and appropriate task responses were met with silence. The rationale for such a strategy had several aspects. First, the majority of individuals participating in these studies exhibited extreme deficiencies in their language repertoires. Many attempts to teach severely handicapped people combine remediation of language deficits with skill instruction. In our view, this practice results in inefficient development of stimulus control over both classes of target behavior involved. There is a lack of clear communication to the learner of what he is expected to do in these situations, and failure often results. The general rule proposed is that language and skill training should be provided separately, with verbal cues included in the instructional process only so far as they are inherently involved in the target behavior. Several qualifications about this rule are needed. The vocational tasks described in this chapter are ideally suited for nonverbal training because criterion performance involves no receptive or expressive language. In most tasks, there is more ambiguity concerning the extent to which language is involved. Also, under certain conditions, verbal cues can function efficiently in training. Caution should be taken, however, to insure that they consistently control the responses that they are intended to control.

The second aspect of the rationale for a nonverbal emphasis comes from a literature commonly called analyses of social reinforcement (Stevenson, 1965). Many studies have investigated the effects of positive and negative verbal feedback (usually presented to children by adults) on rate of simple motor responses, persistence at relatively simple tasks, and discrimination learning. Such feedback can exert a great deal of control over behavior, but it has generally not had strong effects in studies that employ measures of discrimination learning (Cairns, 1967; 1970). Intuitively, it seems probable that high frequencies of praise and criticism lead to increased reliance on the trainer at the expense of active formulation of general problem solving strategies. Zigler (1966) indicates that retarded persons, due to their histories of failure in evaluative situations, are much more likely than matched MA normals to depend on external cues for solving discrimination problems. By minimizing the amount of feedback (particularly verbal) that is provided in training, we hope to force the learner to confront the "rules" of the task. Another consistent and relevant finding of social reinforcement studies is that negative feedback has greater impact on rate, persistence, and learning than do positive evaluative comments (Stevenson, 1965). One explanation for this phenomenon is that criticism is delivered less often, more contingently, and with greater reliability for predicting further consequences than is praise in the social environment (Paris and Cairns, 1972). Finally, this literature indicates that children interpret adult nonreaction as positive or negative feedback if it is alternated with either praise or criticism alone (Spence, 1966; Hill et al., 1974). Thus, learners in the bicycle brake training situation should interpret silence as an indication of good performance.

The third basis for designing nonverbal instructional procedures was the kind of atmosphere that resulted in the training setting. The quiet, business-like nature of the sessions may have helped communicate the kind of social interaction that we tried to offer: The learner is treated as a dignified adult developing vocational competency, and is expected to act accordingly. Constant praise for correct task responses was seen as violating this unspoken agreement.

Judging by the quality of acquisition data accumulated in brake training studies (Gold, 1972), the feedback strategy was effective in providing information to the learner and maintaining on-task work behavior. Adolescents and adults tended to "ask for" feedback during the early trials by looking up at the trainer and hesitating after each correct response. Such behaviors rapidly extinguished because trainers continued to look down at the task and did not return eye contact. The learners appeared to genuinely enjoy working on the brake assembly, and disruptive behavior problems were rarely encountered. In general, the children's performance was excellent in the early stages of training. Although their teachers reported that they had deficient attention spans and would not sit still during classroom activities, the children remained consistently on-task throughout the relatively long assembly cycle (cycles ranged from 5 to 12 min), and were able to complete two or three cycles per session. One child did not respond well under the original training procedures. He did not stay seated for more than a minute at a time, and he did not maintain the constant manipulations needed to complete the assembly task. However, this pattern was reversed by providing play time with the trainer contingent on completion of a full cycle assembly. Eventually, this subject would finish two cycles (approximately 20 min of work) without interruption before the play opportunity was provided. In general, we recommend reliance on natural contingencies in vocational and prevocational training in order to enhance transfer to many diverse work situations. Extrinsic reinforcers are programmed into training only when their necessity has been demonstrated.

Several significant problems were encountered in the later stages of training. Typically, children learned the discriminations, and most of the manipulations involved in the task, but did not improve on one or two crucial manual responses. Although the troublesome manipulations were not identical across subjects, they all were related to inability to hold the brake still as it became uncomfortably larger and heavier with the addition of each part. As the number of trials without improvement increased, the children began to consistently make errors on parts of the assembly that they had clearly learned much earlier in training. Also, at this point in the training process, a significant increase in inappropriate, off-task behavior was noted. These data have led us to search for alternative tasks for which prevocational training techniques can be developed. Such tasks will retain the characteristics of the bicycle brake that we consider important. They will involve detailed, complex assemblies which can be disassembled so that they can be used in ongoing training programs. The assembly cycle will be shorter and the task itself smaller and lighter than the brake.

JOB ENLARGEMENT AND THE SEVERELY HANDICAPPED

If the adult severely handicapped are to succeed in the sheltered or unsheltered world of work, that world must be understood by those who prepare them. The discussion below is meant to contribute to that understanding. The issues which are relevant to the concept of job enlargement are central to both the training of the severely handicapped and to their integration into the labor force.

Gold (1973b) has already pointed out the possible relevance of the job enlargement concept and literature to the vocational habilitation of the retarded. In that chapter, a brief description is given of the concept and a few of the findings from that literature. With the recent trend towards the habilitation of the severely handicapped (Rehabilitation Act of 1974), the concept seems to take on additional meaning: There is now, for the first time, an organized, explicit movement toward their inclusion into the labor force. An optimistic conceptual framework might help such a movement. The concept of job enlargement is reviewed in detail here for several reasons: (1) to provide the reader with some background in an area of industrial psychology that can provide some meaningful "buzz words" and issues for consideration; (2) to point to the complexity of motivational systems, discussing affective as well as cognitive variables; (3) to provide the reader with an expanded in-depth awareness of the context into which the severely handicapped find themselves when entering competitive employment; and (4) to discuss directly the application of the concept to the severely handicapped. If we are going to efficiently and effectively integrate the severely handicapped into industry, we must know a great deal about industry, how it works, how it thinks and, perhaps more importantly, an awareness of recent literature in industrial research so that we can keep up with advances in technology.

The trend in industry since early in the Industrial Revolution has been to simplify jobs. The process of simplification that developed from the scientific management approach of Fredrick Taylor (1895, 1903, 1916) still prevails in many industries. The method involves the analyzing and breaking down of jobs into their simplest components. Jobs are standardized and made routine with workers limited to performance on small components of the total job. This procedure was thought to be the most efficient and economical way to produce.

Management's function under this system is to break the task down and to establish the production process. The worker provides the energy to run the system. As a result of simplification, jobs are reduced to elemental components requiring less skill from the worker, are highly repetitive, and allow little or no flexibility or autonomy from the routine.

The process of job simplification has been linked to worker dissatisfaction by many industrial investigators (Argyris, 1964; Davis, 1957; Guest, 1955; Herzberg, 1966; Kornhauser, 1965; Walker, 1950; Walker and Guest, 1952). The position taken is that simple, routine, nonchallenging tasks remove supposed intrinsic sources of personal satisfaction from the job leading to worker dissatisfaction. This, in turn, results in undesirable behaviors, from a management point of view, such as absenteeism, personnel turnover, and lower productivity.

An explanation for worker motivational problems resulting from simplification can be found in the writings of Maslow (1954). Maslow developed a hierarchy of needs beginning with lower level physiologic needs such as hunger, thirst, and sleep, and progressing towards higher order needs which include achievement and self-actualization. It is suggested that in today's society, most workers have their lower-level needs satisfied and are motivated toward the fulfillment of their higher-level needs. One way of attaining the desired results is through the work situation. A complex responsible job might allow the worker to experience a feeling of achievement and self-actualization, while a simple repetitive job would not. Workers not fulfilling their higher order needs would become frustrated and dissatisfied.

Argyris (1964) proposes that the organization that follows the simplification model causes frustration, a feeling of failure, and conflict in the individual worker. He believes the individual should be integrated into the organization. Evaluating factory workers for mental health, Argyris found them to score low on his positive mental health dimension (richness of self, self-acceptance, growth motivation, investment in living, unifying outlook on life, regulations from within, independence, and adequacy of interpersonal relations). The results confirmed his expectations leading him to conclude that simplified jobs contribute to poor mental health. The state of the workers' mental health before entering employment was not determined, thus obscuring his interpretation.

In another study, Argyris (1959) compared highly skilled workers to semiskilled and unskilled workers. He found that semi- and unskilled workers expressed less aspiration for high quality work, less need to learn more about their work, more emphasis on money, lower estimates of ability, less desire for variety and independence, fewer friends on the job, and less creative use of their leisure time. His position was that their needs and attitudes were a result of the workers' maturity being stifled by their jobs. An alternate point of view would be that the individuals brought the needs and attitudes into the work situation, rather than the job causing them. Since a pretest of the workers' attitudes before they began their jobs was not made, it is difficult to attribute the effects to job simplification.

Kornhauser (1965) maintains that poor mental health may be attributed to the simplification process. He defines mental health as "those behaviors, attitudes, perceptions and feelings that determine a worker's overall level of personal effectiveness, success, happiness, and excellence of functioning as a person." Adhering to the Protestant work ethic principle that work is the most prominent factor in men's lives, he believes that fulfillment must be achieved through the job. Kornhauser doubts whether other aspects of workers' lives, such as their family relationships and recreational activities, could compensate. He questions whether workers who are satisfied with a simplified, repetitious job are experiencing good mental health. After interviewing 655 factory workers, he determined that there was a decrease in good mental health and satisfaction commensurate with decreases in job level. Kornhauser concluded that the simplified job was the cause of the workers' poor mental health, and generalized from the sample to all blue collar workers. His definition of good or poor mental health involved the value judgment that striving for personal betterment is important, whereas a realistic evaluation of one's situation may not be. The assumption that all people should have the common goals of a desire for material possessions, social esteem, influence, and security is unfounded. People differ greatly in their value structure. To place a high value in a job content that allows for greater use of ability is surely a characteristic of some people, but not all. To say those who do not value it are experiencing poor mental health is not justified. Despite the criticisms, there was enough interest in the statements that Kornhauser and others were making to warrant industrial action.

In an effort to combat the presumed effects of job simplification, a contrasting organizational structure called job enrichment has developed. One form of job enrichment frequently used is job enlargement. There are many definitions of job enlargement (Ford, 1969; Guest, 1957; Hulin and Blood, 1968). The definition of Hulin and Blood (1968) seems to incorporate most of the conceptualizations of the other definitions, and is most universally used. They define job enlargement as "the process of allowing individual workers to determine their own working pace (within limits), to serve as their own inspectors by giving them responsibility for quality control, to repair their own mistakes, to be responsible for their own machine setup and repair, and to attain choice of method." The purpose of job enlargement is not simply to increase the individual's duties, but to allow him to do work that requires a higher level of skill. It is designed to incorporate a varied amount of work content and a relatively high degree of autonomy.

Lawler (1969) suggests that jobs can be enlarged along two dimensions, which he terms horizontal and vertical. When a job is enlarged on the horizontal dimension, the number and variety of the operations that a worker performs is increased. Enlarging the job vertically increases the degree to which the individual controls the planning and execution of his job. The amount of participation that the worker is permitted in the determination of company policies would also be included in the vertical dimension. Lawler proposes that for job enlargement to be successful in increasing worker's motivation, both dimensions must be enlarged. There has been a paucity of studies investigating jobs enlarged on only one dimension; therefore, it is difficult to verify Lawler's proposal.

An aspect of horizontal job enlargement that is of particular interest to this chapter is the task. The question to be considered is how significant is the task itself in motivating workers? Ford (1969) considers this issue in his definition of job enrichment. He defines it as "changing the task itself so that it becomes a source of motivation." A discussion of why the task could be a source of motivation will be addressed later in this chapter.

In an attempt to eliminate the high rate of absenteeism, turnover, and lower productivity, industry has turned to the job enlargement concept as a possible solution. There have been numerous studies reporting positive effects from job enlargement (Biganne and Stewart, 1963; Conant and Kilbridge, 1965; Davis and Werling, 1960; Ford, 1969; Guest, 1955, 1957; Pelissier, 1965; Walker, 1950; Walker and Marriott, 1951).

Walker (1950) reported on a job enlargement program at IBM. Four small and distinct jobs that were currently being done in their general machine shop were combined into one enlarged job. The reported results were improved quality, less idle times, and increased worker satisfaction. The study failed to present adequate data to support the findings, and, as in many of the studies to be presented, there was no control for a Hawthorne effect.

Using an interviewing procedure, Walker and Marriott (1951) interviewed 976 men from two automobile assembly plants and one metal mill. The results showed that, in one automobile assembly plant, 35 percent of the workers complained of boredom, and, in the other, 35 percent also had the same complaint. In the metal mill, only 8 percent of the workers complained of boredom. The difference in worker satisfaction between the two types of plants was attributed to the metal mill having very few repetitive jobs. They also found that, within the automobile plants, workers on conveyor-paced jobs were less satisfied than workers who were not. They interpreted the results as a strong argument against repetitious and simplified work, suggesting that it leads to a higher degree of dissatisfaction. The authors failed to acknowledge the possible difference between the work forces as a contributing factor, rather than differences in production techniques. Also, the fact that two-thirds of the automobile workers did not complain of boredom was not emphasized.

Another study investigating job enlargement in an industrial setting was reported by Biganne and Stewart (1963). Intensive and comprehensive attitude surveys of workers at the Maytag plant in Iowa were carried out prior to enlarging jobs. Subsequently, 25 job enlargement projects were carried out over a 6-year period. The results of the projects were improved quality, lowered labor costs, relatively quick majority acceptance of enlargement, and initial costs recovered by tangible savings within 2 years. Some of the positive effects of job enlargement were seen to be improved job satisfaction, additional responsibility, quality improvements, uninhibited pace, and versatility of skills.

The majority of empirical studies considering job satisfaction as it relates to job size have been attacked by Hulin and Blood (1968) as being poorly controlled, and by MacKinney, Wernimont, and Galitz (1962), who maintain that studies indicating detrimental effects of job simplification are methodologically weaker than research to support simplification.

The assumption that job simplification universally leads to worker dissatisfaction is unfound. MacKinney, Wernimont, and Galitz (1962) maintain an individual difference point of view and take exception with those who believe all workers will react in the same way to an enlarged job. They feel that satisfaction with a job is more than a function of the job itself. Rather, it is a function of both the man and the job, or, the man–job interaction.

Smith (1955) found that feelings of monotony were not merely a function of job content, but were related to characteristics in the worker. Workers who were content with a repetitive task generally were characterized by "placidity" and possibly "rigidity," but were not "stupid" or "insensitive." They appeared to be accepting of things as they were. Smith's study establishes an awareness of individual differences, and of the interaction between job content and personal characteristics of the worker.

Results have been reported that link simplified and repetitive tasks to high worker satisfaction (Kilbridge, 1960; Smith and Lem, 1955; Turner and Miclette, 1962). In their paper, Turner and Miclette (1962) describe an industrial setting where less than 20 percent of the workers complained about being bored on an extremely repetitive job. They reported that they derived satisfaction from the work itself.

Baldamus (1961) has also suggested that highly repetitive work may have a positive motivating effect. He proposes a traction effect, a feeling of "being pulled along by the inertia inherent in a particular activity," resulting in a pleasant feeling. This view has been verified experimentally in an industrial setting by Smith and Lem (1955).

It appears that some work populations respond to job enlargement and others do not (Hulin and Blood, 1968; Scott, 1973; Susman, 1973; Turner and Lawrence, 1955). Turner and Lawrence (1955) tested the job enlargement hypothesis on a sample of 470 workers. They investigated 11 industries who provided on 47 different jobs and found nonsignificant results betwen level of job and satisfaction. Analysis of the data showed a number of curvilinear relationships which led Turner and Lawrence to conclude that the workers studied had been drawn from two separate and different populations. They interpreted their data to mean that workers from urbanized factories responded differently to similar jobs than workers from small town factories. The workers from small town factories responded positively to job enlargement, while workers from the urban factories did not.

Hulin and Blood (1968) argue that workers in large urban industrialized communities are alienated from the middle-class work values and respond negatively to an enlarged job. They contend that workers from small communities with low standards of living but with few slums would accept middle-class work values and respond positively to job enlargement.

It appears that a wide range of individual differences exists in regard to what workers find satisfying about a job. Not all workers react in precisely the same way to the same job. Some may find a particular job highly satisfying; to others, the same job may be boring, repetitious, and nonchallenging. Shepard (1972) points out the necessity to determine empirically those characteristics that differentiate workers who will respond to job enlargement from those who prefer more simplified tasks. From the perspective of one concerned with the integration of the retarded into industry, an alternative approach to the study of individual differences is desirable. Rather than studying the characteristics of workers, we might focus on the characteristics of training and intervention programs needed to bring each retarded individual up to acceptable levels of motivation and performance.

Another area of inquiry which might prove fruitful is the relationships between task characteristics and worker motivation. One line of research that has concentrated on the task as a determinant of satisfaction and performance is called activation theory. Having its foundation in physiology, the theory explains task behavior in terms of stimulation of the reticular formation (Scott, 1966). The reticular formation is a dense network of neurons involved in general stimulation of the cerebral cortex. It does not provide the cortex with information, but it helps to maintain the organism at a high level of arousal or activation. According to the theory, individuals who are subjected to repetitive, simplified, dull tasks experience low levels of arousal and will tend to seek stimulus imputs to raise their level of activation.

Variables that are thought to affect activation level are stimulus intensity, variation, complexity, uncertainty, and meaningfulness. Properties such as complexity and meaningfulness are difficult to deal with, since they vary greatly with the individual's perceptions and interpretations of external stimuli. A highly complex interaction between the external properties of stimuli and the individual's cortical processes appears to exist.

Activation theory predicts that when tasks are simple, unvarying, and require the constant repetition of a very few responses, certain behaviors can be anticipated. After an individual learns the responses of a simple repetitive task and becomes familiar with its setting, a decrease in activation level will probably occur. If the individual is forced to stay in the situation, he will develop a negative affect and attempt behaviors that will increase the activation level and decrease the negative feelings. The effect on task performance would be a decline in productivity.

In that situation, the individual may attempt to leave the task setting or engage in other behaviors to increase activation level. He may engage in daydreaming activity or attempt movements such as changing positions or stretching. Leaving the work situation frequently to get a drink or visit the restroom might also be indications of attempts to increase activation level. Another way to increase the activation level is engaging in social activities with fellow employees, such as conversations or horseplay. These behaviors are frequently observed with mentally retarded workers in sheltered workshops, where the tasks are almost always of a highly simplified and repetitive nature. It would appear that, if greater variety and complexity were incorporated into the task, long-run productivity might be sustained and satisfaction for many workers increased.

Hulin and Blood (1968) question the attempt to generalize the theory from studies conducted with vigilance tasks in controlled settings to industrial tasks in factory settings. The different types of stimuli impinging on workers in industrial settings, such as noise, lighting changes, and the interaction and movement of other people do not present the same conditions as the controlled laboratory. They suggest that the tasks used in the vigilance studies are so different from industrial tasks that attempts to link industrial work motivation to a physiologic base could create a valid theory, but further investigation with industrial tasks in industrial settings is warranted. A possible environment for studying these problems is sheltered workshops for the handicapped. In that environment, the research could investigate industrial tasks in a quasi-industrial setting, while maintaining greater control of the variables. Workshops also would allow for more flexibility than industry.

A look at sheltered workshops for the mentally retarded reveals a situation in which workers are relegated to a simplicity previously unheard of. The tasks are almost always the most menial found in any work situation. The work demands placed upon workers are minimal, and nonproductive behavior can be observed in most shops.

When considering the retarded, the assumption usually made is that their limitations only allow them to engage in simplified tasks. Gold (1969, 1972) has clearly demonstrated that moderately and severely retarded individuals are capable of performing much more complex work than has ever been thought possible (e.g., bicycle brakes and electronic circuit boards). Gold's research strongly suggests that, with the proper training techniques, severely retarded people can acquire skills necessary to produce complex industrial assemblies, and not only under conditions involving very short cycle times.

People working with the mentally retarded have not, even conceptually, made use of the job enlargement concept. Perusal of the literature reveals only one study that investigates job enlargement in a sheltered workshop environment. Bishop and Hill (1971) were concerned with enlarging job content as opposed to merely changing it. They also attempted to determine the effects of enlargement and change on contiguous but nonmanipulated jobs and the function played by worker status. The dependent measures were job satisfaction (determined by the use of the Job Description Index), job performance (quality and quantity of output), and tension (measured by the Anxiety Differential Test, used to identify a possible underlying correlate of changes in job satisfaction and performance).

The simplified task consisted of sorting either nuts or bolts while, with the enlarged task, subjects were asked to sort both nuts and bolts. In addition to the sorting, the enlarged groups were also asked to assemble the nuts and bolts and place them in a container. The job change consisted of assigning bolts to subjects that were sorting nuts and vice versa. The task chosen is another indication of the expectancies society has for the retarded. Assembling nuts and bolts does not seem to constitute an enlarged or complex task.

The results showed no changes in quantity of output for the three tasks, but a decrement in quality with the enlarged task. Bishop and Hill suggest that error frequency was a partial function of a greater complexity of the enlarged task. The authors present no information regarding how subjects were trained on either task. With retarded people, the quality of their production is often a function of their initial learning. If they are trained to a rigid criterion, then errors in production are minimal (Gold, 1973a). Without additional information, the assumption could be made that they never really learned the enlarged task. Bishop and Hill further conclude that change is as effective in influencing production and satisfaction as job enlargement. They also determined that manipulated groups (receiving experimental treatment) showed positive effects, while non-manipulated groups demonstrated negative effects.

Although there are questions as to whether the study truly investigated job enlargement at all, Bishop and Hill's discussion of the population and work setting for future investigations is relevant to this discussion. They acknowledge the problem of generalizing the experimental results from a special workgroup to a more normal one. Our concern here is in the other direction, that is, how the notions of job enlargement and the findings in the literature might generalize to the population of concern in this chapter. One might postulate that many of the tasks now performed by normal workers, if performed by the severely handicapped, would constitute, in a sense, the epitome of job enlargement. That is, severely handicapped persons working on tasks which are dramatically enlarged from their current work might show all of the benefits shown by normal workers on enlarged jobs. The retarded, given the opportunity to perform tasks of a much higher complexity and cycle time than they have ever done, might prove to be an ideal labor force. This possibility has significant implications for both sheltered workshops and industry. While there have been no systematic attempts to look at job enlargement with the severely handicapped performing on complex long cycle tasks, subjects working on production in our research program consistently show a willingness and interest in working at the task, even in the absence of external reinforcers such as pay, food, or social praise (Gold, 1973a). The job enlargement concept, then, might provide us with a conceptual basis for further investigation of complex work by the severely handicapped, and also a mechanism for opening up meaningful dialogue with industry for the inclusion of the severely handicapped into their labor force.

ELECTRONIC PRINTED CIRCUIT BOARD
ASSEMBLY TRAINING

Related to the concept of job enlargement is the issue of community perceptions of an individual and how they develop. In our society, what a person does vocationally and how much he earns often determines his value and the level of respect he holds with its other members. The severely handicapped have rarely participated in the labor market because they were thought incapable of making a significant contribution to it. They have been perceived as a surplus, along with the aged, hardcore unemployed, and others (Farber, 1968), without the training or skills necessary to fill existing jobs. Consequently, the retarded constitute one of the largest segments of the nonemployed population with a great deal of energy and money spent on their maintenance. Gold (1972) states, "Some of the energies presently used for *maintenance* of this unproductive portion of the population should be directed toward *training* the retarded to somehow effectively compete in the labor market with other members of the surplus population who are not additionally stigmatized by the label 'retarded'."

Many of the procedures developed in our program and those of others, such as those described throughout this text, are being successfully employed by agencies serving the retarded. Most of the work tasks currently available to the retarded, however, are of a highly simplified and repetitive nature and do not require sophisticated training techniques. Studies to develop training procedures for one particular kind of complex work task which could be available as real subcontracts for rehabilitation agencies are currently being undertaken. The tasks are electronic printed or etched circuit boards (P.C. boards). P.C. boards were selected because of their apparent feasibility as a source of highly remunerative work for this population. Preliminary studies by Merwin (1973, 1974) indicate the ability of moderately and severely retarded persons to perform this type of work.

Merwin investigated the effects of pretraining upon the training and transfer of P.C. board assembly utilizing a match-to-sample training procedure. The initial study utilized 45 adult residents of a state institution. Their mean I.Q. was 55 (range 23–92).

Learning to assemble a circuit board is considered to be primarily a discrimination task. Form, size, and color of the individual components, as well as their position on the board, are the relevant dimensions to be learned. Consistent with the Attention Theory of Zeaman and House (1963), the purpose of the pretraining was to help direct the subject's attention to those relevant dimensions. It was believed that prior knowledge of the relevant dimensions might enhance the learning and transfer of the discrimination skills required in assembling the boards.

Conditions of visual discrimination pretraining was varied for three groups, using an automated multiple-choice visual discrimination apparatus (Scott, 1970). After completing the pretraining, all subjects were trained on the assembly of two similar P.C. boards.

In pretraining one group (group I) was asked to solve match-to-sample problems containing multidimensional junk stimuli (e.g., pictures of a dog, tree, etc.). The purpose of the junk stimuli problems was to familiarize the subjects with match-to-sample type problems, and was not intended to systematically direct attention to the color and form dimensions. After pretraining, they began training on the board itself. The second group (group II) also was trained to solve junk stimuli problems. After learning the junk problems, they were presented with problems involving electronic components as stimuli, and finally sets of problems of P.C. boards with increasing numbers of components. When they were able to discriminate pictures of boards containing 12 different components, training on the actual boards was begun. The purpose of the problems containing the components was to direct the subjects' attention to the color and form dimensions. The P.C. board problems included the dimension of position, as well as color and form.

The final group (group III) first received problems consisting of geometric form stimuli which differed in color and form. After learning the geometric form problems, the subjects were presented with the component problems, followed by the circuit board problems. The intention of the geometric form problems was to make the dimensions of color and form more salient.

Thirty nine of the 45 subjects, 88.6 percent, learned to assemble both the training and transfer P.C. boards each to a criterion of five consecutive correctly assembled boards (60 consecutive correct insertions). The mean number of trials to criterion across both boards was 16.5, and the mean total time for pretraining, training and transfer was 170 min. The effects of pretraining on task assembly training were inconsistent. In accordance with the theoretical assumptions of the pretraining, group III (geometric forms) had superior performance in training and transfer, as predicted. Since group II received identical pretraining, except for the junk stimuli problems in place of the geometric form problems, it was predicted that their performance would be close to group III. Group II had the poorest performance, with group I (junk stimuli only) falling between groups II and III. Although differences between groups occurred, the differences did not reach statistical significance.

Suggested interpretations are that the geometric forms pretraining had a slight effect on assembly acquisition, that experience with match-to-sample problems is facilitative in learning the circuit board task, or there was no pretraining effect at all, and direct training on the board would have been as facilitative. Since there was no control group that received only direct training, the latter interpretation could not be addressed.

A significant transfer effect on the second board was obtained for all groups. Whether this was due to pretraining effects, to the training on the first board, or to the combination of the two could not be resolved from those data.

In her next study, Merwin attempted to resolve the unanswered questions. The second study utilized 60 institutionalized adults. Their mean I.Q. was 40, with a range of 18–77. As with the first study, the type and amount of pretraining were varied between groups. The first group received only direct assembly training on a 12 component circuit board. Following criterion, they were presented with a second board with different components in different positions (transfer). The second group was given matching pretraining in the form of match-to-sample slide problems (components and circuit boards), which was followed by training and transfer. The third group received the matching pretraining (the slide problems), followed by placement pretraining, and finally training and transfer on the two boards. Placement pretraining consisted of manipulation and insertion of six of one type of component in a board. By using identical components, color and form dimensions were held constant, with only position allowed to vary.

Forty-eight out of the 60 subjects, 80 percent, reached criterion on both boards. The data failed to show a significant pretraining effect. It appears that direct training on the task is as effective and efficient as the forms of pretraining employed in the study. As in the first study, a strong transfer effect was found for all three groups. Since most P.C. boards are similar with regard to the relevant dimensions (color, form, position) for the discriminations necessary for assembly, the generalizability of the transfer effect to most other P.C. boards seems probable. The mean total time for all three groups to reach criterion was 246 min.

The training techniques generated from these two studies indicate that retarded workers can learn to insert electronic components into a P.C. board using a match-to-sample strategy. The procedure consists of picking up a component, matching it to its counterpart on the sample board, finding the correct holes on the board being assembled, orienting the component (not reversing it), and placing the leads in the holes. The P.C. boards assembled in the electronics industry usually contain many more components than subjects in the prior studies were required to do, although job stations in industry sometimes call for insertion of only 10 or 12 components. The assembly of the boards also entails additional steps such as bending, cutting, and crimping the leads, and in some cases soldering the components in place. The Merwin studies provide sufficient encouragement to investigate whether retarded workers can do these other steps and how many components they can assemble.

Pilot work addressing these issues has been started using a circuit board consisting of 45 components. The P.C. board task being used is one that is currently produced by an electronics company in the midwest. The components include resistors, capacitors, and diodes. For each component, two leads must be bent, inserted in a specific place on the board and in a specific position, and cut and crimped. In addition to the insertion components, there are parts that must be mounted and riveted into place, and others that require mounting with small screws and nuts.

Four subjects from a sheltered workshop in Champaign, Ill., have been selected to pilot our procedures: (1) a 25-year-old male with an I.Q. of 48; (2) a 28-year-old female with an I.Q. of 35; (3) a 22-year-old female with an I.Q. of 45, and (4) a 19-year-old male with an I.Q. of 45. The etiology of three of the four is Down's syndrome; . . . the fourth is unknown. All subjects were chosen because they were described by their supervisors as functioning in the trainable range with no gross motor or sensory problems, and as being cooperative individuals. It was decided that individuals with those characteristics would best serve to answer the initial questions being asked in the pilot work.

A question being investigated is, can they learn to assemble a large number of parts, using the match-to-sample training procedure? The initial task consists of the insertion of 32 prebent components into their appropriate positions on the board. In this task, they are also required to insert the parts with the markings on the components in identical positions, as found on the sample. Some parts have letters, or numbers, or both facing in a specific direction. Some of the other components have color bandings. If a part is inserted upside down, it is considered an error and the subject must correct it. In actuality, many components function appropriately with either lead in either hole but, because the markings on some of the components must be readable and some components do have specific polarities, we require constant positioning of all components.

At the present time, two subjects have reached our criterion of five consecutively correct assemblies of the part of the board assembled in Job Station I (32 components), that is, 160 consecutive insertions without error or assistance. The total amount of trials (boards) to reach criterion for subject I was 19, which took seven training sessions, one per day. The total time to criterion was 141 min, averaging 7 min 44 sec per trial. The subject was run 19 trials past criterion to determine the validity of our criterion, consistency, and also to get a feel for production. In the 19 trials, which consisted of 608 insertions, he made four errors. The mean time per trial was 5 min 32 sec, decreasing over trials.

An interesting incident took place with this subject during the post-criterion trials. On the table where the subject was engaged in the task was a correctly assembled circuit board with all 45 components. After completing his work, the subject, who is almost nonverbal, pointed to the completed board. He was told that he would soon learn to assemble the est of the board in addition to the parts he already knew. The subject then proceeded to point to each of the new parts on the complete board and correctly showed the experimenter where they went on his board, without ever having been directed toward it.

Another interesting event occurred during the postcriterion period. While assembling a board, he got out of sequence and had six parts in wrong places. He seemed to know something was wrong and expressed concern. The experimenter said "That isn't correct, Francis, fix it." Using the sample board as a guide, he proceeded to correct the mistakes.

Subject II has not yet reached criterion. She has had 83 trials to date, and her number of position errors has gone down from approximately 18 per trial to one or two on her last three trials. The time per trial has also decreased from over 20 min initially to about 10 min currently. Her problem is in attending to the writing or color coding on the parts (reversal errors). If reminded to attend, she will insert the part correctly;—if not, the part will go on correctly or incorrectly, depending on how it was picked up. Use of a magnifying glass did not decrease these errors.

Subject III reached criterion in nine trials. On her first trial, she made no position errors and two reversal errors. That is, with one partial demonstration trial by the experimenter, she proceeded to place all 32 components into their proper places the first time she attempted the task. On trials one through four, she made one position error on all four trials combined, while committing one to two reversal errors per trial. On trials five through nine, she was errorless. Her total time to criterion was 90 min 16 sec, with times per trial decreasing from 15 min to approximately 8 min. She was run three trials past criterion, during which she remained errorless, and her time decreased to under 5 min 30 sec.

Subject IV has had 46 trials to date. His initial trial took over 39 min, and decreased gradually over succeeding trials. His current time is approximately 10 min. Errors over trials have dropped from 28 to 3. This subject had difficulty with the fine motor movements required to insert the parts. As his experience with the task increased, his dexterity improved and insertion no longer presents a problem.

All subjects learned the sequence and positions of the components relatively easily. With two of the subjects, letter and number discriminations (reversal errors) were difficult to achieve. New and more powerful training procedures are being developed in an attempt to facilitate learning.

Two experiments and work with four pilot subjects have been discussed. These data strongly suggest that additional investigation is warranted. Current plans include: (1) the running of additional subjects to verify the findings to date; (2) developing training procedures for lead bending, small tool usage, and soldering; (3) doing the circuit board used in the present pilot work as a remunerative subcontract; (4) obtaining several other subcontracts and training workers in order to validate the training procedures; and (5) creating an electronics factory for the purpose of documenting and marketing the skill competencies of the severely handicapped.

The severely handicapped should be granted the right to full participation in society. An important area of participation is work. Determining their true capabilities in this area and giving them the means for reaching those capabilities is providing an option previously not available. Whether or not they will be able to exercise that option remains to be seen. Today's society will have to undergo major modifications for the full integration of the handicapped to occur. Helping them to develop sophisticated manual work skills may be the most effective means to accomplishing that goal.

CONCLUSION

Data have been presented to document the competency of the severely handicapped in terms of their ability to do high quality complex work. The concept of job enlargement has been presented in detail to provide a conceptual base for their inclusion into industry as a previously untapped labor force with, perhaps, some characteristics that are needed but presently unavailable. In addition, pilot work with younger children was presented to indicate the feasibility of pursuing the development of complex work skills in younger children. All of this is seen as providing the field with a highly optimistic stance towards full development of the skills of the severely handicapped.

For this to happen, we must first be convinced that they are, in fact, capable, and then we must get rid of the many barriers that seem to hold us back. Current testing and evaluation practices, preconceived notions about intelligence, poor preservice and in-service training programs for teachers and other service personnel, and continued reliance on heartstring diplomacy must all give way to the development of sophisticated training procedures, and a commitment to genuine major change in the skill functioning and life functioning of the severely handicapped. As competence by the severely handicapped is demonstrated, current expectancies and benevolent feelings should give way to genuine respect and revised expectancies so that, at some point, virtually all severely handicapped individuals will be given the training and support to become our peers instead of our charges.

REFERENCES

Argyris C: The individual organization: An empirical test. Admin Sci Quart 4:145–167, 1959

Argyris C: Integrating the Individual in the Organization. New York, Wiley, 1964

Baldamus W: Efficiency and Effort. London, Travistock, 1961

Baroff GS: Mental Retardation: Nature, Cause, and Management. Washington, D.C., Hemisphere, 1974

Biganne JF, Stewart PA: Job Enlargement: A Case Study. Research Series No. 25, State University of Iowa, Bureau of Labor and Management. 1963

Bishop RC, Hill JW: Effects of job enlargement and job change on contiguous but non-manipulated jobs as a function of workers' status. J Appl Psych 55:175–181, 1971

Brown L, York R: Developing programs for severely handicapped students: Teacher training and classroom instruction. Focus Except Child 6:1974

Cairns R: The information properties of verbal and non-verbal events. J Person Social Psych 5:353, 1967

Cairns R: Meaning and attention as determinants of social reinforcer effectiveness. Child Develop 41:1067, 1970

Conant EH, Kilbridge MD: An interdisciplinary analysis of job enlargement: Technology, costs, and behavioral implications. Indust Labor Relat Rev, 18:377–385, 1965

Davis LE: Job design and productivity: A new approach. Personnel, 33:418–430, 1957

Davis LE, Werling R: Job design factors. Occup Psychol 34:109–132, 1960

Farber B: Mental Retardation: Its Social Concept and Social Consequences. New York, Houghton Mifflin, 1968

Ford RN: Motivation Through the Work Itself. New York, American Management Association, 1969

Gilhool TK: Education: "An Inalienable Right." Except Child, 39:547–604, 1973

Gold MW: The acquisition of a complex assembly task by retarded adolescents. Final Report, University of Illinois at Urbana–Champaign, May 1969

Gold MW: Stimulus factors in skill training of the retarded on a complex assembly task: Acquisition, transfer and retention. Am J Ment Defic 76:517–526, 1972

Gold MW: Factors affecting production by the retarded: Base rate. Ment Retard, 11:41–45, 1973a

Gold MW: Research on the Vocational Habilitation of the Retarded: The Present, the Future, in Ellis NR (ed): International Review of Research in Mental Retardation, Vol. 6. New York, Academic, 1973b. pp 97–147

Gold MW: Vocational Training, in Wortis J (ed): Mental Retardation and Developmental Disabilities: An Annual Review, Vol. 7. New York, Brunner/Mazel, 1975, 254–264

Guest RH: Men and machines. Personnel, 496–503, 1955

Guest RH: Job enlargement–A revolution in job design. Personnel Admin 20:9–16, 1957

Herzberg F: Work and the Nature of Man. Cleveland, World, 1966

Hill KT, Emmerich HR, Gelber ER, et al: Children's interpretation of adult nonreaction: A trial-by-trial self report assessment and evidence for contrast effects in an observational context. J Exp Child Psychol 17:482–494, 1974

Hulin CL, Blood MR: Job enlargement, individual differences, and workers response. Psychol Bull, 69:41–55, 1968

Kilbridge MD: Do workers prefer larger jobs? Personnel 37:45–48, 1960

Kornhauser AW: Mental Health of the Industrial Worker: A Detroit Study. New York, Wiley, 1965

Kunin T: The construction of a new type of attitude measure. Personnel Psych 8:65–77, 1955

Lawler EE: Job design and employee motivation. Personnel Psychol, 22:426–434, 1969

MacKinney AC, Wernimont PF, Galitz WO: Has specialization reduced job satisfaction? Personnel, 39:8–17, 1962

Maslow AH: A theory of human motivation. Psychol Rev 50:370–396, 1954

Merwin MR: The use of match-to-sample techniques to train retarded adolescents and adults to assemble electronic circuit boards. Unpublished master's thesis, Urbana, University of Illinois, 1973

Merwin MR: The effect of pretraining upon the training and transfer of circuit board assembly skills of retarded adults. Unpublished doctoral thesis, Urbana, University of Illinois, 1974

Paris SG, Cairns RB: An experimental and ethological analysis of social reinforcement with retarded children. Child Develop 43, pp 717–729, 1972

Pelissier RF: Successful experience with job design. Personnel Admin, 28:12–16, 1965

Scott KG: A multiple-choice audio-visual discrimination apparatus with quick interchange display and response panels. J Exp Child Psychol 9:43–50, 1970

Scott RD: Job enlargement—The key to increasing job satisfaction? Personnel J 52:313–317, 1973

Scott WE Jr: Activation theory and task design. Organ Behav Human Perform 1:3–30, 1966

Shepard JM: Organizational Issues in Industrial Society. Englewood, N.J., Prentice-Hall, 1972

Smith PC: The prediction of individual differences in susceptibility to industrial monotony. J Appl Psychol 39:322–329, 1955

Smith PC, Lem C: Positive aspects of motivation in repetitive work: Effects of lot size upon spacing of voluntary rest periods. J Appl Psychol 39:330–333, 1955

Spence JT: Verbal-discrimination performance as a function of instructions and verbal-reinforcement combination in normal and retarded children. Child Develop 37:269–281, 1966

Stevenson HW: Social reinforcement of children's behavior, in Lipsitt, Spiker (eds): Advances in Child Development and Behavior, Vol. 2. New York, Academic, 1965 pp 97–124

Susman GI: Job enlargement: Effects of culture on workers responses. Indust Relat J Econ Soc, 12:1–15, 1973

Taylor FW: A piece rate system. Transactions of the American Society of Mechanical Engineers, June 1895, Paper 647

Taylor FW: Shop management. Transactions of the American Society of Mechanical Engineers, June 1903, Paper 1003

Taylor FW: The Principles of Scientific Management. New York, Harper, 1916

Turner AN, Lawrence PR: Industrial Jobs and the Worker: An Investigation of Response to Task Attributes. Boston, Harvard University, Graduate School of Business Administration, 1955

Turner AN, Miclette AL: Sources of satisfaction in repetitive work. Occup Psychol 36:215–231, 1962

Walker CR: The problem of the repetitive job. Harvard Bus Rev, 28(3):54–59, 1950

Walker CR, Guest RH: The Man on the Assembly Line. Cambridge, Mass., Harvard Univ Pr, 1952

Walker CR, Marriott R: A study of some attitudes to factor work. Occup Psych 25:181–191, 1951

Zeaman D, House BJ: The role of attention in retardate discrimination learning, in Ellis NR (ed): Handbook of Mental Deficiency. New York, McGraw-Hill 1963, pp 159–223

Zigler E: Personality structure in the retardate, in Ellis NR (ed): International Review of Research in Mental Retardation, Vol. 1. New York, Academic 1966 pp ■■■

Dennis E. Mithaug and
Norris G. Haring

E

Community Vocational and Workshop Placement

INTRODUCTION TO REHABILITATION FOR THE HANDICAPPED

Since the 1920s, concern for the needs of the disabled has developed into a national commitment to provide the handicapped with the opportunities for self-development and fulfillment afforded able-bodied citizens. Following the establishment of the Federal Vocational Rehabilitation Agency to help disabled veterans of World War I and industry casualties in the 1920s, the passage of the Barden–LaFollette Act to open vocational training opportunities for the mentally ill in 1943, and the Vocational Rehabilitation Amendments that provided for the modern Vocational Rehabilitation Administration in 1954, a legislative and bureaucratic framework was developed to implement a comprehensive set of services for the handicapped. These included vocational evaluation, vocational training, job placement, vocational counseling, and follow-up (Katz, 1968). The rehabilitation efforts that evolved from this legislation gave rise to a number of community workshops that evaluated a client's employability while providing a training ground to improve his work habits and work skills. These sheltered workshops have served clients with a wide variety of handicapping conditions, ranging from severe disabilities which may significantly delay clients from obtaining full-time employment to mild handicaps requiring relatively short periods of training and adjustment, prior to securing a position in the competitive labor market. The severity of the disability and its effect on the client's potential for employment have a direct effect on his placement in the community. For example, those who can be served in a community workshop include: "(1) those who may be placed in industry after a short period of training in a sheltered workshop; (2) those who may be placed in industry, but will probably need a more or less prolonged training period; (3) those who will probably be able to work in the sheltered workshop environment only and be able to achieve self-support; (4) those who will probably be able to work in the sheltered workshop environment only, but on a marginally productive basis." (Jacobs, Weingold, and Dubrow, 1962; in Katz, 1968, pp. 195–197).

Tobias (1960) classified approximately 200 retarded young adults who applied for sheltered employment as falling into one of four comparable groups: those readily placeable, placeable with special help, sheltered workers I, and sheltered workers II. Sheltered workers I were characteristically emotionally unstable, of low physical stamina, and socially isolated from fellow workers. Although these clients' potential for work resembled those in the immediately higher category, their level of performance did not match this potential. For clients in the sheltered worker II category, work was considered as a constructive and satisfying activity rather than "a symbol of adult status and self-sufficiency." (Tobias, 1960, p. 123)

Vocational training for handicapped adults who do not meet standards for the sheltered worker II category is limited to work-oriented activities occasionally available in independent living programs or activity centers. Tobias and Cortazzo (1963) reported an independent-living program that serves clients who could not adapt to a workshop environment because of their severe deficiencies in independent-living skills. Activities in the program included travel training, grooming, community orientation, remunerative work, food preparation and handling, recreation and sports, camping, speech therapy, homemaking, and group discussions. The remunerative work experience provided improved discipline, decreased distractability, increased self-direction, and client satisfaction for work accomplished.

Activity centers also provide services for the least capable retarded adults. Occasionally a work experience is provided, although the major emphasis is on music, drama, arts and crafts, dancing, trips, and day camping (Katz, 1968, p. 164).

A PROGRAMMATIC SEQUENCE

In many communities, services of one form or another are available for virtually all disabled adults, regardless of their handicapping condition. The activity centers and independent-living programs provide activities and training for the least capable and lowest functioning adults, while the short-term workshops, transitional workshops, and the on-the-job training programs serve those individuals who demonstrate greater potential for immediate and competitive employment.

These community programs could be coordinated to facilitate rehabilitation by establishing an orderly "graduation" of clients from one program level to another as clients gain proficiency in a given service component. Individuals in activity centers and independent living programs who improve significantly during their stay may achieve a level of development and performance acceptable for entry into a long-term workshop. This workshop serves "less able retarded adults who cannot meet the demands of competitive employment" (Katz, 1968, p. 143). Client salary could be as low as 10 cents an hour, commensurate with their low rate of productivity, which may be a fraction of the nonhandicapped workers' wage. Satisfactory progress in the long-term workshop should determine a client's entry into a short-term workshop, which is designed "to place the client in competitive employment after a relatively short period of evaluation and training" (Katz, 1968, p. 127). The next step is direct entry into competitive employment or into an on-the-job training program, which provides the specific job skills necessary for full-time work.

Adopting an optimistic outlook regarding each client's potential for development, regardless of his level of impairment (Olshansky, 1973), should intensify a search for procedures that will promote client progress within each program and will facilitate transfer of successful clients from one program level to another. Rehabilitation should be the principal goal for all levels of client training. When rehabilitation ceases to be the primary object of vocational training, clients remain stationery; few move upward into training opportunities provided at more advanced stations. For example, when the short- or long-term workshops, attempting to survive in a business community, devote too much time and energy to the production of goods, the training activities essential for rehabilitation deteriorate (Wollinsky and Kase, 1973). And when rehabilitation activities are not closely related to specific jobs and skills that the client will eventually be expected to perform, effectiveness in training and accuracy in evaluation is reduced. Improvements in the workshop rehabilitation model may include at least the following: "(1) making the training situation resemble the terminal behavior (employment) as closely as possible; (2) clearly identifying and systematically changing the behavior that renders the client unemployable; and (3) keeping data so the effectiveness of assessment and modification procedures can be evaluated" (Brickey, 1974, p. 16).

OBSTACLES TO REHABILITATION AND PLACEMENT

The training situation should resemble the job situation in terms of the normative behaviors required for success, as well as the specific skills required to do the job. Normalization in the workshop may mean that expectations for the trainee's progress coincide with behavior patterns and work habits required for a targeted job. Also, the successful modification of behaviors contributing to a client's employability requires effective programming techniques for developing relevant job skills and appropriate motivational systems to reduce inappropriate responses and increase worker productivity; and, finally, data on the client's responses to the job situation and his productivity while on-task is essential for determining the effectiveness of the treatment effort. When the data collection system is sensitive to daily and weekly changes in behavior, we can determine when one approach fails or another succeeds.

Skills and Expectations

Power and Marinelli (1974) point out that today, our society's response to deviance in all its forms is one of "stopping and controlling, rather than creating environments for building of positive, healthy behavior." Based upon Wolfensberger's belief that role expectancy influences the behavior of the role performer (Wolfensberger, 1972), these authors suggest that the work environment in sheltered workshops and the associated "subhuman expectancies" have a stultifying effect on rehabilitation. This problem can be avoided, however, when the training situation, including both job skills and role expectations, is similar, if not identical, to terminal placement.

PAST RESEARCH ON EMPLOYABILITY FACTORS.

This consideration may be a timely one, considering the direction and success of past research that relates general factors or variables to employability. While this research has been pursued diligently (Ladas, 1961; McCarron and Dial, 1972; Meadow and Greenspan, 1961; Tobias, 1960; and Wagner and Hawyer, 1965), the results gleaned from extensive literature surveys of the field have been contradictory (Chaffin, Smith, and Haring, 1967).

While some studies report a positive relationship between intelligence and success on the job (Abel, 1940; Baller, 1936; Collmand and Newlyn, 1956; Jackson and Butler, 1963; and Phelps, 1956); a comparable number found no relationship (Baer, 1961; Bobroff 1956; Cowan and Goldman, 1959; Hartzler, 1951; and Madison, 1964). Similarly, studies investigating the relationship between chronological age and employability have shown the following contradictory views: positive, showing a relationship (Minneapolis, 1965; and Hartzler, 1951); negative, showing an inverse relationship (Kolstoe, 1960); and some studies have shown no relationship (Neff, 1959; and Shafter, 1957). When school achievement was related to successful employment, the majority of studies found no relationship (Cowan and Goldman, 1959; Green, 1945; Madison, 1964; and Shafter, 1957), while some (Voelker, 1962; and Kolstoe, 1960) found a slight reverse relationship, and one study found a positive relationship (Erickson, 1966).

Two factors consistently related to successful employment have been family influence and personality. Most investigators are in agreement about the salutary effects of the family on employment success (Abel, 1940; Green, 1945; Jackson and Butler, 1963; Voelker, 1962; Neff, 1959; and Madison, 1964). The personality correlates of employability have included emotional stability (Bronner, 1933; Hay and Cappenburg, 1931), gregariousness (Hegge, 1942; and Whitcomb, 1961), obedience and truthfulness (Shafter, 1957), ambition and self-respect (Abel, 1940), and attitude and motivation (Thomas, 1965).

Unfortunately, general characteristics are not sufficiently differentiated to provide for specific programs of corrective instruction. "And measurement of personality variables, especially with the mentally retarded, is virtually impossible. Altering home conditions, the other factor possibly related to employability, seems unlikely, especially at the senior high level" (Chaffin, Smith, and Haring, 1967). While home conditions and personality factors are related to employability in some global fashion, this information is of little use in determining appropriate objectives for treatment. Even when personality characteristics are specified with referent behavioral descriptors, the reliability of observations from one test situation to another is lacking (Chaffin, Smith, and Haring, 1967).

Contributing to this problem may be the absence of a unifying variable across all job categories that defines successful performance. What contributes to success on one job may contribute to failure on another, or otherwise be unimportant to success (Kolstoe and Shafter, 1961). The search for a general employability factor may have been unproductive because such a factor does not exist. The possibility remains that, aside from productivity, i.e., doing one's required task within acceptable standards of efficiency and effectiveness, the critical associated work patterns are different from job to job.

How, then, does productivity affect employability? Considering the extensive research conducted on variables associated with worker productivity, surprisingly little information is available on production itself (Windle, 1961). Kilstoe (1960) points to the absence of criteria for what constitutes acceptable quality and quantity of work, while Neff (1959) reports one of the few studies showing the importance of production to job success. Regarding associated work patterns, investigations by Loos and Tizard (1955), Gorton (1966), and Lent (1964) suggest ways in which associated variables such as inappropriate social behaviors, social interaction, and reinforced appropriate social behaviors may significantly affect production. Following their own suggestion that "production rate and its interaction with different social variables may affect the vocational success or failure of the educable mentally retarded," Chaffin, Smith, and Haring (1967) conducted a study demonstrating how employer estimations of worker success or failure were a function of changes in worker productivity. When manipulated worker productivity increased, employer estimations of that worker's success increased, and when the productivity decreased, success evaluations correspondingly decreased.

EMPLOYABILITY AND TRAINING

These findings suggest that success on the job may be (1) a function of productivity, and (2) a function of social patterns and work habits as they impinge upon and affect production. Being deviant within a work group and an isolate during lunch and coffee breaks may not lead to job termination. But when this social difficulty diminishes the worker's capacity to produce, his job may be in jeopardy. Kolstoe and Shafter (1961) describe a range of social deviance that cannot be adjudged good social adjustment but, at the same time, does not spell job failure:

> . . . a person may take his place in a factory production line by becoming an accepted, interacting part of the work group. On the other hand, he may withdraw from group participation and still be tolerated as a working member of the group or he may be the butt of the heckling of the others and thus gain a dubious acceptability. All of these behaviors may enable a person to be successfully employed, but it is difficult to classify all three types of behavior as "good" social adjustment or to classify the variations under the single classification of "successful." (Kolstoe and Shafter, 1961, p. 288).

When rehabilitation efforts are based upon employment characteristics, training activities, in fact, represent conditions of the job. If standing alone at a bench for long periods and working at a high rate of production is necessary to hold a job, the client seeking employment in that position must be prepared to meet those particular standards. If the client cannot stand while working, cannot work alone, or work rapidly, he is not employable. Each job requires specific skills and role expectations. If a client is trained in the skill but not the supporting behavior patterns expected by the supervisor, his adjustment on the job may suffer, just as work habits unaccompanied by the skills required to complete the job will probably lead to maladjustment.

Rehabilitation and placement cannot be considered separately. Effective goal-directed rehabilitation depends upon the type of placement intended for the client, and the type of placement that is appropriate depends upon the progress achieved during rehabilitation. Considered separately, the effectiveness of each is reduced; placement personnel find positions for which the client has no training, and the training program prepares the client in areas of little consequence for his or her immediate or long-term employment. Rather than preparing clients to be generalists, i.e., adequately equipped to handle most jobs, the goal-directed program pinpoints the skills and role expectations of a specific job and then provides activities that will enable the client to meet those requirements.

Applied at each level in the rehabilitation sequence, this approach should facilitate client progress within and between programs. Clients in activity centers and independent living programs could be prepared in job skills, production standards, and work habits required for entry into long-term workshops, whose clients in turn, might be prepared for the job skills and work expectations required in the short-term workshop. Finally, the short-term workshop clients might be trained for specific jobs in the competitive work force. Such an effort would require individualization of vocational training programs to fit the particular needs of each client.

Normalization in vocational training and placement means that clients at one level are expected to behave and perform according to standards or norms operating at the immediately higher level. These expectations are specific goals or objectives for worker behavior and job performance. The degree to which client progress approximates these standards determines his readiness for placement at the next higher level. Performance standards and role expectations for jobs in competitive employment become the rehabilitation objectives for short-term workshops and on-the-job training programs. Norms in short-term workshops become the objectives set for clients working in long-term workshops. Standards for acceptable performance and worker behavior in long-term workshops become the objectives for the vocational training programs in the activity centers and independent living programs.

Programming and Motivating

After specifying appropriate behavioral objectives from which to individualize an efficient training program for each trainee, task environments must be programmed "to maximize the likelihood that the trainee will emit the proper behaviors in the proper sequence and at the proper rates" (Crosson, 1969). Rather than matching work according to what the client "can do," Crosson suggests that the client be trained for the work that is available.

That is, rather than to "find work" to match the abilities of those who can be productive in a sheltered environment, the emphasis should be to "find ways" to train retarded youth to perform the available work (Crosson, 1969, p. 814).

This approach reinforces the importance of deriving vocational training and rehabilitation objectives from the normative conditions existing at higher level work environments. Instead of setting expectations for client performance based upon past successes or failures, this method identifies objectives from real work situations and then develops effective training procedures to achieve progress toward those goals. Crosson (1969) demonstrated such a procedure in his analysis of how complex skills may be broken into component subskills.

The first step in programming the task environment requires the specification of the functionally integrated units of behavior (operants) making up these response sequences. A staff member can accomplish this by performing the task while carefully identifying and noting each of the discrete response units (Crosson, 1969, p. 814).

In the drill press operation, Crosson specified 16 operants in sequence which led the trainee from the simplest level of assuming an appropriate position in front of the drill press to the final movement of returning the drill to its original position after drilling a hole. This analysis included the programming of verbal and gestural cues and those naturally associated with the task. The trainer supplemented difficult steps in the sequence with additional cues, which facilitated responding correctly on the first and succeeding occasions. The training sequence also required the delivery of immediate and continuous reinforcement following the successful completion of each step or topography of responses approximating the terminal response. Once the skill sequence was performed reliably and under appropriate cueing conditions, i.e., those inherent to the task rather than artificially supplied by the trainer, the schedule of reinforcement was altered gradually until feedback and praise came after the completion of an entire sequence or several sequences.

When the trainee's performance stabilized, as evidenced by increasing consistency in rate of emission of the correct sequence of responses, reinforcement is gradually phased to higher order schedules, eventually matching the "natural" incentive program of the work environment (Crosson, 1969, p. 816).

These procedures have proven successful in developing complex skills (Barloff and Tate, 1967), with special focus upon cueing procedures that increase the probability of correct responding (Gold, 1972; Haring and Mithaug, 1970). In one study, the cueing procedure involved color coding to facilitate assembly of a 15-piece bicycle brake (Gold, 1972), while the other employed a programmed sequence of pictorial cues to facilitate assembly, start, and repair of a ten piece 0.049 gas engine (Haring and Mithaug, 1970).

Programming sheltered workshop environments for errorless learning must be complemented with an appropriate method for promoting performance and production once the skill has been developed. In addition, the procedures must be effective in decreasing inappropriate responses and increasing work patterns required for the job.

Studies on incentives and worker production suggest that productivity can be altered by manipulating the consequences of the activity. When producing a product or completing a task leads to tangible and immediate consequences which are valued by the trainee (i.e., praise, food, candy, or monetary rewards), production rates increase; when those consequences are not forthcoming, work activities decrease. Studies supporting this general finding have investigated a variety of incentive procedures such as goal setting and encouragement (Gordon, O'Connor, and Tizard, 1954; 1955; O'Connor and Claridge, 1955); praise (Brown and Pearce, 1970); interval and piecemeal pay (Evans and Spradlin, 1966; Brown et al., 1972); social contingencies and monetary reward (Huddle, 1967); and tokens (Zimmerman et al., 1969).

The consequences of failing to employ appropriate motivational or programming procedures such as those described here may include, for example: (1) decreased capacity to train clients in marketable skills; (2) diminished success in developing appropriate work-related behavior and in decreasing or eliminating behavior incompatible with employment; and (3) a low, variable, and seemingly unalterable production rate that renders the client ineligible for remunerative employment.

Client progress during training and client graduation from one employment level to another may require the judicious use of the educational technology presently available. Laboratory findings and applied research in a wide range of settings, including workshops and rehabilitation centers, have demonstrated what is possible. The obstacle to effective treatment is not the lack of knowledge about the effects of variables or the application of procedures, but rather the lack of systematic implementation of these techniques in vocational rehabilitation settings. When educational technology is applied systematically, training and graduation through progressively higher levels of employment become realistic goals.

Measurement

The topic of measurement is usually subsumed under the more generic term evaluation, which denotes the process by which we observe, measure, compare, and then draw conclusions about the effectiveness of our efforts. In vocational rehabilitation, Hoffman (1973) differentiated between vocational evaluation and evaluation that occurs during work adjustment. In vocational evaluation, the objective is:

> To assess a wide range of factors and to make recommendations for rehabilitation. Such recommendations may include: (1) direct placement; (2) education; (3) on-the-job training; (4) work adjustment; (5) placement in such programs as extended sheltered employment, work activity, or day care; or (6) not feasible for continued rehabilitation services (Hoffman, 1973, p. 26).

This is distinguishable from evaluation at the program level, which determines the effectiveness of the work adjustment process. Here the objective is to:

> (1) observe behavior and performance; (2) determine progress towards the goals of the adjustment program; and (3) recommend needed changes, or termination when work adjustment is completed (Hoffman, 1973, p. 26).

The evaluation procedures required to monitor client progress in skill development, behavior control, and production capabilities follow this latter outline. The measurement employed at this level must be specific to the response or behavior pattern being treated, and must be employed frequently enough to detect day to day changes in behavior. One alternative to response-specific measures collected continuously (daily) is indicator measures which rely on observer judgments. This method can be unreliable and, when administered intermittently, can increase the chances of client failure going undetected between evaluation periods.

When a rater observes and rates a client on a number of dimensions, each requiring a conclusion or judgment, evaluation becomes difficult. This difficulty increases as the frequency of the evaluation increases. When uncertain about a client's abilities on a given dimension, an observer may score a client in the middle or average category of the rating scale. This does not occur when observing and tabulating specific behaviors. Subjective judgments are minimized. Furthermore, the frequency of employing a tabulation system does not affect the observer's sensitivity in day-to-day evaluations. In fact, it increases accuracy as the observer becomes more skilled in the tabulations. This success, however, depends upon the precision with which the assessed behavior is pinpointed, i.e., defined behaviorally.

Behavioral evaluations may occur continuously, all day and every day during program time, once or twice daily, or once or twice a week. Intermittent evaluations require more time to determine whether an exceptionally good or bad evaluation result is indicative of success or failure, or whether it is due to a sampling error (observations at a time not representative of how a client usually performs). This problem does not occur with data collected continuously, as the behavioral observations are not samples, but are the universe of responses occurring during the program period.

A PROPOSAL FOR REHABILITATION AND PLACEMENT

In the foregoing discussion, we have suggested that the activities involved in training and job placement are interconnected in such a way that success or failure in one area may affect progress in the other. When a client fails to adjust in his new job, he may have been unable to generalize skills and work patterns established during training, or he may have never learned the duties and responsibilities expected for this particular job. Both problems can be avoided when training objectives are specifically related to client-targeted job opportunities. This approach to vocational training and placement follows general behavior analysis procedures which require a precise specification of targeted behaviors prior to treatment and evaluation. Once a behavior is pinpointed and its level of occurrence is monitored, assessments of excesses and/or deficits are accurate, and the identification of appropriate behavioral objectives are forthcoming. The targeted behaviors to pinpoint in vocational training and placement are job requirements including both skill and work habit requisites. This information focuses client assessments on job relevant behaviors, so that subsequent treatment objectives are appropriate and progress toward the long-term goal of placement is assured.

Outlined below are training and job placement procedures which employ behavioral pinpoints to specify job requisites and behavior principles to promote progress towards subsequently derived training objectives.

1. Analyze the skills required to complete the job task; pinpoint the behaviors expected by the supervisor as necessary adjuncts to performing those skills; and specify the motivational system employed on that job to maintain performance, encourage conformity to rules, and discourage deviant behavior.

2. Assess the client's levels of skill development relevant to the job, supporting work patterns, and motivational control needs.

3. Specify behavioral objectives for each of the deficiencies identified in 2 above.

4. Develop and implement a training program to achieve each of these objectives by employing behavioral principles that specify appropriate procedures for cueing and reinforcing the target behaviors.

5. Continuously evaluate 'through direct measurement' progress towards behavior aims. These measures may include, for example, the number of cues required to elicit the response during acquisition, the elapsed time following a cue before the response is emitted, the time interval between correct responses, the number of correct or incorrect responses per unit of time, the duration of a response, and the percent of correct or incorrect responses per response period.

6. Place the client on the job for a trial period with maximum follow-up support, while continuing to monitor and evaluate his behavior on all relevant dimensions specified during training.

7. Increase on-the-job training if performance maintains.

8. Gradually decrease follow-up support.

Pinpointing Skill Areas, Supervisor Expectations, and Motivational Systems

An example of one procedure for job analysis will illustrate its process and results. The vocational training program for the severely handicapped at the Experimental Education Unit serves a population of clients similar to those served by developmental programs and activity centers in the area. Significantly different is the Experimental Education Unit's focus upon the work skills and supporting behaviors necessary for client employment, usually sheltered employment. The training emphasis in activity or developmental centers is more diverse, including areas such as recreation, social activities, etc. In order to formulate appropriate behavioral objectives that specify work skills and supervisor behavior standards, the Experimental Education Unit staff conducted a survey of the job skills and behavior expectations required in the workshops likely to serve the target population. This information provided a basis from which to build a first-stage curriculum—first-stage curriculum in the sense that clients who achieved these levels should then be considered for more advanced skill development and job placement. This would require a second-stage curriculum based upon job opportunities elsewhere in the community.

Each workshop supervisor contacted by the EEU for graduate placement was asked to respond to behavioral criterion questions regarding the standards minimally required for a client's entry (not maintenance) into that workshop. The supervisors responded to each criterion question from their own perspective and the standards established for their workshop. The interview form consisted of 110 behavior criterion questions covering a wide range of work-related behaviors, which required approximately 1 hour to complete. The interviewer requested that the supervisor identify the behavior criterion for each question topic which he or she considered essential or important for entry into that particular workshop. For example, if expressive language were considered important or essential, the supervisor then specified what language level was required: one to two, three to five, or five to ten-word sentences.

A job analysis survey, also conducted by an Experimental Education Unit staff member, provided information on the specific skills required in workshop subcontract jobs. A sample data sheet (Fig. 1) illustrates the data collection format. The observer recorded the job number in the space to the far left and then checked the corresponding subtasks or skills required for that job. For example, job No. 1 involved skills of counting (with an aid), boxing, sealing, taping, and measuring. Data for each skill were totaled to yield a frequency distribution indicating the skills most often and least often employed at each workshop. Collected frequently over a period of time (sample of many jobs), this information can be used to prepare prospective clients for specific job skills.

Illustrative data from this pilot survey exemplify the method further. Table 1 lists the criterion questions that all four workshop supervisors regarded as nonessential or unimportant for entry into their workshop. Table 2 lists the criterion questions that all supervisors specified as either essential or important. For the remaining questions, three supervisors agreed that 16 percent of the questions were essential, two agreed that 13 percent were essential, and none agreed on the remaining 29 percent of the questions.

Table 1 is informative in specifying what *not* to emphasize in training, just as Table 2 identifies what *should* be included. Clearly, training activities could be misdirected either by focusing upon areas not critical for entry into a workshop, or by not implementing activities considered essential. Table 1 tells us that for entry into any of the four workshops, there are no limitations imposed as a function of the client's ability to read, write, compute, speak, stand, his nut–bolt assembly skills, matching or sorting rates, ability to use money, his verbalizations, learning capacity for complex tasks (requiring more than five responses), verbal reaction to corrections from supervisor, verbal reaction to corrections from peers, or social initiative with fellow workers. Table 2 suggests that those skill areas considered critical by employers include: personal hygiene; promptness; responsiveness to instructions; mode of learning new tasks; on-task endurance; distractability when working alone, when working independently in a group, or when working on an assembly line; minor and major deviances from shop behavior standards; social contact patterns with supervisor; supervisor attention required when working independently; and the effects of supervisor corrections on the client's performance.

Although all supervisors agreed upon the importance of these criteria questions, there was considerable variance regarding the specific

Activity	#1	#2	#3
Bending			
Erasing			
Blotting			
Cutting	✓		
Gluing	✓		
Gluing with gum			
Filing by name			
Filing by number			
Box assembly			
Rubber Banding			
Counting w/ aid	✓		
Sorting	✓		
size			
shape			
color			
quality	✓		
quantity			
Assembly	✓		
one			
two			
three	✓		
four			
five			
Collating		✓	
one			
two			
three			
four		✓	
five			
Boxing	✓		
Bagging		✓	
Wrapping			
Labeling		✓	
Sealing	✓	✓	
Stapling			
Stamping		✓	
Tagging			
Tieing			
Taping	✓		
Stringing			
Weighing			
Measuring	✓		
Filling			
liquid			
powder			
particles			
Capping			
Stuffing			
Soldering			
Wire harnessing			
Wire crimping			
Wire stripping			
Wire wrapping			
Disassembling			
Unpackaging			
Opening			
Screwing			
Pliering			
Pinching			

Figure 1

Table 1.

Items Specified by All Workshop Supervisors as Being Unimportant
or Nonessential for Entry Into Sheltered Employment

---

1. Read full name, home address, telephone number, age, name of employer, address of employer.

2. Write full name, home address, telephone number, age, name of employer, address of employer.

3. Recognize from list: full name, home address, telephone number, age, name of employer, address of employer.

4. Read: 1–2, 3–5, 6–8, 9–15, or 15 or more-word sentences.

5. Write: 1–2, 3–5, 6–8, 9–15, or 15 or more-word sentences.

6. Respond verbally to social greetings, such as hello, with hello, etc.

7. Initiate verbally with statements such as help! I'm lost!, etc.

8. Add sums to 5, 10, 20, 50, 100, or more than 100.

9. Subtract one–, two–, three–, four–, or five– or more digit numbers.

10. Multiply: one–, two–, three–, or more than three–digit numbers.

11. Divide: one–, two–, three–, or more than three–digit numbers.

12. Speak at the rate of 250 or more, 200–250, 100–200, 50–100, 25–50, 10–25, or 1–10 words/min.

13. Have gross-motor coordination and endurance to stand at job station for: 0–30, 30–60, min; 1–2, 2–3 hr.

14. Have fine-motor coordination to assemble 1¼" nuts and bolts at average rate of: 1–2, 3–4, 5–10, 10–20 or 20–30/min.

15. Match and sort items on two variables at 0–10, 10–20, 20–30, 30–40, 40–50, 50–75, or 75–100% of normal production.

16. Match and sort items on three variables at: 0–10, 10–20, 20–30, 30–40, 40–50, 50–75, 75–100% of normal production.

17. Match and sort items on four variables at: 0–10, 10–20, 20–30, 30–40, 40–50, 50–75, 75–100% of normal production.

18. Use money appropriately to purchase items.

19. Initiate (verbally) appropriate safety signals such as look out! danger!, etc.

20. Learn to minimum proficiency new job tasks requiring five to ten responses in sequence in: 0–15, 15–30 min: 1–6, 6–12, 12–24, or 24 or more hr of instruction.

21. Receive each correction from supervisor: with no comment, constructive comment, or inappropriate comment.

22. Receive one out of two corrections from supervisor: with no comment, constructive comment, or inappropriate comment.

23. Receive one out of ten corrections from supervisor: with no comment, constructive comment, or inappropriate comment.

24. Receive corrections from fellow workers with no comment, constructive comment, or inappropriate comment.

25. Respond appropriately to corrections from fellow workers with no comment, constructive comment, or inappropriate comment.

26. Initiate contact with fellow worker when: client needs help on task, needs task materials from fellow worker, needs evaluation on work completed, or never.

Table 2.
Items Specified by All Workshop Supervisors as Being Important
or Essential for Entry Into Sheltered Employment

1. Maintain proper personal hygiene.

2. Appear at job station on time and without prompting: in the morning when work begins, after each coffee break, and/or after lunch.

3. Respond to an instruction to be followed immediately after: 0–30, 30–60, 60–90, 90–120 sec; or 2–3, 3–5, or 5 or more min.

4. Learn to work at new job tasks when supervisor explains by: physically prompting, modeling (doing the job in front of client), or verbally describing how job is to be done.

5. Correct work on task after: first, second, third–fifth, fifth–tenth, or after tenth correction from supervisor.

6. Work at job station continuously for 0–15, 15–30, 30–60 min; 1–2, or 2–3 hr.

7. Not leave job station inappropriately during work period more than: 0, 1–2, 3–5, 6–8, 9–15, or 15 or more times a day.

8. Work independently alone at a table without discontinuing work for more than: 0, 1–2, 3–5, 6–8, 9–15, or 15 or more times per day.

9. Work alone continuously without disruption for 15-min period with: 0, 1–2, 3–5, 6–8, 9–15, 15 or more contacts from supervisor.

10. Not display minor disruptive behaviors (e.g., interruptions) more frequently than: 0, 1–2, 3–5, 6–8, 9–15, 15 or more times per week.

11. Not display major disruptive behaviors (e.g., tantrums) more frequently than: 0, 1–2, 3–5, 6–8, 9–15, or 15 or more times per week.

12. Not initiate contact inappropriately with supervisor more than: 0, 1–2, 3–5, 6–8, 9–15, 15 or more times per day.

13. Work on independent tasks with all clients working on similar tasks in 2– to 3–person group situations (where all clients work at same table) with 0, 1–2, 3–5, 6–8, 9–15, or 15 or more inappropriate work disruptions per day.

14. Work on assembly line tasks (all clients doing different tasks) in two– to three– person group situations (where all clients stand at same table) with client making: 0, 1–2, 3–5, 6–8, 9–15, or 15 or more inappropriate work disruptions per day (client stops working or stops others from working).

15. Work on independent tasks (with all clients working on similar tasks) in four– to six–person groups (all clients work at same table) with client making 0, 1–2, 3–5, 6–8, 9–15, or 15 or more inappropriate work disruptions.

16. Work on assembly line tasks (all clients working on different but related tasks) in four– to six–person group situations (where all clients work at same table) with client making: 0, 1–2, 3–5, 6–8, 9–15, or 15 or more inappropriate work disruptions per day.

criterion chosen as an acceptable entry level requirement. All four supervisors agreed that responsiveness to instructions was important, but three of them allowed 30–60 sec for the client to respond, while one supervisor allowed 0–30 sec. All four indicated that the client ought to learn a new skill after the supervisor demonstrated how the task was to be done, i.e., without physical prompting or verbal instruction to complete the task. One supervisor considered all three modes important. Regarding responsiveness to corrections from supervisor, one employer indicated that the client would be expected to make the proper adjustment after the second contact from the supervisor, two specified a criterion of three to five contacts, while the fourth supervisor indicated that behavior change might come after as many as 10 or more attempts by the supervisor to change the client's method of working on the task. Two supervisors indicated that the client should be able to work continuously at the job station for 30–60 min, one supervisor required a 1–2 hr period, and the fourth required a 2–3 hr period. Regarding distractability, one supervisor allowed one to two inappropriate work disruptions per day with the client leaving his job station, two would permit three to five a day, and the fourth would permit from six to eight. Two supervisors felt that no supervisor contact should be required for a 15-min period, while the other two would allow one to two contacts by the supervisor. For tolerance to minor behavior disturbances there was similar variability, with one supervisor allowing from one to three minor disturbances per week, two allowing three to five per week, and the fourth permitting 15 or more a week. This variability dropped significantly for major disruptions; one supervisor specified that the client would be allowed zero to one per week and still be considered eligible for entry. Two specified a one to two per week criterion, and a fourth would allow from three to five major disruptions per week.

The variability in responses to criteria questions is not matched by variation in job tasks at the workshops. Table 3 ranks the subtask skills in decreasing order of frequency for each workshop and for all workshops combined. For workshop No. 1, the most frequently employed subtask skill was assembly; for workshop No. 2, weighing; workshop No. 3, bagging; and for workshop No. 4 it was placing (including inserting and affixing). The subtask skills common to all or most of the workshops included, for example, assembly, cutting, sorting, boxing, labeling, sealing, measuring, box assembly, stapling, and stacking.

These data assist in identifying the pinpoints necessary to specify job characteristics, which include work skills (e.g., assembly, cutting, etc.) and work expectations (e.g., endurance, tolerable work disruptions, etc.). What remains to be analyzed is the motivational system employed to insure production and behavior control. All workshops employed similar

Table 3.
Subtask Skill Rankings for Each Sheltered Workshop

Workshop No. 1	Workshop No. 2	Workshop No. 3	Workshop No. 4	Total Task Frequency	
Assembly	Weighing	Bagging	Placing	Sealing	12
Sealing	Boxing	Stacking	Stapling	Assembly	12
Bagging	Box assembly	Taping	Cutting	Boxing	11
Labeling	Filling	Measuring	Boxing	Placing	11
Cutting	Sorting	Cutting	Assembly	Bagging	10
Box assembly	Labeling	Assembly	Sorting	Cutting	9
Collating	Sealing	Boxing	Labeling	Labeling	9
Taping	Taping	Sealing	Sealing	Taping	8
Folding	Measuring	Placing	Measuring	Weighing	8
Bending	Punching holes	Glueing	Wire stripping	Measuring	8
Machine use	Wrapping	Rubber banding	Cleaning	Box assembly	7
Stuffing	Bagging	Counting	Machine use	Stapling	7
Stacking	Capping	Labeling	Drilling	Stacking	6
Rubber banding	Unpackaging	Stamping	Glueing	Sorting	5
Counting	Cleaning	Unpackaging	Stamping	Machine use	5
Sorting	Machine use	Painting	Weighing	Folding	5
Boxing	Placing	Sizing	Wire crimping	Counting	5
Stapling	Painting	Punching holes	Wire wrapping	Cleaning	5
Weighing	Use of hand truck	Picking from	Stuffing	Collating	3

Measuring

Cleaning

Coiling

Rolling

Dipping

Sizing

Drilling stack

Painting

Use of air

Uncapping

Writing numbers

Wrapping

Wrapping	3
Drilling	3
Punching holes	3
Painting	3
Stuffing	3
Filling	3
Glueing	3
Bending	2
Rubber banding	2
Stamping	2
Wire striping	2
Unpacking	2
Sizing	2
Capping	1
Wire crimping	1
Wire wrapping	1
Use of hand tools	1
Rolling	1
Dipping	1
Use of hand truck	1
Picking from stack	1
Use of air hose	1
Uncapping	1
Writing numbers	1

systems of piecemeal pay for products completed. One workshop provided monthly visual displays depicting the relationship between amount
of work and the size of the paycheck, but this was an exceptional practice.
Usually, clients receive payment for completed work without the benefits
of special instructional devices to demonstrate this relationship.
Piecemeal pay delivered intervally is contrasted with methods of immediate reward deliveries contingent upon production or appropriate behavior. This difference should be considered in developing a training program with terminal objectives of job placement.

Assessing Client's Job Skills, Work Habits, and Motivational Control

Behavioral assessments may require that an observer record: (1) the
time a client spends performing; (2) the number of times he performs a
given activity or deviates from a norm or rule; or (3) the number of times
an event or activity occurs during a specified period of time. These measures can assess such worker variables as responsiveness to instructions;
the time elapsed from the termination of the instruction to the onset of the
required activity; responsiveness to supervisor corrections; the number of
corrections required to change a client's responses to task; and the
number of supervisor contacts required to maintain productivity during a
specified period of time. The behavioral criteria questions employed to
analyze job expectations permit direct comparisons between client skills
and requirements on the job.

Job task assessments may require the use of job samples that are as
identical as possible to those present in the workshop. Skills in box assembly and taping, for example, might be assessed by providing a com-
pressed, unassembled box and allowing the client to assemble the box by
folding two ends first, then the other ends, and finally applying the tape.
While some clients acquire this skill within a few trials, others have
difficulty with one or more of the several steps. This opportunity to complete a real job task or a close approximation of one identifies needs for
skill development.

Assessing motivation requirements involves a comparison of the systems employed during training with those used at the job site. When the
two systems are comparable, little may be needed in the way of preparing
the client for those conditions on the job. On the other hand, if the training
method to control behavior and maintain performance consists of immediate delivery of reinforcers for responding appropriately, a program
should be developed that gradually changes reinforcement to a system
more comparable to the one in effect in the employment situation.

Specifying Behavioral Objectives

This step is a natural consequence of the preceding one. The deficiencies identified in the assessment procedure suggest objectives around which to focus a training program. At one workshop, for example, clients were expected to work continuously at a task for periods of from 30 to 60 min. When assessment reveals that a client's work attention span is 5 min, an appropriate behavioral objective to meet this need might be to increase his uninterrupted time on task to 10, 15, 20, 25, and then 30 min.

Regarding skill acquisition objectives, the same procedure applies. In a workshop, clients could be required to collate two or three items in a booklet, label the booklet, place it in a bag, and heat-seal the bag, a complex operation for which a client may demonstrate no skills. The several training objectives possible may include: teaching a client to collate one, two, and then three items into a booklet at a specified rate; to tear off a label from the sticker backing, center the label on the book with the aid of a jig, and then affix the label in that position at a specified rate of items labeled per hour; or to pick up a plastic bag, open the bag, insert the booklet correctly, and then heat-seal the open end at a specified number of bags per hour.

Finally, the objectives deriving from the motivational assessment may require that the reinforcement schedule change from immediate and continuous schedules to interval schedules more characteristic of the terminal employment situation. The goal would be to maintain low rates of inappropriate responses and high rates of productivity under schedules of interval pay.

Developing and Implementing a Training Program

The training programs emerging from this approach necessarily depend upon the particular needs of each client. While some clients may have long attention spans but low rates of productivity, others work infrequently but rapidly while on task. Still others have frequent inappropriate outbursts which reduce their potential as employees, even in sheltered workshops. Training programs must be individualized in terms of the objectives specified for each client and the treatments employed to reach those objectives. What works for one client may not work for another.

Although specific tactics are required to deal with unique problems of a given client, the principles governing his response probabilities are the same as for other clients. This knowledge should significantly affect our approach to rehabilitation. We know, for example, that, for all trainees, and especially those afflicted with the most severe disabilities, the time interval between the client's successful response and the delivery of reinforcing feedback or rewards will effect his rate of acquiring new skills. When the delivery of reinforcing consequences for correct responses is immediate, i.e., a fraction of a second following a correct response, the probability of continued correct responding is increased. We also know that the frequency or schedule of delivering reinforcers significantly affects response rates. Continuous schedules, during which a reinforcer is delivered after each response, are effective during the acquisition of a new skill or response, but intermittent schedules, requiring reinforcers delivered after several correct responses, are more effective to maintain high response rates once the skill is learned.

Regarding the procedures appropriate for eliciting responses not currently in a client's repertoire of behavior, we must employ instructional procedures that program cueing events to shape the client's existing response repertoire towards successively closer approximations to the terminal response. Once stimulus control is established with one set of cues, the trainer can rearrange the instructional materials, gradually adding or deleting cues, while continuing to maintain high levels of correct responding. This gradual alteration in instructional requirements and gradual shaping of client responses leads to the final response pattern specified in the behavior aim. For Crosson (1969) for example, the terminal response aim was successful operation of a drill press. The initial responses required in the instructional format were the proper body position facing the drill press, moving one shoulder in line with drill, and extending one hand to obtain drill materials. The final responses were rotating the drill press forearm downward, returning the forearm to the original position, and finally releasing the handle, thus completing a drill press movement cycle.

Evaluating Client Progress Through Direct and Continuous Measurement

Every opportunity to learn a new skill is also an occasion to succeed or fail in the learning process. When performance measures are continuous and direct, the trainer has current, up-to-date information about client progress at all times. When difficulties in the training sequence occur, when the client makes more mistakes or works more slowly than usual, for example, data collected on these dimensions signal the trainer to provide needed program changes. This may be in the form of additional or substitute cues for responding, or a different type of behavior consequence or schedule of reinforcement.

Data measures are continuous when the trainer collects the evaluative information on every occasion that the client has an opportunity to perform the specified skill. If he works a drill press 1 hr each day, a continuous measure would require data collection throughout that period every day. Direct measures of performance occur when the trainer observes, counts, and records the client behaviors required to perform the skill. By contrast, trainer estimations about quality or quantity of work completed only indirectly assess client progress; they rely upon judgments and conclusions based upon intermittent observations, and, consequently, are vulnerable to sampling and estimation errors. The evaluator may observe the client at times not representative of his total performance, and/or he may inaccurately estimate the client's progress by exaggerating observed excesses or deficits.

There are several types of direct measures, each focusing upon a specific behavioral dimension. These include counts or tabulations of client responses, response tabulations over a specified time period, and response duration measures indicating the amount of time that a client responds in a given manner. Each measure should be judiciously employed to evaluate progress toward different behavioral aims. For example, when a precise accounting is needed regarding a client's response rate variations within a small time period, interresponse times may be useful. By recording the intervals between responses and then analyzing results over the period in question, the trainer can identify the time section during which the interresponse times (IRT) are the shortest, i.e., the client is responding at his highest rate. This information may prove useful when analyzing peaks in production, those periods of the hour or day when the client hits his highest levels of productivity.

When a client's skill acquisition is evaluated to assess the rate at which new responses are learned or to analyze the cueing events necessary to reduce errors, the trainer records the number and/or type of cues required to evoke a correct response, as well as the time intervals between the cueing events and correct responses. A detailed analysis of cueing data is helpful in isolating procedures that work. The trainer can then specify those events that increase correct responses and decrease errors. For acquisition rates, the trainer records reaction times to obtain a response-by-response accounting of the client's acquisition rate. When confronted with a new task, the client's reaction times are long initially, but shortened gradually and then more rapidly as the trainee responds more quickly to programmed events.

In some cases, percent measures are adequate to assess client progress toward prescribed behavioral objectives. An indicator of worker concentration might be the percent of time he spends working appropriately. In any training or work situation, one would expect percent of time on task to increase to a maximum level when program procedures are having the desired rehabilitative effect. A gradual decrease or leveling off at a lesser level would signal need for a program adjustment.

In general, the basic data for evaluating skill acquisition are the client's correct and incorrect responses to the cueing events presented in the training sequence. Employed effectively, measures such as those described above—frequency, rate, duration, interresponse time, reaction time, and percent—allow the trainer to analyze progress both in terms of the quality of client performance and quantity of his output. Information on both dimensions is essential for a comprehensive assessment.

Trial Placement

Often, a client needs a transitional step between what we formally consider training and placement. On-the-job training programs provide additional flexibility between the training situation and full-time employment. Additional steps may be necessary in the form of trial placement, whereby the training station maintains control and responsibility for the client as he spends a period of time each day on the job. During this period, evaluation of relevant behaviors continues. The trial placement provides an opportunity to evaluate the long-range effects of training as the client works in a new situation. Maintaining the same system for monitoring deviant behaviors, work patterns, and job skills provides the information necessary for determining whether placement is appropriate, or further training is in order.

Placement and Decreased Followup Support

The final step in the sequence depends upon the success of the preceding one. If the trial placement has been successful and the period of employment is extended to a full day, follow-up monitoring and support is replaced with spot checks at decreasingly frequent intervals. If the client transfers from a work activity program, activity center, or development training program to a long-term sheltered workshop, or from a long-term workshop to a short-term workshop, the training-placement process continues again at the higher level. The content of the job analysis, client assessments, behavioral objectives, and treatment programs may be different from one level to the other, but the approach remains the same. Placement criteria specify the training objectives, and training activities represent the targeted job conditions.

SUMMARY

In this chapter, vocational training services for the handicapped were outlined briefly as they developed from the early 1920s to their present-day form, with emphasis upon the range of treatment settings and procedures potentially available. The authors suggested a reorganization of these services to focus upon job-related skill development during training, and upon graduation from one program to more advanced training activities as client skill levels increased. This coordination of community services would allow clients in activity and developmental centers to graduate to long-term workshops, clients in long-term workshops to graduate to short-term workshops, and clients there to transfer into on-the-job training programs, or directly into competitive employment. The authors pointed out and discussed obstacles to this proposal, stemming from rehabilitation requirements that training objectives be related to specific skills and work behaviors necessary for client-targeted jobs. Proposed solutions to these difficulties included: (1) an analysis of skills, work patterns, and motivational requirements of the prospective job; (2) an assessment of client skills, work patterns, and motivational needs vis-a-vis this analysis; (3) a specification of behavioral objectives designed to remediate client deficiencies; (4) the development and implementation of a training program to meet these objectives; (5) continuous evaluation of client progress toward each objective; (6) trial job placement for short periods with maximum follow-up support and evaluation; (7) increased time spent on the job if performance is maintained; and (8) gradual decrease of follow-up support.

This approach to vocational training and placement follows general behavior analysis procedures which require a precise specification of targeted behaviors prior to treatment and evaluation. Once a behavior is pinpointed and its level of occurrence monitored, assessments of excesses and/or deficits are accurate, and the identification of appropriate behavioral objectives forthcoming. Applied to vocational training and placement, the targeted behaviors to pinpoint are job requirements, including both skill requisites and work habit necessities. This information focuses client assessments on job-relevant behaviors, so that subsequent treatment objectives are appropriate and that progress toward the long-term goal of placement is assured.

REFERENCES

Abel TM: A study of a group of subnormal girls successfully adjusted in industry and the community. Am J Ment Defic 45:66–72, 1940

Baer CJ: Factors Associated With School Holding Power for Educable Mentally Retarded Adolescents. School District of Kansas City, MO., August 1961

Baller WR: A study of the present social status of a group of adults, who when they were in elementary schools, were classified as mentally deficient. Genet Psychol Monogr 18:169–244, 1936

Barloff GS, Tate BG: Training the mentally retarded in the production of complex production: A demonstration of work potential. Except Child 33:405–408, 1967

Bobroff A: Economic adjustment of 121 adults, formerly students in classes for mental retardates. Am J Ment Defic 60:525–535, 1956

Brickey M: Normalization and behavior modification in the workshop. J Rehabil 40:15,16,41,44–46, 1974

Bronner AF: Follow-up studies of mental defectives, procedures and address. Am Assoc Ment Defic 38:258–267, 1933

Brown L, Fox L, Voekler R, et al: Effects of interval payment, task choice and high rate reinforcement contingencies on the production rate of trainable level retarded and severely emotionally disturbed students. Train Sch Bull 69:58–59, 1972

Brown L, Pearce E: Increasing the production rates of trainable retarded students in a public school simulated workshop. Edu Train Ment Retard 5:15–22, 1970

Chaffin J, Smith JO, Haring NG: A selected demonstration for the vocational training of mentally retarded youth in public high school. (RD 1548 Final Report) 1967. Program sponsored by the Vocational Rehabilitation Administration Dept. H. Ed. & Welfare.

Collmand RD, Newlyn D: Employment success of educationally subnormal ex-pupils in England. Am J Ment Defic 60:741, 1956

Cowan L, Goldman M: Selection of the mentally deficient for vocational training and the effect of this training on vocational success. J Consult Psychol 23:78–84, 1959

Crosson JE: A technique for programming sheltered workshop environments for training severely retarded workers. Am J Ment Defic 73:814–818, 1969

Erickson RC: Part II, The relationship between selected variables and success of the retardate in the cooperative work-study program: An analysis of predictive power. (Final Report of Project NIMH 1139) National Institute of Mental Health (1966) 1–69

Evans GW, Spradlin JE: Incentives and instructions as controlling variables of productivity. Am J Ment Defic 71:129–132, 1966

Gold MW: Stimulus factors in skill training of retarded adolescents on a complex assembly task: Acquisition, transfer, and retention. Am J Ment Defic 76:517–526, 1972

Gordon S, O'Connor N, Tizard J: Some effects of incentives on the performance of imbeciles. Br J Psychol 45:277–287, 1954

Gordon S, O'Connor N, Tizard J: Some effects of incentives on the performance of imbeciles on a receptive task. Am J Ment Defic 60:371–377, 1955

Gorton CE: The effects of various sheltered workshop environments upon mental retardates' performance of manual tasks. Unpublished doctoral dissertation, Nashville, Tenn., George Peabody College for Teachers, 1966

Green CL: A study of personal adjustment in mentally retarded girls. Am J Ment Defic 49:472–476, 1945

Haring NG, Mithaug DE: A planning project to increase employment opportunities of handicapped youth by increasing the number of educational opportunities. (Final Report) Division of Vocational Education, Office of State Superintendent of Public Instruction through Vocational Education, Seattle School District No. 1, Seattle Wash., 1970

Hartzler E: A follow-up study of girls discharged from Laurelton State Village. Am J Ment Defic 55:612–618, 1951

Hay L, Cappenburg B: The social adjustment of children of low intelligence, Part III. Northampton, Mass., Smith College of Student Social Work 2:146–174, 1931

Hegge TG: The significance of measurement of adjustment in the institutional and school situation. Am J Ment Defic 47:58–69, 1942

Hoffman PR: Evaluating workshop evaluations: A critical response. Rehabil Rec 14:26–28, 1973

Huddle DD: Work performance of trainable adults as influenced by competition, cooperation and monetary reward. Am J Ment Defic 72:198–211, 1967

Jackson SK, Butler AJ: Prediction of successful community placement of institutionalized retardates. Am J Ment Defic 68:211–217, 1963

Jacobs A, Weingold JT, Dubrow M: The Sheltered Workshop: A Community Rehabilitation Resource for the Mentally Retarded (ed 2): New York, New York State Association for the Help of Retarded Children, 1962

Katz E: The Retarded Adult in the Community. Springfield, Ill., Thomas, 1968

Kolstoe OP: The employment evaluation and training program. Am J Ment Defic 65:17–31, 1960

Kolstoe OP, Shafter AJ: Employability prediction for mentally retarded adults: A methodological note. Am J Ment Defic 66:287, 1961a

Ladas PG: Work sample learning rates of the mentally retarded trainee as indicators of production in a work-training center. Personnel Guid J 39:396–402, 1961

Lent JR: Reduction of negative social behaviors in a work setting. Unpublished paper, American Association of Mental Deficiency Convention, Miami, Florida, 1964

Loos FM, Tizard J: The employment of adult imbeciles in a hospital workshop. Am J Ment Defic 59:401, 1955

Madison H: Work placement success for the mentally retarded. Am J Ment Defic 69:50–53, 1964

McCarron LT, Dial JG: Neuropsychological predictors of sheltered workshop performance. Am J Ment Defic 77:241–3, 1972

Meadow L, Greenspan E: Employability of lower level mental retardates. Am J Ment Defic 51:623–628, 1961

Minneapolis Public Schools. Retarded youth: Their school rehabilitation needs. Final Report of Research and Demonstration Project 681, 1965

Neff WS: The success of a rehabilitation program. Monograph No. 3. Chicago, Ill., Jewish Vocational Service, 1959, 1–37

O'Connor N, Claridge G: The effects of goal setting and encouragement on the performance of imbecile men. Quart J Exp Psychol 7:37–45, 1955

Olshansky S: Evaluating workshop evaluations. Rehabil Rec 14:22, 1973

Phelps HR: Post school adjustment of mentally retarded children in selected Ohio cities. Except Child 22:58–62, 1956

Power PW, Marinelli RP: Normalization and the sheltered workshop: A review and proposals for change. Rehabil Lit 35:66–72, 1974

Shafter AJ: Criteria for selecting institutionalized mental defectives for vocational placement. Am J Ment Defic 61:599–616, 1957

Thomas V: Curricular implications of work experience. Unpublished paper, Council for Exceptional Children Convention, Portland, Oregon, April 1965

Tobias J: Evaluation of vocational potential of mentally retarded young adults. Train Sch Bull 56:122–135, 1960

Tobias J, Cortazzo AD: Training severely retarded adults for greater independence in community living. Train Sch Bull 60:23–27, 1963

Voelker PH: The value of certain selected factors in predicting early post school employment for white EMR males. Unpublished doctoral dissertation, University of Michigan, 1962

Wagner EE, Hawyer DA: Correlations between psychological tests and sheltered workshop performance for severely retarded adults. Am J Ment Defic 69:685–691, 1965

Whitcomb MA: A comparison of social and intellectual levels of 100 high-grade adult mental defectives. Am J Ment Defic 66:213, 1961

Windle CD, Stewart E, Brown SJ: Reasons for community failure of released patients. Am J Ment Defic 66:2, 1961

Wolfensberger W: The Principle of Normalization in Human Services. Toronto, Canada, Canadian National Institute on Mental Retardation, 1972

Wollinsky D, Kase H: Human resource credit—A product marketing aid to the rehabilitation and sheltered workshop. J Rehabil 39:41–2, 1973

Zimmerman J, Stuckey TE, Garlick BJ, et al: Effects of token reinforcement on productivity in multiply handicapped clients in a sheltered workshop. Rehabil Lit 30:34–41, 1969

Adjunctive Intervention Tactics (Procedures)

Robin Beck

A

The Need for Adjunctive Services in the Management of Severely and Profoundly Handicapped Individuals. Part I: A View From Primary Care

Effective comprehensive management of the severely handicapped infant or child should be based in public school programs and coordinated by educators. This is the case not only for children who are delayed in acquiring behavior, but also for those who have acquired bizarre behavior, regardless of its etiology.

To begin a chapter on the need for adjunctive services for the severely handicapped with the above statement accomplishes the following: First, and most important, it stresses the value judgment which must precede the application of an effective intervention technology—that every individual in our society has a right to education, and that education must help him/her to achieve his/her behavioral potential. While different values can be applied to different behaviors in any large group of children, *individually,* the development of self-feeding skills may be as important for one child as the development of "mathematics behavior" is for another child. By individualizing values as they relate to individual potential, we can make difficult decisions about individual educational goals, and we can apply effective technology to reach those goals. Because the public schools are *public,* and because they must now accommodate the widely varying educational needs of their clientele, they are the logical places in which to provide services needed by severely handicapped children.

Second, the statement provides a basis for planning services through the public schools to remediate any recognized developmental delay. For most children at risk, the chance for early recognition of their delay is dependent on "teacher" behavior—pinpointing developmental level, using appropriate curriculum design; and, if necessary, the periodic measurement of the child's rate of acquiring new behaviors. Indeed, for the infant or child with poor developmental prognosis, or for one who is at risk for such a prognosis, the optimum environment is the classroom where diagnosis and remediation are a single function. Moreover, since daily acquisition rates in a classroom are curriculum-dependent and not necessarily a result of the etiology of the child's delay, unusual changes in rate may in fact signal a "medical" problem requiring immediate attention. For instance, a Down's syndrome child's behavior may change because his hearing is affected by inflammation of the middle ear; a phenylketonuric child may show behavior changes with dietary indiscretion; or a hydrocephalic child may have behavioral changes with shunt blockage that has caused increased pressure within the cerebral spinal fluid space surrounding the brain. The classroom manager who spots these unusual changes in behavior and immediately refers the child to appropriate professionals for care is performing an important function and may prevent serious impairment to the child.

Third, the public school is community based, and provides continuity in the educational experience of the infant or child through his/her period of development. It can be the "primary" resource for carrying out prescriptive intervention strategies from diagnostic centers which may be remote from the community in which the child lives. Indeed, it will be useful to think of both educational and "medical" or "adjunctive" services available to the severely handicapped individual in terms of their level within a hierarchy of sophistication, periodicity of contact, and often physical remoteness from the community in which the handicapped individual lives. Secondary and tertiary services are characterized by their increasing specialization and sophistication.

Finally, still another reason to look to the classroom as an effective intervention base in managing severely handicapped children is the ready acceptance by parents of the "school" or "classroom," and by their enthusiasm for being involved in the remediation process with the teacher.

In this chapter, we will do the following: with early identification and remediation for severely handicapped children as our goal, we will look at the characteristics of one segment of this population—severely mentally retarded children—and the role of the community based or "primary" care physician (pediatrician or family practitioner) in relationship to this goal.

Because we look to the classroom as the intervention base for the severely handicapped infant or child, we will also look at the impact of the prevention strategies presently available to the primary care physician on the numbers of children with severe retardation entering the classroom. The point is this: if it were possible to prevent most of the severe handicapping conditions that render infants likely candidates for classrooms such as the one we will discuss, these classrooms would be virtually unnecessary. Certain obvious questions then arise. How effective is our present technology in preventing severe handicapping conditions? Given this technology, are there now, and will there be in the forseeable future, sufficient numbers of severely handicapped infants to justify the specialized kind of intervention we now propose? How "realistic" is it to plan such programs in the face of rapidly changing technology? We will address these questions later in the chapter.

Then, after defining the role of the primary care physician, we will examine the adjunctive services available at the secondary and tertiary levels of health care and their relationship to the management of the severely retarded child within the community.

In the second part of this chapter, with other staff members from the Child Development and Mental Retardation Center at the University of Washington, we will return to the primary or community-based intervention strategy, describing an interdisciplinary "classroom" emphasizing early identification and remediation for the infant or child with poor developmental prognosis. This classrom is a resource to the primary care physician and a base from which to plan the comprehensive management of the severely handicapped individual with utilization of secondary and tertiary level adjunctive services.

CHARACTERISTICS OF CHILDREN WITH SEVERELY HANDICAPPING CONDITIONS INVOLVING MENTAL RETARDATION

The interest in explaining the causes of severe mental retardation (I.Q. below 50) in recent years has led to the accumulation of an overwhelming body of information about severely retarded persons. Development of centralized data collection and standardized nomenclature has required international cooperation. Frustrating as it has been to understand this heterogenous population, the recent publication of three compendiums using standardized nomenclature should make the task easier. These not only establish and describe specific syndromes, but also provide the basis for developing a rational approach to the early diagnosis of severe retardation. Such an approach may in turn have impact on future progress in basic research, as well as on intervention. Bergsma (1973) has compiled a list of 842 major and minor anomalies related to birth defects, with an atlas of 641 pictures. Holmes (1972) has compiled an atlas of syndromes in which mild and severe retardation occur. The most recent edition of Smith's compendium on the recognizable patterns of human malformations (1976) lists 222 syndromes—most of which are associated with mild to severe retardation—utilizing as closely as possible the international terminology for syndromes established in February 1975 (Smith, 1975a).

Given the heterogeneity of the severely retarded population and the fairly recent appearance of these compilations, whose contents could change almost as rapidly as printers can prepare revised editions, what has been accomplished? We find the most encouraging approach to diagnosing severe mental retardation early is one suggested recently by Smith (1975b), which is based on data by Crome (1960), and on a recent study by Kaveggia (1973), reporting the incidence of malformations in a large population of severely retarded individuals. While this approach to diagnosis and categorization may not be ideal for everyone working with severely retarded persons, it is very useful in the context of this discussion, which evaluates ''medical'' intervention strategies from the primary care base, and their effect on the prevalence of severe retardation.

Smith's approach to diagnosing severely retarded children emphasizes collecting detailed family, prenatal, perinatal, and postnatal information, and performing a thorough physical examination, especially for major and minor malformations of noncentral nervous structures. (Hereafter, we will use the common abbreviation for central nervous system: CNS.) Smith suggests that, after collecting the history and performing the physical examination, it is possible to assign the child's disorder to a category based on the probable timing of insult to the CNS. (There is a category for ''unknowns''—not the largest—and there are a few special disorders which fit multiple categories, discussed separately by Smith.) Only then does Smith suggest that further studies be considered, although, interestingly enough, most severely retarded children require no further diagnostic studies. Table 1 lists some of the categories used for sorting syndromes in which mental retardation is a component.

We expect that there will be shifts within this framework as we gain further understanding of the biochemical, genetic, and environmental factors which influence CNS development. The approach outlined above—collecting data, examining the child, and sorting his/her problem into the appropriate category according to the probable age of onset of the disorder—emphasizes primary care physician behavior, with addition of more complex diagnostic tests when appropriate, tests that are often available only at secondary or tertiary medical facilities. The actual need

Table 1.
Categories for Classifying Mental Retardation by The Timing
of Insult to the Brain

---

1. *Prenatal problem in morphogenesis* 44% of population (Kaveggia)
   A. One-third, single defect in brain morphogenesis
   B. Two-thirds, multiple major and minor malformations of non-CNS
      structures
      a. 40% chromosomal abnormalities
      b. 20% recognized ''syndromes''
      c. 40% unknown patterns of malformation

2. *Perinatal (birth related) insult to the brain*
   Direct medical complications of the birth process or medical complications
   in the immediate period following birth including hypoxemia, hyper-
   bilirubinemia, infection (meningitis), disturbances of fluid or electrolyte balance, hypoglycemia, etc.

3. *Postnatal onset of brain dysfunction*
   Normal appearance at birth and, after a variable period, deterioration either
   secondary to medical complications or expression of an inborn metabolic
   error, e.g. PKU.

4. *Unknown age of onset* 35% of population (Kaveggia)

This information is adapted from Smith, 1975b.

to refer children to sophisticated care facilities for further diagnostic work
is in fact unusual, even for the population identified as severely handicapped. It is important, however, to distinguish between secondary and
tertiary facilities whose function is to manage the complex and interre-
lated problems of children with multiple handicapping conditions, and
those facilities which are primarily concerned with diagnosis of developmental delays and their etiology. We will examine these adjunctive services later in this chapter.

In the next section, we will look at medical intervention strategies
with emphasis on prevention. These strategies are arranged to correspond
to the categories described by Smith (1975b). A more comprehensive
review of prevention tactics—that is, prevention involving nonmedical as
well as medical interventions—can be found in a previous chapter in this
volume by Alice H. Hayden and Valentine Dmitriev.

Prenatal Intervention

The ability to aspirate amniotic fluid and amniotic cells from the gravid uterus has been a recent major technological advance. Late in pregnancy, analysis of the amniotic fluid can give information about fetal distress and about the adaptability of the fetus to extrauterine life. This information has allowed the physician to maximize the infant's chances for survival and healthy development when early delivery is necessitated for various medical reasons.

Very early in pregnancy (12–13 weeks), fluid and cells can be aspirated for quite a different reason. The cells aspirated at this early stage of pregnancy can be cultured for chromosomal and biochemical analysis (Nadler, 1975). While the procedure is technically much more difficult at this stage of pregnancy, the risk of harming the mother or the fetus with the aspiration (called amniocentesis) has been much less than 1%. Should the presence of an abnormality be discovered through cell analysis, there is still time to terminate the pregnancy safely for the mother, if she agrees to termination, and before the fetus meets the "legal" definition of viability, approximately 26 weeks' gestation. Legal and moral issues related to elective termination of pregnancy are beyond the scope of this chapter and will not be discussed. We would like to refer readers to a recent article by Fletcher (1975), which discusses this issue at length.

While the risk to the mother and fetus from amniocentesis is low, the technical difficulty inherent in this procedure, when it is performed early in gestation, makes it unlikely ever to be incorporated into routine prenatal care. However, there are women for whom this small risk is negligible compared to the risk of their bearing a child with an enzymatic, structural, or chromosomal defect which precludes normal growth and development. These defects are found within Smith's first category in the table, some of which we will discuss in more detail below with regard to their impact on the prevalence of severe mental retardation.

Perinatal Intervention

Optimizing the timing and place of delivery of infants at risk for perinatal complications has had significant impact on the infants' survival. Regional centers now provide comprehensive care to prematurely born and other high-risk infants. Indeed, infants born remote from these facilities can be transferred to them quickly if necessary, with full life-support systems. The rapid and rewarding growth in knowledge and technology in neonatal medicine has improved high-risk infants' survival (Ellis, 1972), and, most important, reduced the number of severe CNS sequelae (after-effects) in selected weight groups within this population (Alden, 1972). Interestingly, the most recent significant reduction in general perinatal mortality, a more crude statistic, occurred following liberalization of abortion laws (Glass, 1972). And in New York, an even more important finding has been reported: the number of premature and high-risk newborns has also decreased following liberalized abortion laws (Smith, personal communication, 1975).

It is impossible to guess what impact perinatal intervention strategies have had on the prevalence of severe retardation. One must ask whether the increased numbers of infants surviving through comprehensive care at regional centers have offset the reduction in sequelae in this population, so that the number of impaired persons is stabilized or perhaps even increased.

Postnatal Intervention

The early diagnosis and treatment of bacterial CNS infections, prevention of viral diseases known to cause CNS damage, and the control of environmental toxins detrimental to the developing CNS will certainly contribute to reducing the number of children at risk for severe mental retardation from these causes.

But there are many reasons to believe that significant reduction in the population of severely retarded children from intervention strategies in this category will not be easily or quickly forthcoming. For example, the incidence and severity of CNS insult from bacterial meningitis, for which medical intervention now exists, may depend on socioeconomic factors (i.e., late diagnosis and inadequate treatment are more likely to occur in low socioeconomic groups), host factors (e.g., poor nutrition, anemia, etc.), or environmental factors (crowding, poor sanitation). With newer bacterial vaccines, some types of meningitis can be prevented; however, lower socioeconomic groups may be at risk because they may fail to receive adequate immunizations due to insufficient access to information about their availability.

Except for the small percentage of children with metabolic errors— for instance, PKU—that can be treated postnatally, intervention strategies to prevent severe mental retardation from disorders in this category will be extremely difficult to implement or evaluate.

Unknown Age of Onset

There is simply not enough known about individuals within this category to speculate about the potential for intervention. Certainly, as knowledge increases, the causes of some disorders for individuals assigned to this category will become identifiable, and this should lead to development of appropriate intervention strategies.

The Impact of Intervention Strategies on the
Prevalence of Severe Mental Retardation

Our discussion of intervention strategies for disorders categorized according to probable timing of CNS insult is far from exhaustive. But it is sufficient to permit a more detailed look at two syndromes and one type of CNS malformation all in the prenatal onset category, for which there is reason to believe that safe and effective prevention is, or soon will be, possible. One cannot overestimate the importance of these interventions in their relief of human suffering, and their lessening of the economic burden placed on a family or community caring for severely handicapped persons. To give only one example of the cost effectiveness of certain intervention measures: preventing the deleterious effects of phenylalanine in the diet of individuals with PKU, while affecting fewer than 1% of the severely retarded, not only saves the cost of long-term medical or institutional care that would be needed for these persons if they were not treated, but also is inexpensive enough to justify mandatory screening for PKU of the total population of newborn infants.

The three disorders with prenatal onset that we will discuss here are Down's syndrome (mongolism), fetal alcohol syndrome, and dysraphism.

Down's Syndrome

This well-recognized chromosomal abnormality was first described by J. Langdon Down in 1866. It is the most common autosomal abnormality compatible with survival of the affected fetus. The physical abnormalities characterizing the syndrome in the newborn, with incidence within the Down's population, are listed (Smith, 1976) in Table 2. The incidence of mental retardation with Down's syndrome is 99%. This syn-

Table 2.
Physical Abnormalities Characterizing Newborn Down's Syndrome Infants

Physical abnormality	Incidence
Hypotonia	80%
Poor Moro reflex	85%
Hyperflexibility of joints	80%
Excess skin on back of neck	80%
Flat facial profile	90%
Slanted palpebral fissures	80%
Anomalous auricles	60%
Dysplasia of pelvis	70%
Dysplasia of midphalanx of fifth finger	60%
Simian crease	45%

drome probably accounts for about 10% of the severe retardation in our population (I.Q. less than 50). Down's syndrome occurs in approximately one out of 750 live births, but the risk factor varies trememdously with maternal age (see Table 3). Since the women at highest risk for bearing Down's syndrome children are identifiable, it has been estimated that approximately 33% of Down's syndrome could be prevented if women over 35 underwent amniocentesis at 12 to 13 weeks' gestation. Chromosomal analysis could thereby be performed on the amniotic cells in time for therapeutic abortion if an affected fetus were discovered.

Fetal Alcohol Syndrome (F.A.S.)

Although the adverse effects of alcohol on the fetus have been known since antiquity, the syndrome was initially reported in the scientific literature by Lemoine in France and subsequently identified in this country independently by Jones, Smith, and Ulleland (1973). The characteristics include a history of chronic alcoholism in the mother. The abnormalities present in the affected newborns and percentage of incidence within the population studied by Jones and Smith (1973) are in Table 4.

Table 3.
Relationship of Maternal Age and Incidence of Down's Syndrome

Maternal Age	Incidence of Down's Syndrome
Less than 20	1:2500
More than 40	1:75

Table 4.
Physical Abnormalities Characterizing Newborn F.A.S. Infants

Abnormality	Incidence
Prenatal growth deficiency	100%
Short palpebral fissures	100%
Microcephaly	90%
Altered palmar crease pattern	70%
Joint anomalies	70%
Maxillary hypoplasia	60%
Cardiac anomalies	60%
Epicanthal folds	40%
Anomalous external genitalia	40%
Capillary hemangiomata	40%
Micrognathia	30%
Cleft palate	20%

The incidence of retardation is apparently well over 60%, and severe retardation probably occurs in 10% of the children with this syndrome. The incidence of the syndrome within the general population is difficult to estimate, but from estimates of the number of alcoholic women of child-bearing age, it is certainly not rare. From Kaveggia's study (1973), the group in Smith's first category, which included multiple non CNS malformation syndromes which were nonchromosomal but of known cause, accounted for 20% of the total. For the sake of later discussion, we will assume that about 33% of these were FAS, and that this syndrome accounts for approximately 2.5% of the severely retarded population.

If pregnancy could be prevented in women of childbearing age who suffer from chronic alcoholism—that is, if they could be persuaded to delay childbearing until after their alcoholism has been effectively treated, or if they were provided with therapeutic abortions—there is reason to believe that this syndrome would be completely prevented.

Dysraphism

In CNS development, the anlage (the first signs in an embryo of organ development) folds to form a tube-like structure which closes at approximately 4 weeks' gestational age. Abnormal tube closure leads to malformations including anencephaly (absence of the cranial vault and reduction in cerebral hemispheres); encephalocele (hernia of the brain); meningomyelocele (protrusion of part of the meninges and spinal cord through a defect in the vertebral column); spina bifida (defective closure of the bony spinal canal); and spina bifida occulta (defective closure in the posterior bony wall of the spinal canal, but without associated abnormality of the spinal cord or meninges). Severity of retardation varies with the neurologic deficit present at birth and the subsequent complications, the most common one being hydrocephaly (abnormal accumulation of fluid in the head). Anencephaly is incompatible with survival beyond the newborn period. The other defects in neural tube closure may not be lethal and the CNS insult varies, depending on the lesion and the effectiveness of medical intervention in preventing complications (Shurtleff et al., 1974).

In 1972, Brock and Sutcliffe discovered an elevated protein in the amniotic fluid of embryos who were later born with severe neural tube defects. In later studies, the same protein elevation was also found in maternal serum during these abnormal pregnancies. With the establishment of standards for this protein throughout gestation, it is now possible to identify from 50 percent to 60 percent of severe dysraphism in time to terminate the pregnancy safely. While this identification test is being routinely performed on mothers at risk (i.e., when there is at least a 3 percent chance of recurrence), it may become a routine part of prenatal care in certain populations where these malformations occur more frequently (such as in Great Britain).

The contribution of this malformation of the CNS to the prevalence of severe retardation is difficult to estimate. It occurs about once in every 500 births. If 50 percent of these infants were severely retarded, then dysraphism would account for approximately 2 percent of the severe retardation in our population.

Summary

The brief discussion of these three disorders was presented to emphasize the importance of Smith's approach to the diagnosis of severe retardation. These three disorders are among the most common causes of retardation for which at least partial prevention is now possible. But another reason for presenting these data is to dispel a misconception which is unfortunately held by many. Let us assume that the above intervention tactics were implemented nationally. Assume also that termination of pregnancy was accepted by all mothers known to be at risk, and that there was a proportionate reduction in the birth of children with severe and mild retardation: 3.3 percent of severe retardation due to Down's syndrome would be prevented; 2.5 percent of severe retardation due to fetal alcohol syndrome would be prevented; and 1 percent of severe retardation due to dysraphism would be prevented. Stated differently, 93.2 percent of the severely retarded population from all of the categories mentioned earlier would remain. A more reasonable guess would be that 95–97 percent of that population would still require appropriate diagnostic workup, medical management, and special educational intervention. (J. Hanson, personal communication, 1975). The important factor to remember is that for the teacher, the number of severely retarded students entering the classroom is not likely to change appreciably during the rest of this century, and probably not until well into the next. Therefore, to answer the questions raised earlier about the current and future prevalence of severe retardation and the corresponding need for classes for severely retarded infants and young children: our present medical technology is not likely to reduce the critical need for postnatal, educational intervention strategies for the forseeable future. It is all the more imperative, then, that these strategies be planned not for any impossibly "ideal" situation, or ivory tower where, presumably, anything can be planned and implemented, but for feasible application to needs and resources within the larger community. Later in this chapter, we will describe a program having that potential.

ADJUNCTIVE SERVICES OUTSIDE THE PRIMARY CARE COMMUNITY

As noted earlier, these are the basic characteristics of severely handicapping conditions associated with the risk of significant developmental delay:

1. Historically, there may be prenatal, perinatal, or postnatal events which place the infant at risk.

2. Physically, there may be major or minor abnormalities of noncentral nervous system structures, some of which will fit recognizable patterns of malformation with known etiology, which again place a child at risk.

Certainly, the recognition of these risk factors is in the realm of primary physician (pediatrician or general practitioner) behavior. But once the physician determines that an infant or child is at risk for handicapping conditions including severe developmental delay, he or she must identify resources for help in the child's medical and educational management. In Part II of this chapter, we will describe the development of a resource which we believe can be based within the primary care community and within the public schools in that community. First, however, we will look at the more sophisticated and usually physically remote resources that are presently available.

Tertiary Levels of Care

Tertiary levels of care include the institution (e.g., university) based facilities where teaching and research are major components of the facilities' duties. Typically, more expensive and less routine procedures are available at these centers, and care is provided by specialists whose patient population is referred. Care is almost always periodic, and continuity is provided through consultation to the primary care resource within the community. Usually, two different types of tertiary resource are identifiable at state or regional centers:

BIRTH DEFECTS CLINICS

The largest percentage of severely handicapped children have multiple problems besides developmental delay. One of the most easily identifiable types of resources for these children, the birth defects clinics are almost always at tertiary care facilities, but may include services at secondary levels of care as well.

To illustrate the kinds of services provided by these clinics, we will look at a clinic presently operated by the University of Washington at Children's Orthopedic Hospital and Medical Center in Seattle. Patients referred to this clinic have disorders encompassing the whole spectrum of congenital defects and handicapping conditions, including mental retardation. The clinic is a multidisciplinary facility in the ultimate sense. For any individual patient, professionals from as many as 22 specialties may be called upon to help manage the child's problem. Indeed, to coordinate this complex task, a "nurse coordinator" is assigned to each patient. The nurse coordinator's sole function is to arrange appointments with the varying specialists and to help preside at the case conference which summarizes the diagnostic and intervention strategies, including the plan for follow-up and coordination with the primary care physician. The types of subspecialties available in this clinic include the following:

Medical subspecialties:
Pediatrics
Neurology
Biochemical genetics
Dysmorphology
Cardiology
Hematology
Dermatology
Psychology
Psychiatry
Rehabilitative medicine
Nutrition

Surgical subspecialties:
Pediatric surgery
Neurosurgery
Urology
Orthopedics
Otolaryngology
Dentistry

Others:
Developmental therapy
Social service
Nursing service
Education
Audiometry
Speech pathology

UNIVERSITY AFFILIATED FACILITIES OR CHILD DEVELOPMENT CENTERS.

The second readily identifiable resource at the tertiary level includes the child development centers located at seven universities throughout the country. Staffs in these centers study mental retardation and learning disorders and serve retarded or learning disabled children. They provide a multidisciplinary team approach in the diagnosis of the individual child. The team usually includes a pediatrician, psychologist, psychometrist, developmental therapist, communication disorders specialist, audiologist, and neurologist; but professionals in any of the subspecialties listed under the birth defects clinics may also be called upon in the comprehensive evaluation of any of the patients. The primary mission is not only to provide service to the population of severely handicapped children with significant developmental delay, but also to develop programs in basic research and to train professionals within the subspecialties available in each particular facility.

The workup completed by the team includes prescriptive recommendations for the individual child on his or her referral back to the primary care physician, who is almost always remote from this type of tertiary facility. Indeed, this remoteness and the lack of facilities within smaller communities to carry out the intervention strategies recommended by the diagnostic teams has been a source of frustration in this kind of diagnostic and prescriptive workup.

Secondary Levels of Care

Most of the subspecialists in the tertiary facilities category can also be found at secondary levels of care. These are generally specialists practicing in more urban centers whose specialty patients are almost always referred. Certainly, secondary levels of care may be less remote from the primary care community and physician. However, the specialists are usually more loosely organized, working independently or in small groups, and they may or may not be associated with a university or other teaching facility. Indeed, if their services are utilized, the primary care physician is faced with the task of coordinating the patient evaluation by referring the child to the separate subspecialists, as well as attempting to organize the child's follow-up care and management.

Georgia Adams, Robin Beck,
Lynn Chandler, and Sandra Scott Livingston

Part II: The Infant Diagnostic Classroom—A Community Resource

We would like to reiterate several points from the earlier discussion:

1. The earliest identification of children with severely handicapping conditions or at risk for significant developmental delay is dependent on physician behavior, that is, on the physician's obtaining a complete medical history and performing a physical examination with emphasis on patterns of malformation of both CNS and non-CNS structures.

2. Accurate diagnosis of developmental delay is a function of "teacher" behavior, with ongoing (as opposed to periodic) developmental assessment, and accurate behavioral observation over time of the child's rates of acquiring new behavior.

3. Remediation, to be effective, must begin early, with continuity and long-term commitment provided at the primary or community level of care in a facility which can be identified as a "classroom," with appropriate interdisciplinary input for the teacher.

At present, there is no facility at the primary care level which combines these functions for the young infant or child. Interestingly, the basic skills for meeting these needs are usually present within the primary care community and/or the public schools within those communities. It was these circumstances which led to the concept of an infant classroom. We view this classroom as a resource not only to the primary care physician in the diagnosis and remediation of severely handicapping conditions, but also to implement the prescriptive intervention tactics for individual children after their referral and evaluation at secondary and tertiary facilities.

The concept of the classroom as the intervention base for these infants and children has some important implications:

Operationally, the classroom is in most instances truly interdisciplinary rather than multidisciplinary; that is, the input to the classroom from
the various specialists involved in remediating the infant's or child's handicap is through the teacher rather than through direct long-term involvement by the specialist within the classroom. Indeed, if direct intervention
is necessary by the specialist, it is within the classroom with the teacher
and the parent(s) present. It is also interdisciplinary rather than multidisciplinary according to the distinction recently made by Tarjan. The various professionals work together on a problem of common concern rather
than on separate, although related, problems (Tarjan, 1975).

Administratively, the classroom concept encourages planning by the
school district for the types, numbers, and geographic distribution of the
different specialists who have direct relevance to the classroom teacher's
needs.

Economically, the plan permits optimal utilization by the school district of specialists in such fields as developmental therapy, communication disorders, and psychology.

Finally, the tertiary level resources discussed in Part I can be viewed
in a perspective which places these services in a truly adjunctive role to a
long-term community-based interdisciplinary program. This should certainly lead to more appropriate and economic utilization of these services.
For instance, instead of referring a child with the question, "What is
wrong, and what do we do?" one can well envisage a time when referrals
will be accompanied by questions like this: "Here is where we are with
this child, here is where we are going, how can you help us get there?"

In the spring of 1975, through the cooperative efforts of staffs from
the Department of Pediatrics and both the Clinical Training Unit and
Experimental Education Unit of the University of Washington's Child
Development and Mental Retardation Center, a project was started which
we hope will be a model transferable to the primary community and fulfill
the above objectives.

The function of the infant classroom is to provide dynamic assessment (measurement of infant performance across time) in order to help
diagnose infants at risk for significant developmental delay, and to direct
intervention for those infants with handicapping conditions, including
poor developmental prognosis. In the classroom, the parent is involved
with the teacher in every aspect of the infant's curriculum, particularly in
remediation tactics, if appropriate.

ACCESS TO STUDENTS

Referrals to the infant classroom are being sought from primary care
practitioners within the geographic boundaries of King County. The satis-

factory development of these referral sources will be a measure of the infant classroom's ability to meet the needs of these practitioners' patients, and the physicians' acceptance of the classroom as a resource for the high risk infants and children in their care.

Of more immediate interest in developing the program and identifying eligible children is the presence of the Maternal and Infant Care Project run by the Washington State Department of Health and the Seattle-King County Department of Public Health. The project provides comprehensive health care to mothers and infants through the first year of the infant's life. Multidisciplinary care is provided by pediatricians, public health nurses, social workers, nutritionists, and others. Some of the criteria used in assigning a mother or infant to the program are:

1. Prenatal History
   Maternal age (under 16, over 35)
   Maternal medical problems (including those related to fetal risk, drug abuse, psychiatric problems)
   Social–economic factors (single mother, inadequate income, no prenatal care, history of child abuse or abusing parent, history of previous relinquishment of infant or child)
2. Perinatal History
   Low birth weight
   Prematurity with or without complications
   Medical complications (associated with CNS sequelae)
3. Postnatal History
   Failure to thrive
   Neglect or abuse
   Medical problems

The program is extremely flexible, and when the risk factors are recognized, families can be placed on the program at any time. Likewise, when the family is doing well, the infant is thriving, and the Maternal and Infant team resources are no longer needed, alternative health resources can be found for the family. It should be stressed that, while this project does concentrate on high risk infants, the care is provided by primary care pediatricians and pediatric trainees. Routine physical examination, immunizations, and care for illnesses are provided. Developmental assessment is performed by the physicians or nurses. However, when a child has multiple risk factors, or questionable developmental progress, referral is made either to the developmental therapists for more accurate assessment or to the infant classroom.

THE TEAM APPROACH: ROLES AND ACTIVITIES

Professionals who work in this interdisciplinary program have had very different specialized training; yet almost all of them have had experience in working as members of a team. In one sense, a new venture of this kind demands such practical experience in team management almost as much as it requires the various skills. We are all learning from each other. There are no fixed, immutable rules about our team procedures. In most cases, they derive from the specific needs of the individual infant. For instance, there are some children who need to have ongoing therapy sessions with the developmental therapist, rather than periodic consultation; for other children, consultations followed by prescriptive programs that can be carried out by the teacher or parent are sufficient. So, too, input from nutritionists, communication disorders specialists, pediatricians, neurologists, and other specialists available to the team will vary in intensity and duration. The teacher is responsible for coordinating all of the activities, as well as for implementing many of the remediation strategies developed by the whole team.

Perhaps one of the most distinguishing features of this program is that parents of enrolled infants are bona fide members of the team. One of the underlying principles is that continuity of care is critical, and that continuity can best be achieved if the parents, who spend so much more time with the infant than do the other team members, participate in assessment and remediation.

Of all the team members besides the parents, those who maintain the closest association with the children over time are the teacher and the developmental therapists. For that reason, our discussions about the work of the team will be restricted to their activities.

Assessment

One of the first considerations in the educational management of infants is specifying their development in precise behavioral terms. As in many other areas of study, significant progress in the field often depends on the professionals' ability to precisely define and measure the input and outcome variables under consideration. With infants, the significant outcomes of concern are the child's behaviors which indicate his or her progress in developmental areas such as gross and fine motor, social, communication, and early cognitive skills. Generally, it is important to speak about behaviors in terms of "movement cycles"—that is, to specify behaviors which are observable, repeatable, and have definite beginning and ending points. Thus with an infant, one might define "attending behavior" as a movement of the child's eyes from some area of the visual field to fixate on a presented object. In this case, the "movement cycle" begins when the child stops "looking" somewhere other than at the intended object, and terminates when the child moves his eyes away from the object. Different aspects of movement cycles can be noted by recording latency, duration, intensity, or approximations to the movement cycle, or by recording other accompanying behaviors which may correlate with the movement cycle under consideration. Careful and exact specification of behavior is necessary to make an adequate initial assessment and to evaluate a child's subsequent progress in each area of development.

However, the precise definition of behavior in terms of movement cycles is only a beginning step. The behaviors to be considered must be considered in some context. In this regard, the extensive efforts that professionals have made in identifying "developmental progressions" are extremely important. For example, the Developmental Pinpoints collated by Cohen, Gross, and Haring in this volume provide a lengthy series of developmental behaviors against which one can assess a child's early performance. Brazelton's infant assessment scale (1973) includes a series of early behaviors against which one can check an infant's early development. Many other writers attempt to present a developmental sequence through which a child progresses. The importance of such "developmental sequences" is that they provide a reference point or context for measuring an individual child's performance. If a child exhibits extensive and severe deficits in comparison with the presented "norms," the evaluating professional can note these deficits and make recommendations about interventions for ameliorating them.

Behavior must also be viewed in terms of its immediate and long-term consequences to the individual. For instance, the infant who fails to emit any social behaviors, such as eye contact, vocalizations, or motor responses to parental movement and vocalizations, does not reinforce the parents for providing social stimuli. As a result, the parents often decelerate their overtures to the child, and patterns of noninteraction begin, in which the child with deficits receives even less than the usual amount of environmental stimulation. The child who does not learn to fixate visually on an object is more likely to have difficulty later in attending to and discriminating visual stimuli which are intended as learning cues. Such considerations are useful in determining which specific behaviors require assessment and subsequent intervention.

Other notable elements of infant behavior are its regularities and consistencies. To the casual observer, an infant may appear to engage in much random behavior unrelated to immediate events. However, precise and continuing observation of infants suggests that much behavior is periodic in its occurrence and predictable in its relation to environmental stimulation. It is this orderliness of behavior which helps the educational manager know what to look for in assessment and intervention with infant development.

There are at least two important components to the assessment process. First, one wishes to determine what behaviors a child possesses. In this respect, some of the developmental assessment scales are useful. They provide the manager with information about the child's behaviors in reference to a sequence of expected behaviors. But one of the limitations of such assessment is its static nature. Even with older children who respond consistently to environmental cues, the results of a one-time test are regarded as only a tentative indication of performance. This should be even truer for infants, who do not exhibit the same high degree of consistency in responding to environmental stimuli. The results of a one-time measure should be regarded with caution.

Thus, a second vital component of the assessment process is repeated measurement across time. For example, the manager may assess a child's performance on a visual tracking task during several sessions. Such repeated measurement provides a much more reliable picture of child performance than a single measure. If one day's score is very low or very high in comparison with other days' scores, that fact is obvious and the manager is not misled by a single day's extreme score. Repeated measures across time also give the manager an opportunity to observe an infant's behavior in the context of a variety of states. The manager is then able to assess the extent to which a child's performance is likely to vary as a result of sleep cycles, hunger, and other factors.

One of the most important purposes of repeated measurements is that they allow a manager to observe behavior change. Through observation of behavior change, the manager can note whether or not a child is making developmental progress, whether such progress is "spontaneous" or requires intervention, and what interventions result in the most rapid gains in the child's performance.

These procedures are followed when a child enters the Experimental Education Unit's infant program. First, medical and case history information is collected and reviewed. The team then conducts an initial evaluation of behaviors in the infant's repertoire, using developmental scales as indicated previously. Next, the team conducts repeated measures on selected behaviors. One infant, for example, was initially assessed with the Bayley Scale of Infant Development (1969). After analyzing the results of this assessment, the staff selected visual tracking ("to track object with eyes"), and turning to sound ("to turn head to sound"), as behaviors to be measured more precisely and as possible areas for subsequent intervention.

In order to ascertain the environmental events which served as occasions for these behaviors, they were measured with a variety of stimulus events. These are summarized in Table 5. Because the classroom staff were concerned not only with the complete movement cycle, but also with associated behaviors which were likely to precede it, they identified a number of other preceding movement cycles. For example, an infant might inhibit ongoing behaviors in response to a noise, but might not turn his head toward the sound. The measurement of preceding behaviors such as "stilling" does provide the manager with much information about the child's development. For the behaviors specified earlier, to "turn head to sound" and "track objects with eyes," the staff defined the behaviors listed in the following table as approximations to the desired movement cycles. These behaviors are sequential (Table 6). After defining the re-

Table 5.
List of Movement Cycles Subjected to Repeated Measures and Their Associated Antecedent Events

Antecedent Event	Movement Cycle
1. Manager places ball at midline in front of child and moves ball to right or to left.	1. To track ball with eyes.
2. Manager shakes rattle to left side or right side.	2. To turn head toward rattle and focus eyes on rattle.
3. Mother positions her face at midline in front of child and moves to right or left.	3. To track mother's face with eyes.
4. Stranger positions face at midline in front of child and moves to right or left.	4. To track stranger's face with eyes.
5. Mother talks to child from left or right side.	5. To turn head towards mother's face and focus eyes on mother's face.
6. Stranger talks to child from left or right side.	6. To turn head toward stranger's face and focus eyes on stranger's face.
7. Mother positions her face at midline in front of child and talks to child, moving face to right or left.	7. To track mother's face with eyes.
8. Stranger positions face at midline in front of child, talks to child, moving face to right or left.	8. To track stranger's face with eyes.

Table 6.
Some Approximations to Desired Movement Cycles of "Turning Head to Sound" and "Tracking Objects With Eyes"

Movement Cycle	Approximations to Movement Cycle
To turn head to sound and focus eyes on object.	1. To exhibit "stilling" or "startling" response. 2. To turn only eyes toward sound. 3. To turn head and eyes toward sound. 4. To turn head and eyes toward sound and fix on object (corneal reflex).
To track objects with eyes	1. To exhibit "stilling" response. 2. To fix on object (corneal reflex). 3. To track object with eyes part of 60° distance. 4. To track object with eyes full 60°.

sponse categories the staff formulate a data collection format. For the behaviors just discussed, the following type of data collection format was used (Table 7).

Intervention

Once data are collected, intervention programs can be established. It is possible that the child will make satisfactory progress with no specialized interventions. But if the child exhibits little or no progress without intervention, some instructional plan is required.

The major strategy with infants is to base behavioral intervention on the information gleaned from direct assessment of developmental behaviors, utilizing both antecedent stimuli and reinforcing events; and directly and repeatedly evaluating the infant's progress in those behaviors selected for intervention. The first step in intervention is selecting target behaviors—those behaviors that require remediation or development. This is always based on the assessment process of identifying the point in a developmental sequence at which children are performing, or of identifying atypical or pathological behaviors. For example, if a youngster is functioning at a very primitive level, one might select such behaviors as the rooting, grasping, or walking reflexes (Brazelton, 1973). With more advanced infants, one can work with attending behavior, vocalizations,

Table 7.
Data Collecting Format Used With Infant Behaviors

Movement Cycle	Response Categories	Time	1	2	3	4	Trials 5	6	7	8	9	10	Percent
1. See ball: To track with eyes	0. No change in behavior 1. Show stilling response 2. Fix eyes on ball 3. Partially turn head and eyes 4. Track ball full 60°												
2. Hear rattle: To turn and fixate with eyes	0. No change in behavior 1. Show stilling or startle response 2. Turn only eyes toward sound 3. Turn head and eyes toward sound 4. Turn head and eyes toward sound and focus on object												

etc. Major kinds of intervention are manipulation or utilization of organismic variables, antecedent stimuli, and reinforcing events.

Because infants generally are not responsive to the wide range of environmental stimuli that older children respond to, intervention strategies require careful utilization and management of those variables which affect the state of the organism. For example, intervention is usually ill-advised when an infant is fatigued, hungry, or otherwise distressed. But it may sometimes be advisable to have the infant in a mild state of deprivation in order to properly elicit and reinforce a behavior. For example, one might work with the components of the sucking reflex when an infant has not been fed in the last few hours.

In regard to antecedent stimuli, it is advisable to use those objects and events to which the child usually responds. The mother's face and voice, objects from the infant's crib, or a pacifier which the infant uses can often serve to elicit desired responses. Some stimuli such as loud noises and bright objects can often facilitate certain responses.

One also uses reinforcing events to strengthen behaviors. Here, too, it is important to begin with those objects or events that are already reinforcing to the infant, such as the mother's voice and smile, stroking, cuddling, feeding, or a pacifier.

Sometimes the assessment data suggest the intervention to use. For example, if the child tracks his mother's face only when the mother is talking, the first training step might be to practice under these conditions. Once stimuli which are familiar to the child have been used to strengthen target behaviors and the appropriate reinforcement is established, the manager can proceed to broaden the range of stimuli to which the infant will respond, as well as the infant's range of behaviors.

Three courses of action may be taken with children following assessment in the infant program. For those children who progress at an adequate rate, the usual periodic visits to the clinic are most effective. Some children who exhibit delays will require "minimal" intervention, wherein the staff instructs the parents in using those intervention activities necessary to maintain the child's progress. However, some other children will require more extensive intervention, such as daily to weekly programs with the professional staff, to insure developmental progress.

Adjunctive Services from Team Members and Consultants

At all points in the program, the educational staff have access to adjunctive services. As noted earlier, referrals to the program are made from child study clinics, pediatricians, and maternal and infant care programs. Such personnel as physical and occupational therapists, pediatricians, nurses, communication disorders specialists, and psychologists participate in assessment and intervention. Pediatricians, nurses, and social workers can provide follow-up consultation and liaison with parents.

A registered occupational therapist (OTR) or a registered physical therapist (RPT) who has specialized in pediatrics and uses the developmental model as the foundation for evaluation and treatment is often called a developmental therapist. According to Banus in her book on the developmental therapist, the therapist must be "aware of all aspects of development in order to make significant contributions within the framework of his specific knowledge of development and its deviations" (Banus, 1971, p. 3). The work involves preventing disabilities, as well as habilitating/rehabilitating the profoundly and severely involved individual from infancy through adulthood.

The most common referrals received by the developmental therapist are for assessment and programming in fine and gross motor functioning, self-help skills (including feeding problems that need remediation), perceptual–motor abilities, and sensory integration, and for adaptive equipment in these areas. The therapist may use one or more instruments for assessing functioning in these areas: for screening, these might include the Malani-Compretti and the Denver Developmental Screening Test; for diagnosis, the Gesell and the Bobath neurodevelopmental evaluation.

As a member of the team, the therapist has several specific roles. First, in initial assessment, the therapist's knowledge of sequence and quality of normal motor behavior, as well as deviant motor patterns, makes his contribution particularly useful in evaluating the functioning level of the severely handicapped child. Discrepancy in motor behavior is often the first indicator of developmental delay. For example, a 5-month-old child may not bring his hands to midline because of lack of motivation to do so, or he may well be unable to perform this motor skill because he is pulled into extension by a tonic labyrinthine reflex (a primitive reflex), indicating the possibility of cerebral palsy.

After the evaluation and goals-setting by the assessment team (including parents), the therapist may assume one or more roles which are not mutually exclusive. Further, some overlay in roles among the various disciplines is not only appropriate, but will be very likely to occur. As the child progresses, the therapist's role(s) will change to meet new priorities and goals. On the basis of the priorities set for the child, the team decides whether or not the therapist needs to give direct treatment. For example, an older infant with a severe communication problem and with motor delay, but no abnormal motor patterns, will probably need more help from the communication specialist than from the developmental therapist. The therapist, therefore, will play a consultative rather than direct care role, while the communication specialist works directly with the child. The developmental therapist may help the teacher to plan activities appropriate to the child's motor delay, and may plan management techniques for home and school without taking the child's time for individualized therapy. In other cases, the therapist will be directly involved in management. For example, a cerebral palsied child with a strong asymmetrical tonic neck reflex (a normal reflex for infants, but one that is not integrated by cerebral palsied children) urgently needs treatment from the therapist if the reflex is causing a deformity. If this reflex is abnormally present, it may promote scoliosis (abnormal curvature of the spine) and dislocation of the hips. In this case, the therapist takes primary responsibility for the motor program, even though the teacher and parents also need to use appropriate management techniques.

In the first example, the therapist's major role is to provide consultation to the teacher and parents. The teacher and parent then are primarily responsible for carrying out the program which facilitates learning in the classroom and makes home care easier. These programs are not meant to substitute for actual therapy sessions, but to augment them. In the second case, the therapist provides treatment. A child need not be severely physically involved to require the therapist's treatment for a specific problem. For example, an older child with poor trunk control may be sitting in his chair gripping the sides with his hands or wrapping his legs around the chair legs for support, and with this output of energy used for maintaining balance, he has minimal energy left to attend to the teacher. The therapist can first of all suggest to the teacher an alternate method of seating the child which eliminates the child's fear of falling from the chair and allows him to pay full attention to the learning task. But it would also be important for the therapist to work with this child on increasing trunk control.

The therapist can also be a case manager or a liaison person. The case manager role is most appropriate in those cases where a child's physical disability is of primary concern and requires the coordination of medical, rehabilitation, and educational services. The therapist's case management work does not conflict with that of teachers managing within the classroom. With less physically involved children, the therapist provides liaison services between the classroom and the medical rehabilitation services, or between the parent and medical personnel to help in clarifying issues. A therapist can discuss with the parents the implications of a given disability in classroom and home management; for instance, if a child is diagnosed as a spastic quadriplegic, the therapist can suggest the proper positioning of the child in the classroom, the possible perceptual deficits which will affect his performance, and the handling necessary to insure that he will not develop further physical problems, e.g., contractures.

Finally, the developmental therapist performs a training role.

Whether with in-service training to other members of the team concerning procedures to use with a particular child, or in providing a broader perspective in an area of disability or a problem that extends across children, the therapist's role includes teaching adults as well as children.

To reiterate: the developmental therapist on the interdisciplinary team managing profoundly and severely handicapped infants and children must play many roles. He or she evaluates, applies treatment techniques, consults, case manages, can be a liaison between other facilities and the classroom, and provides training.

CONCLUSION

We began this chapter with what we hope will become a platitude: we said that long-term management of severely handicapped infants and children should be based in the community's public schools. Elsewhere in this volume (see particularly the chapters by Norris Haring, by Alice Hayden and Valentine Dmitriev, and by Norris Haring and Diane Bricker), authors have stressed the critical importance of early, continuous, and comprehensive management of this population. We agree completely with that view, and have suggested in this chapter a community-based model for providing such management. We have also attempted to integrate some of the "medical" and educational components of such a model, as well as discuss the rationale for its development. In discussing the behaviors and skills that fall within the separate purviews of professionals who will be involved in comprehensive management, we have emphasized that any such efforts require, and, in fact, would fail without, the skills of all. Finally, because neither medical nor any other technology has yet found the means to reduce significantly the number of children who will require such management, we believe that planning for community-based management programs is long overdue. The new infant classroom for children who are either already identified as severely handicapped or considered to be at risk for severe developmental delay should provide a transportable model for communities willing to implement a truly community-based management strategy.

REFERENCES

Alden ER et al: Morbidity and mortality of infants weighing less than 1,000 gms in an intensive care nursery. Pediatrics 50:40, 1972

Banus BS (ed): The Developmental Therapist: A Prototype of the Pediatric Occupational Therapist. Thorofare, N.J. Slack, 1971

Bayley N: Bayley Scales of Infant Development. New York, Psychological Corp. 1969

Bergsma D: Birth Defects: An Atlas and Compendium. Baltimore, Williams & Wilkins, 1973

Brazelton TB: Neonatal Behavioral Assessment Scale. London, Spastics International Medical Publications, 1973

Brock DJH, Sutcliffe RG: Alpha-fetoprotein in the antenatal diagnosis of anencephaly and spina bifida. Lancet 2:197–199, 1972

Crome L: The brain and mental retardation. Br Med J 1:897, 1960

Ellis WC, et al: The regional newborn center: Effect on neonatal mortality of referring hospitals. Pediatr Res 6:409, 1972

Fletcher J: Abortion, euthansia, and care of defective newborns. N Eng J Med 292:75, 1975

Glass L, et al: Decrease in neonatal mortality following legalization of voluntary abortions. Pediat Res 6:409, 1972

Holmes LB, et al: Mental Retardation: An Atlas of Diseases with Associated Physical Abnormalities. New York, Macmillan, 1972

Jones KL, Smith DW: Recognition of the fetal alcohol syndrome in early infancy. Lancet 2:999–1001, 1973

Jones DL, Smith DW, Ulleland CN: Pattern of malformation in offspring of chronic alcoholic mothers. Lancet 1267–1271, 1973

Kaveggia EG, et al: Diagnostic genetic studies on 1,224 patients with severe mental retardation. Proceedings of the Third Congress of the International Association for the Scientific Study of Mental Deficiency. The Hague, The Netherlands, September 4–12, 1973

Nadler HL: Prenatal diagnosis of inborn defects: A status report. Hosp Prac 10:41, 1975

Shurtleff DB, et al: Myelodysplasia: Decision for death or disability. N Eng J Med 291:1005, 1974

Smith DW: Classification, nomenclature, and naming of morphologic defects. J Pediatr 87:162, 1975a

Smith DW: Rational diagnostic evaluation of the child with mental deficiency. Am J Dis Child 129:1285–1290, 1975b

Smith DW: Recognizable Patterns of Human Malformation. Philadelphia, Saunders, 1976

Tarjan G: Critical issues in interdisciplinary research. Paper presented at the Charles C. Strother–Child Development and Mental Retardation Center Seminar, "The Interdisciplinary Team in Health: Critical Issues in Education, Leadership, Clinical Practice, and Research." Child Development and Mental Retardation Center, University of Washington, Seattle, Washington, May 27, 1975

James W. Tawney

B

Educating Severely Handicapped Children and Their Parents through Telecommunications

The right to education and normalization movements are creating a demand for new delivery systems to educate those who are severely handicapped. Early intervention, home placement, and utilization of community resources are proposed as alternatives to institutionalization of children who manifest severe and multiple handicapping conditions. This means, in brief, that education must be provided to persons who have not been recipients of this right, at an age when educational services have not been rendered, and that additional supportive services must be provided to parents of these students to enable them to manage and educate their children. The magnitude of the task requires the development of innovative and cost-effective delivery systems. This chapter describes the application of telecommunication technologies to home education of severely handicapped children and their parents. Five prototype telecommunications systems are described in this chapter. Multiple functions of a model telecommunications system are listed. Potential combinations of single systems are projected, and recommendations for future system development and utilization are considered, particularly those which relate to the potential for long-term research and curriculum development.

The case of Brown vs. Board of Education precipitated a social revolution which has altered the fabric of American education repeatedly for the past 20 years. The fact of inequality exploded into public view and has remained there continuously, kept current by disclosure of educational

Preparation of this chapter was supported by Contract No. OEC-0-74-7539 and by Grant No. OEG-72-5631, awards from U.S.O.E., Bureau of Education for the Handicapped, School Systems Branch and Division of Innovation and Development.

practices which are discriminatory to children. A commitment to provide equal educational opportunity has generated a variety of experimental programs designed to reduce past inequities and foster maximum intellectual growth in all of society's children. As intervention strategies were developed to provide equal educational opportunities, it became apparent that a social experiment of massive proportions was underway. Preschool programs emerged, to be followed by infant development and home training projects. While the effects of these programs were being debated, parents of handicapped children began to discover that minorities were not defined exclusively by color. An analysis of existing laws and traditional educational practices showed that children with severe handicapping conditions were excluded from public education programs. Through litigation, PARC vs. Commonwealth of Pennsylvania, parents sought and obtained a remedy to the situation. This, and subsequent legal action, established the right to education movement for all handicapped children. This movement has received national attention and served to accelerate changes in practices related to the care and treatment of the handicapped, particularly the mentally retarded.

The contrast between basic human rights and living conditions in institutional settings has increased pressure to remove children from institutions and return them to their home communities. In the next decade, numerous strategies will be employed to bring handicapped and nonhandicapped persons into daily interaction to "normalize" experiences for both groups. These actions have initiated a social experiment equal in significance to the original civil rights movement. If it is successful, handicapped children will no longer be placed in institutions. Instead, they will remain in home settings, receive educational intervention from birth through adulthood, and maintain a degree of independent living with the assistance of community-based service agencies. The dimensions of this social experiment are not confined to the generation of new delivery systems. Instead, the real experiment is a test for social acceptance of human variation. The outcome of normalization and right to education is the presence of individuals in a society which has historically rejected them because of extreme behavioral and physiologic deviations from an inferred cultural norm. This dimension appears to have received little professional attention, an oversight which must be remedied to insure comprehensive planning.

Extreme effort will be required of parents as they work to develop a supportive home environment for their children. An equal effort will be required of professionals as they address the managerial and human factors which will ultimately determine the success of evolving support systems. The magnitude of the task requires that the problems must be fully conceptualized, that sufficient resources must be obtained, and that the most advanced technologies must be incorporated into efforts to develop prototype educational and social service delivery systems to support community placement of severely handicapped children.

This chapter will describe preliminary attempts to utilize emerging telecommunications technologies to teach children and to support parents whose severely handicapped children remain at home. This support is provided in the form of direct instruction to children and parent education. The systems deliver instruction to severely impaired children from birth to adulthood who represent the full range of handicapping conditions. The focus, however, is on severe learning and behavior disorders in children from birth to 6 years of age.

A RATIONALE FOR THE DEVELOPMENT OF TELECOMMUNICATIONS TECHNOLOGIES

Throughout this discussion, it will be important to keep in mind that descriptions of telecommunications systems and their functions have two referents in time: what can be done today and what may be done in the future. This section considers the factors which have encouraged the development of five prototype systems and the immediate goals they are designed to meet. Subsequent sections describe how systems may be used in the future. A critical factor will emerge to link the time referents—the utility of the systems to initiate systematic intervention from birth through the early school years. A brief rationale for early intervention will bridge the gap between present and future.

Immediate Needs for Alternative Educational Delivery Systems

Traditionally, children go to school on foot or by bus. If they deviate to some degree from other children, their destination is a special class placement. If they deviate significantly, they do not go to school at all. For some children with temporary injury or permanent health impairments, school may come to them in the form of homebound instruction or, in extremely rare situations, in the form of a telephone link to a classroom. For children who deviate significantly in intellectual or behavioral attributes, the traditional social response has been to remove them from their homes and place them in institutions where they may or may not have the opportunity to go to "school." Sometimes, when mountains, flooding rivers, or cultural barriers exist between home and school, children simply do not go to school at all. The barriers supersede the issue of deviance. The traditional public view, in summary, has been stated very directly: "You go to school or you do not. If you do not fit, you stay at home. If you do not go to school, you may receive limited home instruction, if it is convenient to do so. If it is not convenient, you will not be served."

However, the practices which were an outgrowth of the traditional view have been declared unconstitutional, and alternative methods must be found to educate those children who have been excluded from school. Concurrently, the number and types of excluded children are becoming increasingly more visible as a result of court-directed identification programs and the efforts of child advocacy projects (see *Children Out of School*, a report by the Children's Defense Fund, 1974). The pressure to alter traditional practices has intensified the search for nontraditional delivery systems. In a society that has become increasingly oriented toward the use of technology to solve major problems, the development of telecommunications systems is a logical strategy to circumvent geographic and political barriers. Similarly, as traditional age restrictions are being changed, telecommunications systems are looked upon as viable alternatives to serve new and younger populations, particularly in the 0–6 age range. The immediate goals of the emerging prototypes are clearly identified, as are the populations they will serve.

A basic objective of a telecommunications system is to deliver instruction to children who are geographically isolated from instruction. Severely handicapped persons are a relatively low incidence population, particularly when they represent combinations of handicapping conditions. When such persons ae located in sparsely populated areas, or in areas which are isolated by geographic barriers, the service delivery problem is intensified. Telecommunications systems offer a variety of ways to link homes in remote locations with a central instructional unit. Telephone or television transmission systems can provide daily instruction of a higher quality than that provided by present itinerant, homebound services.

There are, among the population of excluded children, those whose health is impaired to such a degree that education in traditional public school classes is considered unfeasible. This population is, presumably, heterogeneous in age and level of intellectual functioning. Computer-assisted instruction systems, transmitted via telephone or television, have been developed to provide home instruction appropriate to this heterogeneous group. Several years of work have gone into the development of curricula for CAI systems. These curricula are sufficiently comprehensive to provide a range of instruction in the traditional elementary and secondary content areas. Limited curricula exist, and more are being developed, to deliver instruction to persons who presently function below the traditional content areas. It is unlikely that the content of instruction and existing single delivery systems are adequate to serve this heterogeneous group. However, an immediate goal of the prototype systems is to expand programming capacity to serve those persons who have no other alternative.

Presently, many excluded children remain at home, and that placement is tenuous at best. Some are school age, but have been excluded because they are presumed to be severely retarded or to manifest severe behavior disorders. Others have not yet reached mandatory school age, but manifest such extreme intellectual or behavioral defects that their families may be considering institutional placements. Telecommunications systems will perform three immediate functions for these family units: assist parents in managing their children, teach parents to teach their children, and provide direct instruction to children. It is presumed that these interventions will raise children's functional levels, reduce behavior management problems, and reduce the probability that the child will be institutionalized.

Compensatory education programs began at the preschool level, then worked backwards to infant training, parent training, and home education programs. A similar trend has developed among those concerned with the education of the severely handicapped. For children with sensory impairments in vision and hearing, the necessity for early education has been acknowledged by legislation which permits public education at an earlier age than nonimpaired children. Precedents are being established for all handicapping conditions, from birth to the present mandatory school age (and beyond). However, litigation and legislative actions are too new to be represented as a mandate which will guarantee education from birth for infants with severe and multiple handicapping conditions. The conceptualization of some of the prototype telecommunications systems has been predicated on the anticipated demand for infant learning programs, and systems are being designed to provide direct instruction to infants and to assist parents with the task of maintaining their child at home and in the community. The immediate goals for these systems are to demonstrate that it is possible to communicate with remote stations from a central computer system via telephone transmission lines, and that computer technology can be employed effectively by parents and professionals to shape or build a behavioral repertoire in a severely impaired infant, utilizing systematic, daily intervention continuously from birth through the early school years.

Factors which have led to the development of and funding for telecommunications systems have been described. The immediate general goals for technology-based telecommunications systems have been stated. The activities required to meet these goals will be carried out, and initial support will have been terminated by July 1976. Shortly thereafter, project reports will be available and the effectiveness of the systems will be open to public scrutiny. Those results will reflect short-term effects; the potential for the technology-based telecommunications systems will emerge when they are viewed with respect to their utility in long-range instructional research and curriculum development efforts.

Their application to the development of automated sequential curriculum for infants and young children will emerge as a primary function. Why that should be done, and how it will be accomplished, will emerge in the next section, which sets the stage for a description of what the projects propose to do now. That will be followed by a description of what they may do in the future.

THE BASIS FOR EARLY INTERVENTION THROUGH TELECOMMUNICATION SYSTEMS

The immediate function of the prototype systems has been defined: to provide a variety of educational interventions for existing populations which are heterogeneous in age and level of development. For the most part, these interventions are aimed at the modification of behavioral or intellectual defects of long-term duration. The technologies may be applied more efficiently and effectively in the future to provide systematic instruction to children and support to parents, beginning at birth. Or, as Tawney (1975) noted, to develop model systems for the child of the year 2000.

The basic function of any intervention program is to facilitate or accelerate the course of normal development. Where severely handicapped infants are concerned, early intervention programs are designed to prevent retarded development which might be considered a function of observable biologic defect, or inadequate environments (Bijou, 1966, p. 3). Here, biologic events include sensory impairments, and environmental events refer to the stimulus–response interactions which retard development. Thus, from Bijou's (1966) framework, "a retarded individual is one who has a limited repertoire of behavior shaped by events that constitute his history" (p. 2). This formulation has proved extremely useful in the conceptualization of intervention programs. The task is clearly defined: to design environments which will shape or build a response repertoire (Tawney, 1974). Where severely handicapped infants are concerned, the environment will be the home, and family members will constitute the major class of stimulus events. For severely and multiply handicapped infants, pressure is mounting to develop programs which begin intervention shortly after birth. There is a growing body of literature that supports immediate intervention. Clues to the direction such interventions should take are drawn from the comparisons of structured vs. nonstructured preschool programs. And, within the literature on the experimental analysis of behavior, there are precedents for the design of programmed or prosthetic environments. The potential of the telecommunications system appears greatest as a component of a prosthetic environment, where it is used to deliver instruction to infants and young children on a daily basis, to build or shape a "normal" repertoire through fine grain sequences of instruction. At the same time, the technology creates a service delivery system which can be used to assist parents with the task of facilitating the development of their child.

Support for intervention originating shortly after birth can be found in enabling legislation, BEH priorities for early childhood education, the development of an early education network for preschool education for the handicapped, money set aside in Head Start funding to insure service to the handicapped, and the initiation of research and demonstration programs designed to insure enrollment of children in preschool and day care programs. The empirical basis for early and systematic intervention is fragile, but is growing with the accumulation of evidence which suggests that infant behavior can be modified. White (1971), for example, has reported selected studies from his long-term program of research with normal infants. Recent studies in infant learning have been reviewed by Fitzgerald and Porges (1971) and Hulsebus (1973). These excellent reviews suggest that infant instruction is feasible and, in addition, offer clues for the development of appropriate learning tasks. The empirical basis for long-term intervention with handicapped infants and young children is sparse. However, research efforts such as the recently completed Toddler Research and Intervention Project (Bricker and Bricker, 1972) should provide a rationale for early intervention as data become widely distributed. The long-term, ongoing intervention program for Down's children (Hayden and Haring, in press) provides strong support for early intervention. After 5 years of intervention with infant learning programs, parent training, and support programs, and continuous sequential instruction, Down's children are entering first grade classes with "normal" children. The academic performance of these children refutes the assumption that Down's children are low-functioning. Hopefully, the performance of these children will stimulate special educators to examine the assumptions they hold concerning the potential of all handicapped persons.

The experience in the growth of preschool programs for the disadvantaged suggests the directions that infant learning programs are likely to take, in terms of structured vs. nonstructured programs. Early childhood studies (Karnes, et al. 1968) which demonstrate the positive outcomes of direct instruction, indicate the direction which infant programs might follow. Basic approaches to education for severely handicapped infants will emerge with time. Lambie, Bond, and Weikart (undated) have described three types of curricular approaches for the normal infant: programmed, open framework, and learner-centered. The behavioral characteristics of severely handicapped infants suggest that the programmed approach may hold much promise. This view is supported by the positive results, which are generally reported in the literature of the experimental analysis of behavior. In contrast to the results of large, experimental studies conducted by special educators to test the "efficacy" of special education practices, this literature contains successful demonstrations of the application of fine grained programming techniques to shape academic and social behaviors. Of particular interest are studies which utilize an errorless learning paradigm to shape complex discriminations (Bijou, 1968; Sidman and Stoddard, 1966; Tawney, 1972; Terrace, 1967).

This methodology has been applied to instructional programming for children with severe developmental retardation (Tawney, et al., 1975). The methodology (precise control of environmental events, carefully sequenced instructional steps, immediate and contingent reinforcement of correct responses, arrangement of stimulus presentations to reduce the probability of error) can be applied to the development of instructional programs for infants. Telecommunications systems which utilize home-based computer terminals have the capacity to deliver "errorless" curricula to home settings. The characteristics of prototype systems, described in the next section, illustrate present capacity to provide instructional programming. Later sections describe the function of telecommunications in broadly based alternative educational delivery systems.

FIVE PROTOTYPE TELECOMMUNICATIONS SYSTEMS

The Utah Project

The Exceptional Child Center at Utah State University is establishing a Homebound Handicapped Resource Center as a major component of their telecommunications project. The goal of the project is to serve children in rural areas who are considered severely and profoundly retarded, multihandicapped, or emotionally disturbed.

The telecommunications network links the Resource Center, homes, a local homebound instruction teacher, and the Intermountain Medical Program, a health service unit, by standard telephones equipped with interactive speakers. Once identified, parents are sent instructional packages which are designed to assist them in teaching language, leisure time, arithmetic, and self-help skills to their children. The instructional packages are written specifically for parents, and contain step-by-step instructions to teach skills such as counting objects, naming coins, number skills, and number symbols. They also contain instructions to enable parents to provide verbal assistance, to evaluate responses, and to correct errors.

The interactive telephone speaker system is used to report children's progress, to solve instructional or programming errors, and to assist parents in solving management problems. The system provides low-cost supplementary educational services to parents. The inclusion of the local homebound teacher and a regional health agency increases the base of supportive services to families who are geographically dispersed throughout a large, sparsely populated area.

The Teaching Resources Center Project

Teaching Resources Center at the City University of New York is developing a series of films to teach language concepts to children who are considered to be mentally retarded or who manifest severe behavior disorders. Tape vignettes feature puppets, similar to Sesame Street characters. The dialogue is written to teach and reinforce use of specific language concepts.

Programs are presented on a responsive TV system—a standard television set which has been modified by the addition of an electronic switching device. For this application, a four-button response system is connected to the switching device. Each button contains a picture of one of four puppet characters featured in the video tape lessons.

Each video lesson is programmed to present a single concept, then to test children's knowledge of the concept. After each episode, the characters direct the child to press a specific button to register a discriminative response. A correct response produces an appropriate confirmation/reinforcement from the character. An incorrect response produces corrective feedback from the character whose button is pressed.

This telecommunication system is presently being used in research to test hypotheses related to television instruction. The video programs can be used over the air or on cable systems. The instrumentation required to convert a standard TV to a responsive system appears to be uncomplicated, and will perhaps gain wide usage.

The New York State Department Project

The New York State Department of Education at Albany has initiated a telecommunications project in the Buffalo area which will serve 100 persons, primarily 5–21 years of age, whose physical handicaps are so severe that they are unable to attend public school classes.

Curriculum materials which are available commercially will be transmitted into homes via an interactive television system composed of cable TV and telephone transmission to communicate with the student. A teletype keyboard and acoustic coupler will be placed in the home and integrated with the families' existing television set, creating a CAI terminal.

The system is designed to work in the following manner: the student dials the computer center, places the telephone in the acoustic coupler, and types a message to the computer center on the teletype keyboard. His message will call up a specific instructional program or set of instructions, which will be transmitted over the cable TV system and appear on his television set. His response will call up a program change and the computer–student interaction will continue until the lesson is completed.

The computer control system is designed around a Hewlett-Packard 2000F dual processor computer, modified by MITRE Corporation for use with their TICCIT system. Basically, the systems operate in the following manner. Programs are stored in computer memory. When a specific program is called up, computer signals are generated, fed into the TICCIT system, and transformed into a TV signal which is transmitted over a cable network. The visual display appears on the television set in the home.

A wide range of curriculum programs will be available to users of the system. One set of materials includes reading and language arts programs appropriate for grades 3–6, as well as secondary programs in language, English, reading, arithmetic, and GED preparation skills. Another set contains approximately 350 individual lessons appropriate for all elementary grades, generally known as the Palo Alto materials. A third set of materials is appropriate for secondary level students and includes arithmetic drill and practice and simulation games. This set contains contributed materials prepared by computer users and distributed by the computer manufacturer.

This project will serve approximately 100 families during its development phase, and can provide different programs to ten homes simultaneously. The range of programs will provide individualized instruction and extensive data recording and storing capacity.

The Purdue University Project

The Purdue University Achievement Center for Children has initiated a project which utilizes two television transmission systems to deliver video tape programs to homes of 50 children labeled either severely or profoundly retarded, cerebral palsied and/or physically handicapped, and seriously emotionally disturbed, from birth through 3 years of age. Robert Currie, the director, and his associates are producing a series of 80 half-hour video tapes designed to teach specific developmental skills.

Professional quality video tapes are designed to provide illustrations of three methods for teaching a discrete behavior. A professional actor introduces each tape and carries on an informal dialogue directed toward the parent. A parent trainer demonstrates teaching techniques to a handicapped child, then assists the child's parent as she uses the same techniques. The informal style of the narrator and the use of a living room set establish a relaxed, nondirective instructional format. When the programs are complete, they will be transmitted into homes by midband cable TV or ITFS systems. During the term of the project, the 50 children in the target population will be identified and assessed by Achievement Center personnel. Equipment will be placed in their homes to enable families to receive programs. Instruction will be available to parents 4 hr per week for a 40-week period. Parents will receive a TV schedule indicating when programs specific to their child's needs will be shown. Each broadcast period will last approximately 1 hr. After the videotape is shown, parents will interact through a telephone link to the studio. Professional staff will be present to answer parents' questions and to provide additional suggestions. Since many families may be using the same programs simultaneously, parents will have the opportunity to hear each others' questions and concerns. Children's growth will be evaluated during the project and compared to a control group which does not receive instruction.

The University of Kentucky Project

For 3 years, Tawney (1972) has been involved in the design and implementation of technology in a preschool for children with severe developmental retardation. An INTERACT computer system (BRS/LVE), integrated with solid state equipment, has been used to develop hardware and software for automated teaching programs. The telecommunications project at the University of Kentucky is an extension of ongoing research and development activities initiated by the earlier project, Programmed Environments for the Developmentally Retarded. The goal of the telecommunications project is to design a system which will deliver direct instruction to infants and young children in their home environments. The first objective of the system was to develop a prototype unit which would enable signals generated by the INTERACT system to be transmitted over telephone lines to instructional devices in home settings. The second objective is to determine that these devices can work reliably for extended periods of time, while they provide instruction to children. When completed, this will be the first application of direct computer-generated instruction to remote terminals which are individually designed to register simple responses to complex stimulus presentations. Thus, the Kentucky project is a technology demonstration whose product will be a replicable system with a wide range of applications.

The components of the system are an INTERACT computer system, signal transformation units which convert electronic signals to audio signals, acoustic coupling devices, and a WATS telephone hook-up.

The INTERACT system consists of a Data General Nova 1200 minicomputer which has been modified by BRS to operate with ACT (Automated Contingency Translator), a language designed for the Behavioral Sciences. ACT programs are written in a natural language which is translated into a machine language by the INTERACT system. It can be learned rapidly by a person with little expertise in computer programming, an attibute which makes it especially attractive for educational applications. The first major efforts have been the design and testing of a prototype device (presently called a parallel-to-series unit) which enables the computer signal to be transformed to an auditory signal which can be transmitted over a telephone line. Each unit has two components. One is placed between the computer and the modem which connects to the telephone line, and the other is placed between the acoustic coupler and the teaching machine in the home. An electronic signal is transformed into an audio signal at one end, and converted back to its original form at the other. The learning devices which are placed in the homes range from an automated crib to a teaching machine console which can present and record responses to reading comprehension programs. Presently, the telecommunications system is linked to the state WATS system through the University access lines.

Eighteen families will be served during the second year of the project. They will have access to six lines at the computer so that six children can receive instruction simultaneously for 2 hours per day, for approximately 250 days. Sequential curricular programs will be designed by a home liaison coordinator, and carried out in cooperation with parents.

THE DESIGN AND FUNCTIONS OF A MODEL TELECOMMUNICATION SYSTEM

The birth of an infant with observable and multiple handicapping conditions signals an immediate change in the life cycle of a family unit. The number, type, severity, and incontrovertible presence of handicapping conditions is in direct proportion to the number, type, and duration of contacts the family will have with health, educational, and social service agencies.

Social commitments to home rearing and community services mandate new service delivery models. Preliminary evidence from early intervention programs suggests that it is desirable to begin educational intervention within a few days of birth, and maintain daily, systematic, and sequential curriculum programming continuously through and perhaps beyond the normal schooling period. The nature of handicapping conditions and a presumed range of parents' adaptive behavior dictates that families will come into contact with numerous social agencies as their child matures. The use of technology to assist parents in aiding and educating children is assured by the development of the telecommunications described in an earlier section. The specific function of each of these projects has been described. The purpose of this section is to describe the functions which a composite, model telecommunications system might perform during the first years in the life of a person with severe and multiple handicapping conditions. The basic functions include the use of technology to assist parents to teach their children, to provide direct instruction to children from birth into the early school years, and to assist parents with the additional child rearing demands by coordinating communication with and arranging interventions from the appropriate service agencies. The implications for comprehensive data collection will become apparent and will be discussed in the final section of this chapter.

Components of a Model Center

FACILITIES

The Kentucky telecommunications system will be utilized as the most direct reference for the model, designated simply as the Center, and located on a major university campus. The location provides access to the resources of the university, particularly medical services, which receive damaged infants for emergency treatment.

INSTRUMENTATION

The instrumentation component of the Center is composed of a minicomputer system which is linked by telephone and/or television transmission to homes of handicapped persons geographically dispersed across a service area. Control systems, such as INTERACT and TICCIT, integrated to function as independent or combined systems, will generate a wide variety of signals or displays. An extensive library of software programs will be available to generate instructions from simple discrimination training to preacademic and academic instruction, including regular elementary and secondary curricula. Banks of signal transformation or modulation devices will link the computer systems to the appropriate transmission system. A link-up between the campus computer system will permit data transmission for permanent storage in the larger system. The Center may also be linked to other centers across the country, as computer-to-transmission coupling devices, e.g., the Kentucky parallel-to-series units, move from prototypes to full production systems.

An extensive inventory of television equipment will complete the instrumentation for the Center. Specialty equipment, e.g., TICCIT computer-to-cable signal generator/transformers, videotape recorders, and portable TV units, will send video-taped information into homes and enable field coordinators to obtain video data on child or family performance in the home. Where cable transmission is not feasible and over-the-air transmission is inadequate, loaner video tape recorders may be placed in homes to transmit certain information to parents. The Purdue tape series represents an excellent example of material that might be presented in the home by loaner equipment.

In addition to the instrumentation, the Center will also contain a workshop where individually designed hardware units such as automated cribs and teaching machines are stored or built. This unit might also be responsible for the design and fitting of prosthetic devices for handicapped persons. If devices are available to families on a loan basis, and if they can be modified simply, it may be appropriate for such a unit to develop a "lending inventory," particularly since devices for young children are used for short periods and then outgrown.

STAFF

At a minimum, a Center may be staffed with two people: a field liaison coordinator and a computer/educational programmer. The coordinator's major responsibilities are monitoring children's educational programs and initiating liaison with appropriate service agencies. The programmer's responsibilities include generation of appropriate programs and collection and treatment of the data which those programs produce.

An expanded staffing pattern is entirely contingent upon the financial support base for the Center, the number of children served, the rate of increase in population served per year, and the number of ancillary research and demonstration activities conducted in conjunction with the delivery of services. In short order, it is easy to consider the addition of administrative and secretarial staff, a research coordinator, a full-time social services coordinator, data analysts, hardware design and construction staff, equipment maintenance technicians, a curriculum development specialist (especially critical in the area of infant learning), and additional field coordinators in multiples of n children served. Cost effectiveness data will, of course, be a deciding factor in staffing a Center. It is sufficient here to note that direct service costs must be separated from total costs, to determine cost per unit of instruction and other relevant data.

TRANSMISSION SYSTEMS

Telephone, television, and satellite systems may eventually link the Center with remote (home) sites. Any home may be furnished with specially designed equipment to communicate through one or all systems. The Kentucky system permits voice or computer communication over telephone lines. The Albany project requires both television and telephone transmission to and from the home. In some cases, transmission over bands of a given frequency range will require adaptors for home television sets. These modifications, in a sense, provide the family with their "personal" station or channel, to view material that is specific to their interests.

HOME-PLACED RECEIVING SYSTEMS

The basic task which confronts Center staff is to identify the least obtrusive site for a learning station in the home. The decision is relatively clear-cut if the person is a newly born infant with a room of his own. The task is more complex if the child is one of several children living in a two-room house in the heart of Appalachia. Data phones, electronic/audio signal converters, special television antennae, and television set converters will be installed in locations where the child will receive instruction. Then appropriate instructional devices, e.g., teaching machines, response panels, touch telephone, or teletype keyboards, will be placed in the designated learning environment. Where possible, a learning carrel may be built to insure that instructional sessions can be conducted with a minimum of disruption to the learner or interruption of family routine. Center staff will supervise placement of the appropriate learning devices in the home and arrange for different devices to be built or installed as the learner develops. Center staff may also recommend modifications of the home environment to reduce architectural barriers and to insure maximum mobility within the home.

Service Functions of the Center

The location, history, and public information systems of a telecommunications Center should insure that every newborn child with observable and multiple handicapping conditions who resides within the service region is referred within a few hours of birth. This referral will initiate a sequence of interventions by the Center. The functions which the Center is likely to perform are described in the following hypothetical example. The infant may be presumed to manifest observable biologic defect and multiple handicapping conditions. Without intervention, by school age, under traditional labeling practices, the child would probably be considered severely developmentally retarded, with physical impairments in locomotion, vision, or hearing. The infant's parents are likely to be poor, located in an area which is geographically separated from access to social services, to be relatively uneducated, and to have managed the rearing of other children with at least a marginal degree of success. If they have not yet become known to one or more service agencies, the birth of their handicapped child will target them immediately.

The functions of the Center may be generally classified as inter-agency liaison and coordination, direct instruction, parent training and support, and information collection. Subsequent to the referral, Center staff's first functions will be to enter the infant and family in a registry, to determine if a prior history exists with regional service agencies, and to inform appropriate agencies that the family may be prospective service consumers. These activities should be carried out with procedures and safeguards recommended by the participants in the Project on Classification of Exceptional Children, reported by Hobbs (1975, pp. 222–283). Contact with the family will be initiated while the mother and child are in the hospital. Parent support services may be initiated in the home prior to the infant's arrival, in those instances where extended hospitalization is required. The general objectives of Center staff during this period should be to alert agencies to potential requests for services, to provide technical and personal support to parents, to teach parents child care skills determined by specific health problems, and to develop a basic set of requirements for the first component of a learning environment within the home. These objectives should reduce the impact of the handicapped child on the family, and prepare a support base for a positive learning environment.

Direct Instruction—Child and Parents

When Center staff have obtained extensive information on the infant, the home setting, and the parents' child rearing abilities, a first set of intervention strategies will be written. Then, Center liaison programming and environmental design staff will enter the home to prepare for the installation of the telecommunications linkage systems. The location of the learning environment will be determined, and the first components will be constructed. In this instance, the infant is likely to be a few days or weeks old, and the first learning environment will be his crib. The general objectives for this set of functions are to link the home to the Center by the appropriate set of communication systems, and to design and install the learning environment.

Several types of instructional functions will be initiated simultaneously. Parents must be taught to use the instrumentation and may require instruction in general child rearing practices, as well as specific health-related practices. A sequential instructional program will be written for the infant, and parents may receive specific training when the program calls for parent–child–apparatus interaction. If, for example, the infant showed significant lack of tone or development in the leg muscles, the specific instructional objective would be to strengthen muscle tone using a kick panel crib device and parent reinforcement, contingent upon a computer-generated cue signifying that leg thrust of a specific force had been recorded. The field coordinator would state and describe the rationale for the program to the parents and teach the following skills to enable them to operate the instrumentation: (1) turn the aparatus *on*; (2) if necessary, wait *n* minutes until a *ready* signal appears; (3) place the panel in the crib and set the force adjustment to a predetermined number; (4) dial the Center; (5) wait for the appropriate signal; (6) place the telephone in the acoustic coupler for telephone line transmission.

To participate in the instructional program, the parent might be required to: (1) assist the child to make the first set of responses by gently placing its feet against the panel and pressing; (2) reinforce the child's response with a social response (tummy rubbing, talking, patting) when a computer signal indicates a correct response (made with *n* units of force).

The instructional function is, obviously, the most constant activity of the Center. The field liaison personnel will write short- and long-range programs for children in the areas of language, self-help, motor, concept, and social development. The coordinator, in cooperation with the Center-based computer programmer and instrumentation design staff, will write balanced educational programs that insure the continued development of the child throughout the early years.

As the child matures, instrumentation will be changed, the learning environment will be modified, and prosthetic devices may come and go. When combinations of handicapping conditions necessitate complex instructional programming, Center staff will be able to call upon consultant resources to assist with program writing. The structure and function of the Center, as noted, is based on service to a low incidence, difficult to manage, geographically dispersed population. This presumes that day care, preschool, kindergarten, and early public school programs will not be readily available to the handicapped child. Where they are, however, Center staff will be responsible to see that the child has access to these programs, and may arrange to install learning environments in these settings.

Interagency Liaison and Coordination

The interagency liaison and coordination functions of the Center may be performed continuously through the life of a severely handicapped person. Initial contacts with health and social service agencies will establish a basis for an ongoing communication network. In the case of a marginally adaptive family unit, as in our example, it is likely that the Center may orchestrate interventions by each agency in the Center's service area. After the birth of the infant, first coordination efforts are likely to be with health-related agencies. Infants may require repeated hospitalization or a special health care regimen in the home. Center staff's extensive involvement during this period will enable them to observe significant changes in the infant's condition, to assist parents to follow a specific regimen, or to alert professionals if the family does not carry out recommended procedures. Diagnoses of infant's functional abilities in vision and hearing may remain tentative for an extended period. Center staff may assist parents in obtaining repeated assessment from those few agencies that have the requisite personnel and instrumentation to conduct valid assessments. When Center staff receive the results of these assessments, they may incorporate them into instructional programming changes and transmit results to other agencies. Where health related intervention programs, e.g., physical therapy, are carried out by interventionists from other agencies, the Center will receive their progress reports and consult with their personnel to insure correspondence among concurrent training programs. Home maintenance of the infant may require significant adjustments in the personal health and nutritional habits of the family. When it is evident that public health intervention is required, Center staff may informally monitor the extent to which new techniques are used, and alert public health personnel to increase or reduce intervention. This function has the potential to increase the efficiency and effectiveness of such interventions, and can contribute to more effective manpower utilization.

The marginally adaptive family may require additional financial support to maintain their child in the home. Center staff may assist them in contacting appropriate welfare or social security agencies to determine the types of existing support systems. Providing access to such resources may require coordination and information sharing with legal aid societies and advocacy groups. The Center will maintain a listing of procedures for obtaining financial support to purchase or lease special prosthetic or instructional devices, in much the same way that parents of the blind child might presently obtain a brailler, an Optacon, or other materials.

Finally, Center staff will be able to monitor the family's ability to maintain the infant in the home. All of the listed functions are directed toward that goal, and it is presumed that the suggested interventions will be sufficient to enable the family to raise their child. To increase the probability that they do, Center staff may encourage them to seek support from mental health clinics and parent support groups. Where respite care services are available, Center staff may assist families in utilizing them.

Where they are not available, staff may be instrumental in assisting other agencies to establish them. If it becomes apparent that massive support is insufficient to maintain the home placement, the Center's information base and extensive interaction with the family will enable them to assist other agencies in obtaining a foster home placement in the community. Although the parents may not be able to manage the child on a daily basis, the Center can insure that the first move out of the home is a short one and that sustained efforts are made to reduce the probability of institutionalization.

Information Collection

The education and liaison functions of the Center will generate a comprehensive data base on each family unit. The major portion of the data will be daily records of the child's performance on instructional tasks. Responses to automated curricular tasks will be received and recorded 50 msec after they are emitted. In many instances, the first function of the data will be to signal an automatic, on-line change in the academic program. In other instances, programmers may modify a program after an instructional session has been completed. Parents and the field coordinator may enter the results of nonautomated programs, either through the computer system or by regular telephone transmission. Similarly, physical therapists and others who intervene in the home will transmit a record of child performance to the Center. The daily record will be transferred to permanent storage to become part of a comprehensive cumulative record of each child's educational history. It will be possible to call out data summaries on all, or a portion of, the child's record. These summaries will be helpful in the development of long-range educational programs. The summaries will document what and how well a child has learned over a period of time—information which is critical at this point in history, when few people hold a positive view of the potential of the child with severe and multiple handicapping conditions. The liaison function of the Center will generate a complete history of the family's contacts with service agencies. Kept in a central location and used as a reference by appropriate agencies, these records will contribute significantly to interagency communication and coordination of effort.

This brief description of the multiple functions of the Center clearly emphasizes the unit's role as the primary educational agent from birth to an undefined point in adulthood. At the same time, the description of liaison and coordination functions gives a brief glimpse of the potential of a central agency which serves as a clearinghouse for all social service agencies. The comprehensive data base, coded for confidentiality and monitored continuously, provides a foundation for a level of coordinated service delivery which is unparalleled in history.

The examples and activities given here have been described in the future tense, which tends to give them a sense of unreality. However, certain functions will be initiated on the Kentucky telecommunications project before this chapter appears in print. Whether the project can be transformed into a model Center remains to be seen, but the critical decisions to affect that transformation will have been made before this book is widely distributed. Thus, hypothetical examples will become reality in a relatively short period of time. The integration of technologies, a next logical step, will expand the scope of planned activities. As the Center concept develops, the nature of service delivery systems will be altered drastically. The Center may become a significant factor in radical change of service delivery patterns, and will obviously become a critical factor in the lives of the families it serves. Not entirely by coincidence, the Center has the potential to affect some of the reforms recommended by HEW's Project on Classification of Exceptional Children, namely that:

> The public schools should be the institution with the primary advocacy responsibility for providing or obtaining educational and related services for all children in need of special assistance whose condition or life circumstance does not require their institutionalization. (p. 250)
>
> Funds should be made available to public schools to provide educational or developmental services to handicapped children and youth from birth through the school years . . . (p. 251)
>
> . . . educational programs for handicapped children be carried out in as near to normal settings as is consonant with the provision of specialized services they need. (Hobbs, 1975)

SYSTEMS OF THE FUTURE

Combining Prototype Systems

The telecommunications systems described here are, by and large, prototypes. Once it is determined that they work, it will be necessary to determine whether they work reliably, whether they are utilized to the maximum, whether they produce desired changes in behavior, and whether they do so in a cost-effective manner. As these questions are answered, the systems and their products will undoubtedly be used in different combinations and with yet-to-be conceived technologies.

The teaching packages prepared at the University of Utah are widely exportable and potentially useful in a variety of educational settings. The content of the video language instruction tapes developed in New York City will make them useful, whether transmitted with the responsive TV system or modified for standard presentation. The Purdue University parent training tapes, likewise, will undoubtedly find their way into university training programs, family health care units, etc. The hardware and slide programs developed at the University of Kentucky are adaptable for other instructional environments.

The potential of television as an instructional medium seems assured, regardless of the rate of development of specific systems. Cable networks may or may not expand into every area of the country, and may or may not be heavily subscribed. Where cable TV is available, it may be necessary to subsidize cable payments to families to provide access to home training materials. Or, as television equipment costs drop, it may be reasonable to provide state grant support to enable parents to purchase video tape recorders. The cost per unit, figured on a daily use basis for 5 or 10 years, will be minimal. Tape lending libraries, equipped with facilities for duplicating master tapes onto reusable tapes, can provide large numbers of users with the same material, sent by mail or delivered by a home liaison coordinator. As the cost of small portable video recording units decreases (and when their reliability increases), it will be possible for home liaison personnel to obtain permanent records of parent–child interaction and child response to automated programs. These permanent records may be useful for study by researchers or other interventionists.

Presently, computer systems such as INTERACT and TICCIT are constrained by the unique design characteristics of same-generation computer systems. Programs designed for one computer cannot be used on another without extensive and costly modifications. This problem will be reduced as minicomputer users expand and share software packages. Most computer manufacturers encourage and support the activities of user groups. These groups will undoubtedly grow in size and originality—increasing communications among users and accelerating the development of novel applications of standard programs. The products of these groups will expand the curricular offerings of the projects described here. As noted, a portion of the Albany library comes from this source.

Present design constraints may be removed, making it possible to combine systems like INTERACT and TICCIT so that one minicomputer can drive both systems in succession. It is reasonable to assume that both systems will be used side by side in a model Center, similar to that described in an earlier section. When the first attempt is made to integrate the two systems, the resulting engineering changes are likely to standardize the components on the independent systems.

The technologies described here are relatively earth-bound. They may, however, be combined with projects which have been initiated to determine the feasibility of satellite communication systems which have been under development for the past several years. As the space program has decelerated, NASA has initiated programs to determine the feasibility of earth–satellite–earth communications. Major programs have been initiated in the Rocky Mountain states and in Appalachia. Educational programs may be beamed to a satellite from a central studio, and then directed by satellite to multiple sites within the "satellite footprint." In some instances, relatively low cost antennae enable audiences to receive television signals. In other instances, more expensive sender–receiver units are placed in a central location; these interactive units enable a large audience to communicate with professionals at the television studio subsequent to and even during broadcast. It is too early to tell whether the satellite projects will be cost-effective or whether they can generate sufficient simultaneous broadcasts to serve the many educational needs of the inhabitants of the sparsely populated or geographically remote areas they were designed to serve. In the event that they receive continued support, the program content developed on the telecommunications projects can be transmitted via satellite. At the same time, the programming content they have developed for specific audiences may be added to the tape libraries for the telecommunications projects.

Our society has entered an era of rapid technological development, where today's innovation may be outmoded tomorrow. The telecommunications technologies represent new and exciting ways to deliver instruction to children. Although they may become obsolete within 10 years, they will initiate changes in instructional models which will remain after they have been replaced by more advanced technologies.

Future Manpower Requirements

When the opportunity is presented to engage in a bit of futurism, there is temptation to speculate at length on the potential of technology to create a demand for new types of personnel and to open up new areas of research. There is a tendency to obscure the difference between what *is* possible with the advent of the prototype telecommunications projects and what *may* be possible with a technology-based Center delivery system. It is apparent, particularly with respect to the Center concept, that speculation proceeds on a variety of assumptions about the way the world *ought* to work, rather than the way it *does*. These cautions notwithstanding, the prototypes have the potential to bring about significant change in the lives of families. To do so will require personnel with new sets of competencies and will open up areas of research which have been logistically impossible in the past.

The Kentucky telecommunications project will create the most immediate need for personnel with different sets of competencies. A home liaison coordinator will need to be skilled in: parent training, curriculum development, infant learning and development, operation of instrumentation, and interagency liaison tasks. An educational/computer programmer will need to be skilled in: computer programming, writing software programs, writing long-term instructional programs, data reduction and analysis, reporting child performance.

By themselves, these are not new competencies. Taken together, however, they represent unique job descriptions which few persons are qualified to fill. As technologies are combined to provide long-term and extensive services, additional functions, e.g. social service referrals and follow-up, child/family advocacy, will be added to these basic positions.

FUTURE DIRECTIONS FOR CURRICULUM AND PROGRAMMATIC RESEARCH DEVELOPMENT

The discussion of infant learning tasks would lead one to the assumption that valid curricula do exist, sufficient in scope to cover the age range from birth to approximately 6 years of age. The Kentucky and Purdue projects represent approximations to comprehensive, sequential curricula. One of the highest priorities for research and development is the design of a total curriculum for infants with severe and multiple handicapping conditions. The prototype telecommunications systems are, from one perspective, more sophisticated than the curricula they deliver. It is possible to deliver instructional signals and record responses in a fraction of a second. On selected learning tasks, simple branching is possible. What is lacking is identification of valid learning tasks and the development of fine grain instructional sequences. The literature on infant learning offers some direction for the curriculum developer. A limited number of infant training programs have been published, and there are a few "stimulation" programs in progress at this moment. These will form the working material for, but should not be confused with, a complete, systematic, sequential, and fine grain infant curriculum. Such curriculum may require 10 to 15 years of development and validation. While present technology is sufficient to initiate the task, future developments may accelerate its completion.

Little is known about the early development of the handicapped infant, or of the normal infant either, for that matter. The literature on infant learning is sprinkled with comments on the logistical problems which face the researcher. Consequently, empirical studies of infant behavior are often based on short-term observations. The advent of the telecommunications systems will remove many of the barriers which have hampered programmatic research efforts. Home-placed computer terminals and long-term Center contact with families should guarantee access to a population and enable researchers to obtain data from homes on a daily basis. Research priorities are likely to be addressed to two general questions: "What does the severely handicapped infant do (e.g., how does he behave) when he enters his home environment?," and "How do families behave when they return home from the hospital with their handicapped infant?" Infant learning studies are likely to be integrated with, and form the empirical basis for, a valid, systematic curriculum. One general approach will be to determine the extent to which it is possible to shape or build a behavioral repertoire. The outcome will include a curriculum and a set of studies which describe the effects of specific intervention strategies.

Few researchers have attempted to observe a family's response to a fragile and observably impaired infant. A Center-based telecommunications system, in contact with a family almost immediately after the birth of the impaired infant, will have the capacity to observe family–infant interactions and intervene to increase the quality and quantity of those interactions. With sufficient programming, it may be possible to identify and document those strategies which most effectively help parents maintain their child in the home. Comprehensive record systems collected on heterogeneous family units over long periods of time will contribute to more efficient and effective delivery of services. The growth of computerized telecommunications systems will provide an opportunity to observe the extent to which family units can incorporate an advanced technology into the daily patterns of home living. Computer systems are designed to assist, rather than supplant, parents, and are designed to perform multiple functions. They will be most effective when utilized to the maximum. The presence of these systems in homes, and projected use over a period of several years, will provide a fertile testing ground for the facilitation of man–machine interactions and, more specifically, infant–computer, family–computer, and parent–infant–computer interactions.

A final note is called for to emphasize the ordering of priorities for research with prototype telecommunications systems and proposed automated curriculum. As soon as a system has been conceptualized and designed, a natural first question is often, "Yes, but is it better than 'x' (anything else)?" There is a more logical set of questions which must be directed toward prototype systems, and it is important that policymakers, professionals, and parents learn to address first questions first. Viewing all the systems collectively, a general sequence might be: Does it work? Does it work reliably? Is the system cost-effective? What are the parameters for curricular presentations? How do parents, child, and system interact to carry out an instructional program? What are the "normal tasks of childhood?" What are valid instructional tasks from birth to 6? How do infants respond to specific instructional tasks? Do severely retarded infants learn? Is this approach better than another?

In closing, it should be apparent from the length of the list that the first natural question must be preceded by a more logical set. In 1975, telecommunications systems appear to have the potential to produce significant change in the lives of handicapped infants and in the structure of future delivery systems. In some cases, it may require up to 15 years of research and development to provide answers to each of the questions which are addressed here. It seems appropriate to end with a caution that consumers and consumer advocates address the proper questions in their logical sequence. Failure to do so will consign these innovative programs to the nation's junk heap of grandiose projects which have foundered on the shoals of underfunding and premature evaluation.

REFERENCES

Bijou SW: A functional analysis of retarded development, in Ellis N, (ed): International Review of Research in Mental Retardation, Vol. 1. New York, Academic, 1966, pp 1–19

Bijou SW: Studies in experimental development of left-right concepts in retarded children using fading techniques, in Ellis N (ed): International Review of Research in Mental Retardation, Vol. 3. New York, Academic, 1968, pp 66–96

Bricker W, Bricker D: Toddler Research and Intervention Project Report—Year II. Nashville, Tenn., George Peabody College for Teachers, IMRID Monograph No. 21, 1972

Children's Defense Fund, Children Out of School in America. Cambridge, Mass., 1974

Fitzgerald H, Porges S: A decade of infant conditioning and learning research. Merrill-Palmer Quart, 17:79–117, 1971

Hayden AH, Haring NG: Programs for Down's syndrome children at the University of Washington, in Tjossem T (ed): Intervention Strategies for Risk Infants and Young Children. Baltimore, Md., University Park Press (in press)

Hobbs N: The Future of Children. San Francisco, Jossey-Bass, 1975

Hulsebus R: Operant conditioning of infant behavior: A review in Reese H (ed): Advances in Child Development and Behavior. New York, Academic, 1973, pp 111–158

Karnes M, Hodgins AS, Stoneburner RL, et al: Effects of a highly structured program of language development on intellectual functioning and psycholinguistic development of culturally disadvantaged three-year-olds. J Spec Ed, 2:405–412, 1968

Lambie DZ, Bond JT, Weikart DP: Framework for Infant Education. Ypsilanti, Mich., High/Scope Educational Research Foundation, undated

Sidman M, Stoddard L: Programming perception and learning for retarded children, in Ellis N (ed): International Review of Research in Mental Retardation, Vol. 2. New York, Academic, 1966, pp 151–208

Tawney JW: Programmed Environments for Developmentally Retarded Children: A project for a coordinated program of research, program model development, and curriculum development and dissemination. Project No. 233118 (original proposal), 1972

Tawney JW: Training letter discrimination in four-year-old children, J Appl Behav Anal, 5:455–465, 1972

Tawney JW: Programmed environments for the developmentally retarded, in Mann P (ed): Mainstream Special Education. Washington, D.C.: Council for Exceptional Children, 1974

Tawney JW, Allen MA, O'Reilly C, et al: Developing curricula for errorless learning: A search for order in an unorderly world. Selected papers: American Association for the Education of the Severely/Profoundly Handicapped, 1975

Tawney JW: Prerequisite conditions for the establishment of educational programs for the severely retarded. Proceedings of the NARC conference on education for the severely retarded: National Association for Retarded Citizens, 1975

Terrace H: Stimulus control, in Honig W (ed): Operant Behavior: Areas of Research and Application. New York, Appleton-Century-Crofts, 1967, pp 271–344

White B: Human Infants. Englewood Cliffs, N.J., Prentice-Hall, 1971

Index